Profiles in Achievement

BLISS INSTITUTE SERIES

Bliss Institute Series

John C. Green, Editor

William Hershey and Colleagues, *Profiles in Achievement: The Gifts, Quirks and Foibles of Ohio's Best Politicians*

Joy Marsella, *Creating a New Civility*

William Hershey, *Quick & Quotable: Columns from Washington, 1985-1997*

Jerry Austin, *True Tales from the Campaign Trail: Stories Only Political Consultants Can Tell*

Christopher J. Galdieri, Tauna S. Sisco, and Jennifer C. Lucas, editors, *Races, Reforms, & Policy: Implications of the 2014 Midterm Elections*

Tauna S. Sisco, Jennifer C. Lucas, and Christopher J. Galdieri, editors, *Political Communication & Strategy: Consequences of the 2014 Midterm Election*s

William L. Hershey and John C. Green, *Mr. Chairman: The Life and Times of Ray C. Bliss*

Douglas M. Brattebo, Tom Lansford, Jack Covarrubias, and Robert J. Pauly Jr., editors, *Culture, Rhetoric, and Voting: The Presidential Election of 2012*

Douglas M. Brattebo, Tom Lansford, and Jack Covarrubias, editors, *A Transformation in American National Politics: The Presidential Election of 2012*

Daniel J. Coffey, John C. Green, David B. Cohen, and Stephen C. Brooks, *Buckeye Battleground: Ohio, Campaigns, and Elections in the Twenty-First Century*

Lee Leonard, *A Columnist's View of Capitol Square: Ohio Politics and Government, 1969–2005*

Abe Zaidan, with John C. Green, *Portraits of Power: Ohio and National Politics, 1964–2000*

Profiles in Achievement

The Gifts, Quirks and Foibles of Ohio's Best Politicians

William Hershey and Colleagues

UNIVERSITY OF AKRON PRESS
AKRON, OHIO

ISBN: 978-1-62922-137-3 (paper)
ISBN: 978-1-62922-138-0 (ePDF)
ISBN: 978-1-62922-139-7 (ePub)

A catalog record for this title is available from the Library of Congress.

∞ The paper used in this publication meets the minimum requirements of ANSI/NISO Z39.48–1992 (Permanence of Paper).

Cover photo: Library of Congress, Prints & Photographs Division, photograph by Carol M. Highsmith, LC-DIG-highsm-41852 DLC

Cover design: Amy Freels

Cover illustration: Nadia Alnashar

Profiles in Achievement was typeset in Adobe Caslon with Avenir display by Beth Pratt. *Profiles in Achievement* was printed on sixty-pound natural and bound by Bookmasters of Ashland, Ohio.

To Akron Beacon Journal editors and reporters,
past and present, who have helped readers
understand Ohio politics.

Contents

Foreword

DR. JOHN C. GREEN

Director Emeritus, Ray C. Bliss Institute of Applied Politics,
University of Akron

Political journalists meet some interesting people.

Bill Hershey and his colleagues at the Akron Beacon Journal certainly did, and moreover, they wrote profiles of many of them. Published between 1980 and 2014, the twenty-eight essays republished here cover a wide variety of leaders who "achieved big things" in their careers.

The title of this collection, *Profiles in Achievement*, echoes *Profiles in Courage*, a book about eight U.S. Senators who stood up for what they believed in the face of intense pressure and criticism. Authored by then-U.S. Senator John F. Kennedy (and ghostwritten by speechwriter Theodore Sorensen), the book established a genre of books about good leaders. It soon inspired Richard Nixon's *Six Crises* (ghostwritten by journalist Charles Lichtenstein), chronicling episodes of leaders in action Nixon witnessed—including his own loss to Kennedy in the 1960 presidential election. Recent additions to the genre include U.S. Senator Sherrod Brown's *Desk 88: Eight Progressive Senators Who Changed America* and former Ohio Governor John Kasich's *Courage is Contagious: Ordinary People Doing Extraordinary Things to Change the Face of America*. Some of the best books in this genre were written by journalists, such as David Broder's *Changing of the Guard: Power and Leadership in America*.

Taken as a whole, this genre is an antidote to the popular view that leaders, especially politicians, are self-interested and corrupt. There is, of course, a good bit of truth in this often-overstated conclusion. Indeed, the Beacon Journal writers also profiled poor leaders, often with pre-science. An example is Ohio's Larry Householder, who served twice as Speaker of the Ohio House of Representatives. In 2020, his long-recognized lack of ethics resulted in his indictment and arrest on federal racketeering charges. Reporting on these kinds of interesting people is one of the purposes of a free press, but reporting on successful leadership is of equal interest.

Courage is a feature of the high achievers profiled here, both doing the right thing under fire as well as recovering from the burns of defeat and disappointment. Longevity is clearly an important factor: resilience provides the time necessary for major accomplishments. For example, James Rhodes and Vern Riffe set records for time in their respective offices; Jo Ann Davidson and Eddie Davis life's work broke social barriers and opened the way for the careers of Mary Taylor and Barbara Sykes. The hindsight of experience, the foresight to solve problems, and the insight from building consensus are important features of the people profiled as well.

If political reporting is the first draft of history, then profiles are a second draft. There is an intimacy in these accounts not found in daily reporting. Some profiles sum up a lifetime of achievement, such as Bill Batchelder's years in the Ohio legislature and Johnny Apple's decades of covering presidential campaigns. In other profiles, there is a sighting of what will eventually be achieved. For example, we encounter George Voinovich as mayor of Cleveland, long before he became Ohio's Governor and Senator; we see Maureen O'Connor as a local prosecutor on her way to becoming Ohio's first female Chief Justice of the Supreme Court; we observe John Glenn as a dogged legislator and Sherrod Brown as an ardent policy advocate.

We also learn about high achievers little known today, such as real estate developer John Galbreath and civil rights leader Sterling Tucker, whose impact is still felt in the fabric of everyday life. We also hear about virtues welcome in a time of contentious politics: Republican Ray Bliss tells us, "We should be tolerant of the deeply held convictions of others," while Democrat Louis Stokes reminds us "...while I admire your love for America, I hope that you will never forget that others, too, love America just as much as you do and that others, too, will die for America, just as quick as you will."

Not even high achievers are perfect, of course. All the profiles reveal interesting quirks and foibles of their subjects—some endearing, some infuriating. But these profiles are more than just celebrations of success: they show that the quest for good leaders is not a fool's errand.

This volume is a fine addition to the Bliss Institute's book series with the University of Akron Press, joining Hershey's earlier compilation, *Quick & Quotable: Columns from Washington, 1985–1997*; the collection of his Beacon Journal colleague Abe Zaidan, *Portraits of Power: Ohio and National Politics, 1964–2004*; and the book by fellow political journalist for the Columbus Dispatch Lee Leonard, *A Columnist's View of Capitol Square: Ohio Politics and Government, 1969–2005*.

Please enjoy: you will meet some interesting people.

Introduction
Profiles in Achievement

WILLIAM HERSHEY

Republican Ray Bliss and Democrat Eddie Davis agreed on few things during long and successful political careers, but they had one thing in common:

Both achieved big things.

Starting out as an errand boy in the 1931 Akron mayoral race, Bliss became a nationally recognized political organizer. Over a 50-year career, he led and when necessary rebuilt Republican Party organizations that helped elect mayors, governors and presidents. He earned the title "Mr. Chairman."

Davis broke the color barrier in Akron politics when he was the first Black person elected to city council in 1957, just three years after the landmark 1954 U.S. Supreme Court decision that ruled that state laws establishing segregated schools were unconstitutional. In 1969, Davis' colleagues elected him council president.

They are among the high achievers that my colleagues and I reported on in more than 40 years of covering Ohio government and politics for the Akron Beacon Journal.

This book includes profiles of Bliss, Davis and 26 other men and women who distinguished themselves in the Akron-Canton area, in Ohio and nationally.

The profiles represent the in-depth reporting that good regional newspapers like the Akron Beacon Journal used to produce regularly for their readers. Sadly, the economic changes that have led to the decline of local journalism have made such stories rare, almost museum pieces. Evidence of this trend can be seen in the length of the profiles included—by and large those written more recently are shorter and tailored to specific events.

But whatever the occasion for which these profiles were written, they describe the gifts, quirks and foibles of Ohio's best politicians, people whose careers made a difference in politics and government at the local, state and national levels.

Besides me, the authors include other former Akron Beacon Journal reporters and writers: James C. Benton, Carl Chancellor, Michael Cull, Michael Douglas, Bob Dyer, Steve Hoffman, Doug Oplinger, Brian Usher and Dennis J. Willard.

Bliss and Davis get the profiles started and Republican Mike DeWine and Democrat Sherrod Brown bring them to a close.

DeWine and Brown are the long-distance runners of Ohio politics. I met both in the early 1980s when DeWine, from Greene County, was a state senator and Brown, originally from Mansfield, was in the Ohio House. By 2021, both still were going strong, DeWine in his first term as Ohio governor and Brown in his third term as a U.S. senator.

Each man rebounded from a disappointing defeat. Brown lost his bid for a third term as Ohio Secretary of State to Republican Bob Taft in 1990. That same year DeWine was elected lieutenant governor on the ticket with gubernatorial candidate George Voinovich.

Two years later Brown hit the comeback trail and won the first of seven terms in the U.S. House. That same year DeWine made an unsuccessful attempt to unseat incumbent Democratic Sen. John Glenn. Two years later, DeWine ran for the U.S. Senate again and beat Democrat Joel Hyatt for a seat that opened up when Democrat Howard Metzenbaum, Hyatt's father-in-law, retired.

DeWine was re-elected to the Senate in 2000 and was ousted in 2006 by a Democratic challenger—Brown. Brown was re-elected in 2010 and then to a third term in 2016.

DeWine wasn't out of office for long. He made his political comeback in 2010 when he won the first of two terms as Ohio attorney general. Then in 2018 he was elected governor, achieving a longtime goal.

All but two of the book's subjects were directly involved in politics. There was a political dimension, however, to the career of each exception.

Builder and sportsman John Galbreath, from Mt. Sterling south of Columbus, earned an international reputation for developing projects and rebuilding downtowns in the United States and around the world. In Ohio, he was also was one of the business leaders who supported Bliss as chairman of the Ohio Republican Party.

These business leaders ignored chairman Bliss' advice in 1958 and foolishly put a right-to-work issue on the statewide ballot. Voters overwhelmingly rejected the issue and clobbered Republican candidates. The business leaders retreated to Galbreath's Darby Dan farm west of Columbus where Bliss dressed them down and laid out the blueprint that successfully rebuilt the state GOP.

The other exception was Akron native R.W. "Johnny" Apple. Apple began his newspaper career as a copy boy for the Beacon Journal and later joined the New York Times. Over a 40-year career he became arguably the most influential and most colorful political writer in the United States.

He covered 10 presidential elections and more than 20 national nominating conventions, according to his New York Times obituary when Apple died at 71 in 2006. Besides politics, Apple served as the Times' bureau chief in Moscow, London, Nairobi and Lagos, and for two and a half years led the paper's coverage of the Vietnam War.

Back in Summit County, Jim Williams and Maureen O'Connor developed their own careers as political trailblazers, building on the legacies of Bliss and Davis.

Williams, a Democrat, in 1969 became the second Black person elected to Akron City Council and later became the first Black person elected a councilman-at-large, representing the whole city. He was appointed U.S. attorney for northern Ohio in 1978 by President Jimmy Carter. He became an Akron Municipal Court judge in 1983 and in 1989 became the first African American to serve on the Summit County Common Pleas bench.

Republican O'Connor in 2010 became the first woman elected chief justice of the Ohio Supreme Court. She was re-elected in 2016. Before that, O'Connor had served as a Summit County Common Pleas Court judge, Summit County prosecutor, Ohio lieutenant governor and as an Ohio Supreme Court associate justice.

Two other Akron-area women faced off in an all-Summit County race for Ohio auditor in 2006.

In that race, Republican Mary Taylor of Green defeated Democrat Barbara Sykes of Akron—but just barely—with 50.6% for Taylor to 49.4% for Sykes. Taylor was the only Republican to win a statewide non-judicial office that year.

Taylor began her political career in 2001 as a member of Green City Council and then was elected to two terms in the Ohio House before her 2006 win. In 2010 she was elected lieutenant governor on the ticket with gubernatorial candidate John Kasich, and re-elected in 2014, becoming the first woman to serve two terms in this office. She lost the Republican primary for governor in 2018 to Mike DeWine.

Sykes had done her own trailblazing in 1983 when she became the first Black woman on Akron City Council. She was serving in the Ohio House when she ran against Taylor for auditor. She also lost a race for state treasurer in 1994. If Sykes had prevailed in either race, she would have become the first African American Democrat elected to a state constitutional office in Ohio.

Roy Ray, another Republican, also served both in Akron and Columbus. He was elected Akron mayor in 1979. He was elected to the Ohio Senate in 1986 and served until 2001.

Democrat Tom Sawyer knocked Ray out of the mayor's office in 1983, breaking an 18-year Republican stranglehold on the chief executive's office. Sawyer left the mayor's office after being elected to the U.S. House in 1986 where he served eight terms. Sawyer also served in the Ohio House and the Ohio Senate.

Don Plusquellic, another Democrat, had been city council president and took over as Akron mayor after Sawyer left for the U.S. House and went on to serve as mayor for more than 27 years, becoming the longest-serving mayor in the city's history. Plusquellic combined political vision and courage with a short temper, a combination that left an indelible mark on the mayor's office.

Up the road from Akron, Republican George Voinovich was elected Cleveland mayor in 1979. Voinovich, like Plusquellic, had both courage and a temper, but was known for "doing more with less" rather than for casting grand political visions. He served as mayor until 1989 and in 1990 was elected to the first of two terms as governor of Ohio. He was elected to the U.S. Senate in 1998 and re-elected in 2004.

Voinovich also served in the Ohio House of Representatives and was elected lieutenant governor in 1978 on the ticket with Gov. Jim Rhodes.

Republican Rhodes, a native of Jackson County in southern Ohio, was the only person elected to four four-year terms as Ohio governor, serving from 1963–1971 and 1975–1983. He was a master vote-getter, but his legacy was blemished by the decision to send Ohio National Guard troops to the Kent State University campus in 1970 to quell protests, resulting in the death of four students.

Democrat Dick Celeste, from suburban Cleveland, was elected governor in 1982, and in 1986 became the only Democrat, as of 2021, re-elected to a second four-year term as the state's chief executive. Celeste had lost the 1978 governor's race to Rhodes but avenged that defeat by defeating Rhodes in 1986, effectively ending Rhodes' long political career. Of the group profiled here, Celeste is the only one who is genuinely charismatic. He could seduce politicians and voters, even reporters and academicians.

Republican Nancy Hollister of Marietta had a short but historically significant career as governor, just 11 days. Hollister became Ohio's first and, by 2021, only woman governor when she was sworn in on Dec. 31, 1998. She took over after Voinovich resigned to take the U.S. Senate seat he had won in November. She served until Republican Bob Taft, elected governor in November, was sworn in on Jan. 11, 1999.

Two other Republican women also were history makers. Betty Montgomery, whose political base was in Wood County, was elected attorney general in 1994 and re-elected four years later, becoming the first woman to hold that office. When Montgomery was elected state auditor in 2002, she became the first woman in that position as well.

In 1995, Jo Ann Davidson, from suburban Columbus, took over as speaker of the Ohio House, the first woman to hold that job. She had led Republican efforts to win a House majority in the 1994 elections, ending 22 years of Democratic control. Davidson was speaker until 1999 when term limits forced her exit.

The speaker for 20 of those years of Democratic control was Vern Riffe from Scioto County in southern Ohio, whose tenure made him the longest-serving speaker in state history. Riffe's ability to build a diverse, winning

Democratic caucus has been unmatched since he left the political scene in 1995. Riffe's reputation was tarnished in 2005 when he pleaded guilty to charges of failure to report speaker's fees he received while in office.

Republican Bill Batchelder of Medina also served as speaker but took a circuitous path. He served 30 years in the House from 1969–1999, much of it as a conservative back-bencher. He then became a Medina County Common Pleas Court judge and after that an appeals court judge before his second coming to the Ohio House with a victory in 2006. By then the Republican Party had moved in Batchelder's conservative direction and, like Davidson, he was enough of a pragmatist to win the speakership in 2011, serving four years until forced out of the House by term limits.

The GOP's conservative tilt presented a challenge to Thaddeus Garrett of Akron, a Black man in a party that was becoming increasingly white. An ordained minister, Garrett never gave up on trying to win more Black support for what once was the party of Lincoln. He developed an especially close relationship with George H.W. Bush and worked for Bush when he was both vice president and president.

Sterling Tucker, another Akron man, came to Washington, D.C. in 1956 to run the local chapter of the Urban League and ended up working with eight presidents to advance civil rights and related causes. Along the way, Tucker was elected chairman of the Washington, D.C. City Council.

Tucker was already in Washington when two men from the Akron-Canton area were elected to the U.S. House where both excelled at what members of Congress are supposed to do—work together to pass legislation.

Republican Ralph Regula from Stark County was first elected in 1972 and served 18 terms before retiring. Democrat John Seiberling, the grandson of Goodyear founder F.A. Seiberling, was elected in 1970 and retired after seven terms. Shunning Washington D.C.'s revolving door, through which retiring members of Congress walk to high-paying jobs as lobbyists and consultants, both men returned to Ohio in retirement.

Seiberling's crowning legislative achievement was the creation of what is now the Cuyahoga Valley National Park. Regula played a leading role in the park's creation and used his position on the House Appropriations Committee to secure the money that helped make the park one of northeast Ohio's premier natural attractions.

Democrat Louis Stokes from Cuyahoga County was another U.S. House member from northeast Ohio who, like Eddie Davis in Akron, made a major political breakthrough. Stokes was part of a history-making brother combination. His younger brother Carl in 1967 was elected Cleveland mayor, one of the first Black mayors of a major city.

Louis Stokes was elected to Congress in 1968, becoming Ohio's first Black U.S. House member. He used his seat on the powerful, money-dispensing Appropriations Committee to benefit the Cleveland area and Ohio but also took on vital roles as chairman of the House Ethics and Intelligence committees and as of the committee that investigated the assassinations of Martin Luther King and President John Kennedy.

Most politicians attain fame—or infamy—after being elected to Congress. That wasn't the case with Democrat John Glenn.

Glenn, who grew up in New Concord, had been a Marine fighter pilot in both World War II and the Korean War and as an astronaut became a national hero in 1962 when he was the first American to orbit the earth.

It took Glenn, whose career was marked by understated and dogged determination, several attempts to win a seat in the U.S. Senate. It was in 1974 that he succeeded. He was re-elected three times, becoming the only Ohioan to win four consecutive Senate terms. While other senators headed for the microphones and TV lights, Glenn dug into problems without easy answers such as how to dispose of the radioactive waste from the nation's nuclear weapons plants.

For 18 of Glenn's 24 years in the Senate, his partner was fellow Democrat Howard Metzenbaum of Cleveland. At first there was little fellowship. The two hardly spoke after a bitter 1974 primary won by Glenn. Gradually they became allies, if not close friends.

Metzenbaum deserved the nickname "Headline Howard" but backed up his ability to make news with hard work that produced legislation to protect consumers, workers and the poor and to control the spread of guns. When many Democrats trimmed their progressive sails during the "Reagan Revolution," Metzenbaum defiantly stuck to his liberal commitments.

These achievers had styles. Some like Metzenbaum had a flair for publicity while Glenn was evenhanded to a fault. Some were aggressive like Plusquellic as mayor. Few were as cautious as Sawyer, both as mayor and in the U.S. House.

They all had the discipline, patience and courage to take on opportunities with no guarantees of success. Bliss took over as chairman of a national Republican Party on life support after Republican Barry Goldwater's shellacking in the 1964 presidential election. He helped elect Richard Nixon president in 1968 as other Republicans scored victories at the state and national levels.

Louis Stokes was a successful young trial lawyer in the 1960s and never intended to run for Congress. His younger brother Carl had been interested in that job. When a 1967 U.S. Supreme Court decision led to the creation of a U.S. House district that a Black candidate had a chance of winning, however, Carl already had been elected Cleveland mayor. Louis Stokes ran for Congress, won the election and was re-elected 14 times, earning a bipartisan reputation for hard work and taking on the toughest assignments.

There were other Ohioans who achieved big things along with those whose profiles are included in our book. Former U.S. House Speaker John Boehner, former Governors John Kasich and Bob Taft, and U.S. Sen. Rob Portman—all Republicans—come to mind. So does Democrat Ted Strickland, a former governor and congressman.

In 2021, others were making names for themselves, including Republican Frank LaRose, a Summit County native, who was elected Ohio Secretary of State in 2018. On the Democratic side, Emilia Sykes of Akron was serving as Ohio House Democratic leader, following in the footsteps of her legislator parents Vernon and Barbara, who both served on Akron City Council and in the state legislature. It's not certain, however, that there will continue to be newspapers that comprehensively chronicle their achievements and missteps.

Ray Bliss: The Party's Not Over

*At 73, the Akronite who revived the Republicans is cutting
back—to a six-day work week*

Akron Beacon Journal Beacon Magazine, June 7, 1981
WILLIAM HERSHEY

The party was for Ronald Reagan, but the way Congressman Ralph
Regula tells it, the president shared the spotlight with a septuagenarian
Republican from Akron—Ray C. Bliss.

Regula was in Bliss' box at the Kennedy Center for one of the several
balls marking Reagan's inaugural last January.

Instead of dancing, the Stark County congressman and his wife Mary
just watched as senators, representatives and party leaders—past and
present—filed past, paying tribute to Bliss and his wife Ellen.

"It was like holding court," says Regula. "Ray just stayed in the box.
He knows them all."

At 73, Bliss, the Akron-born son of German immigrants, is the
Republican Party's living legend. This is the 50th anniversary of a political career Bliss started as an errand boy in the 1931 Akron mayoral race—
shortly after he was thrown out of The University of Akron.

Bliss' expulsion stemmed from alleged ballot box stuffing in the
campus May Queen election, an incident Bliss still declines to discuss
in detail.

But he appears to have redeemed himself several times over in the university's eyes.

He received his bachelor's degree in 1935 and was awarded an honorary Doctor of Humane Letters in 1968. In 1965 he received the university's Alumni Honor Award. He is serving his second term on the university's board of trustees, on which he serves as vice chairman.

After his humble beginning in party politics, Bliss went on to serve as Republican chairman at the county, state and national levels. He has played a major role in electing Republican presidents, governors, legislators, mayors, city councilmen, sheriffs—and maybe even dogcatchers.

Republicans got a head start on Bliss' 50th anniversary at last year's national convention. They gave him a solid gold medal, a tribute some thought was long overdue.

Because he generally has worked behind the scenes, his achievements are not as well known to the public as those of other famous Akronites. In his own way, however, Bliss has meant as much to the Republicans— and the two-party system—as Harvey S. Firestone meant to tire-making.

He led the way in the use of public opinion polls, voter surveys and television, and proved that honesty can be the best policy for winning elections. He also knew how to raise money honestly.

Bliss may have left Akron to serve the party in Columbus and Washington, but he never has turned his back on his hometown.

When Bliss resigned from the national chairmanship in 1969, then-President Richard M. Nixon offered him the ambassadorship to Denmark, where there still is royalty.

As Nixon discussed Denmark, Bliss recalls, the president's eyes just "glowed and glowed."

"He attached great importance to what I call the phony things in life," Bliss says matter-of-factly.

Bliss attached more importance to Akron—smokestacks and all— than to Copenhagen.

"I went to school here. I was raised here. The people of Akron helped make me a success. If I hadn't been a success here, what would I be? Nothing."

Akron, of course, had to share Bliss, as W.R. Timken Jr., chairman of the Canton-based Timken Co. and vice chairman of the Ohio Republican Finance Committee, made clear at the party's state convention last year:

"That man is none other than Mr. Ohio, Mr. Republican and truly Mr. America."

National party leaders say Timken wasn't exaggerating.

"The party owes Ray Bliss a lot," says Congressman John Rhodes of Arizona, a former House minority leader, who met regularly with Bliss when he served as national chairman.

Democrats are envious, not grudging, when they talk about Bliss.

"What we're talking about is someone who has the capacity to motivate a grassroots organization," says State Rep. Vernon Cook, D-Cuyahoga Falls, an assistant House majority leader. "He's interested in the historic mission of the political party—to pick winning candidates."

Cook confesses that when the Democrats gathered earlier this year to weep, gnash some teeth and pick a new national chairman, they had one goal: Find a "Ray Bliss."

They picked a Los Angeles lawyer, Charles T. Manatt. If Manatt is to be a "Ray Bliss," there are a couple of political yardsticks he'll have to measure up to.

In 1949 Bliss was called to Columbus as state chairman. Ohio Republicans were as long-faced then as Democrats are nationally today. In the 1948 statewide elections, the Republicans won only one of eight races. The GOP also lost control of both houses of the legislature.

With Bliss in charge, the party bounced back in 1950. The Republicans won five of seven statewide races that year and regained control of both houses of the legislature.

Then, in 1965, Bliss was off to Washington to clean up after another GOP disaster—Barry Goldwater's landslide loss to President Lyndon B.

Johnson. There were premature reports that the two-party system was dead.

This was the same year former President Gerald Ford was elected minority leader in the House of Representatives. Ford says he and Bliss worked closely during the next four years to rebuild the party.

"He was literally drafted to pull a demoralized and discouraged Republican Party together," Ford told Beacon Magazine.

By the time Bliss left Washington in 1969, he had done more than breathe life back into the Grand Old Party.

Nixon was in the White House. There were 31 Republican governors, up from 17 when Bliss took over the national chairmanship. In the Senate, the Republicans had 43 seats, a gain of 11. The size of their minority in the House went from 140 to 192.

Bliss, who believes that a party must build from the bottom up, had not neglected the statehouses, city halls and county courthouses.

When he took the national chairmanship, Republicans controlled seven state legislatures. When he left, they were in charge of 20. Under his leadership, Republicans added 97 mayors—conservatives such as John S. Ballard in Akron and moderates such as John Lindsay in New York. The GOP also added 1,420 county officeholders.

Bliss didn't achieve that kind of success just by making pep talks and buying free beer—although he did both. First, there was his devotion to the job. If you don't like dawn-to-dark politics, you would have had little in common with the pre-1969 Bliss.

(More about the post-1969 Bliss later. He returned to Akron that year to gradually "retire" from politics and devote his energy to his insurance business, Tower Agencies Inc., in the First National Tower.)

(He has *almost* retired from politics, but still sits on the Summit County Republican executive committee and seldom turns down requests for advice from Alex Arshinkoff, the Bliss protégé who now chairs the county GOP executive committee.)

Bliss' friends are short on anecdotes. If you really dig into his past, however, you'll discover that he had one deviation from the grind of running the Republican Party. Bliss liked popcorn.

Former Dayton Congressman Charles Whalen, who was in Washington during Bliss' tenure as national chairman, remembers:

"He had a limousine with a phone in it. When he'd leave headquarters, he'd call his wife and say, 'I'm leaving, get the popcorn ready.'"

As anecdotes go, popcorn after midnight will not make as many headlines as swims in the Tidal Basin or hiring pretty secretaries who can't type.

"He's not the type of person you remember anecdotes about," says Rep. Rhodes. "He doesn't make mistakes. Anecdotes are made of mistakes."

Bliss can distantly remember having hobbies.

"I did play some golf in the 1930s," he recalls. He gave up the game, he says, after taking over as chairman of the county party's central committee in 1941.

He once grew roses.

"I quit that because the beetles beat me to them," he remembers.

Arshinkoff, whose respect for Bliss amounts to hero worship, doesn't think it makes much sense to talk about Bliss' hobbies.

"Ray Bliss' hobby is electing Republican candidates," says Arshinkoff, adding that he's not worthy of being mentioned in the same story with Bliss.

Politics *was* a full-time job for Bliss, but it is the way he pursued that job that produced revolutionary changes in the way candidates are elected.

"Ray was one of the first people to use public opinion polls for guidance," says Democrat Cook, who also is an associate professor of political science at The University of Akron.

"He was doing that (polling) when most of the party chairmen were concerned about who was going to get on the patronage payroll at City Hall."

Bliss did not just experiment with polls and voter surveys; he used them to win elections.

In 1949, for example, he surveyed Republican voters and found that in the state's principally rural areas, 140,000 of them had not bothered to vote in 1948. His survey also showed that at least 150,000 potential Republicans in industrial areas weren't even registered.

By 1950, enough Republicans registered and voted to achieve the statewide comeback Bliss engineered.

Bliss also helped pioneer the use of television in political campaigns nationally.

He got curious about the new medium in the fall of 1949 while taking a train from New York to Philadelphia for an Army-Navy football game. The train went past rows of apartment houses where large numbers of working-class and middle-class voters lived.

"I'm looking out the window and I'm seeing all these aerials, one after another," Bliss recalls.

It dawned on Bliss that television might be a key tool to use in Sen. Robert Taft Sr.'s re-election campaign. That getting Taft on television would get him before a large number of voters was confirmed by a check with bartenders in Akron.

Surveying bartenders was one of the nonscientific techniques Bliss employed. Bartenders are listeners, Bliss says, and by visiting bars in different neighborhoods, he got a pretty good idea of what a cross-section of voters were thinking.

Bliss' bartenders—and unsuspecting field workers—told him people were crowding into the taverns to watch television—whatever was on the tube.

"The beer joints were filled to the gills," Bliss recalls.

It took a little persuasion, but Bliss eventually convinced Taft's handlers that the new medium was what their man needed to get his message across.

Bliss, a confessed perfectionist, did not leave things solely up to the camera. He used a *Meet the Press* format for the Taft television presentations.

He found that Taft, who along with former President Dwight D. Eisenhower was one of Bliss' favorite officeholders, did better if he was challenged by one of the reporters.

"I'd always try to get to one reporter and ask him to get Taft angry," Bliss chuckles.

Taft, of course, won the election, defeating labor-supported Joseph T. Ferguson by 430,000 votes.

Taft was a conservative, as is Bliss.

"I believe those who hold public office ought to be more responsible in spending our public money than we are with our own money," says Bliss. "I'm a fiscal conservative. I've always been that way. I'll die that way."

———

Another key to his success, however, was that he never insisted that other Republicans pass tests of ideological purity.

"Ray's 'secret' was the confidence all Republicans had in his professionalism and his lack of partisanship within the Republican family," says former President Ford, "In other words, he was respected as a tactician who had the confidence of the Goldwater, Rockefeller and all other elements in the Republican Party.

"We knew he was dedicated to Republican principles and the GOP victory."

Bliss was pragmatic, but he also believed in inclusiveness.

"We should be tolerant of the deeply held convictions of others," says Bliss.

This meant that he welcomed candidates like Lindsay, whom he recruited to run for mayor of New York, and Whalen, the former Dayton congressman.

Lindsay and Whalen, to Bliss' dismay, are both Democrats today. If he still were in charge, Bliss says, he would have found room for them. He is almost bitter about the treatment given to moderate Republicans.

Whalen, for example, served in Congress for 12 years until quitting in 1978. He was driven out not by the Democrats—who eventually put up only token opposition to him—but by Republicans who constantly criticized his voting record.

Bliss says it is foolish for Republicans to think the same sort of candidate can be elected from big cities as can win in rural areas. The constituencies are different and have different needs, he says.

Lindsay and Whalen do not say much nice about the Republican Party, but they have only praise for Bliss.

"He was a man who believed deeply in inclusiveness…making room for moderates," says Lindsay, now a lawyer in private practice in New York. "Ray was a real giant in the world of professional politics."

———————

Bliss genuinely enjoyed Lindsay, Whalen and other moderate Republicans, but there was a pragmatic reason for his emphasis on inclusiveness.

"He recognized an important fact," says Rep. Rhodes. "You have to build your party with some diversity. You can't have a monolithic structure. You don't win."

Bliss knew, Rhodes says, that it was better to have a "moderate" like Whalen in the House than any kind of Democrat. On organizational votes, Bliss could count on Whalen and, if the Republicans ever had achieved a House majority, Whalen's vote would have helped elect a Republican speaker.

Bliss is bothered a little by constant references to his pragmatism, his reputation as the party's quintessential "nuts and bolts" man.

"I was probably as interested in the issues as any chairman," he declares. He proved it.

When he went to Washington, he used the Republican Coordinating Committee, which met quarterly, to research complicated issues ranging from human rights to crime and delinquency.

Members of the committee included Eisenhower, Nixon, the Republican congressional leadership and two or three governors.

———————

Bliss, of course, could have used public opinion polls, bartender surveys, television and coordinating committees and still not have lasted. He also used an older, but often unused technique: He told the truth.

"Just remember one thing about politics," Bliss says. "The only thing you have in politics is your word. When your word is not good, you've lost what bargaining power you have.

"I've never broken my word in my life, intentionally."

Democratic state Sen. Oliver Ocasek, former president of the Ohio Senate and dean of the Summit County delegation to the state legislature, testifies to Bliss' integrity.

In 1958, Ocasek was running for the state Senate against eight-year Republican incumbent Fred Danner. Bliss was on the county board of elections.

Unofficial returns showed Ocasek a loser by about 1,400 votes. Ocasek noticed, however, that in Cuyahoga Falls there were more votes for Danner and Ocasek than the total vote cast.

Ocasek called the Democrats on the elections board but says they weren't especially interested. He persisted, however, and a recount showed that through a tabulating error Danner had been credited with about 2,000 more votes in Cuyahoga Falls than he actually received. Ocasek was the winner.

"I have always given Ray Bliss a large part of the credit for looking into that matter and correcting it," Ocasek says. "He's a Republican, but that doesn't interfere with his sense of justice and fair play."

Reminded of Ocasek's 1958 victory, Bliss wants to make one thing clear: He was rooting for Danner. He seems surprised, however, that anyone would think it unusual that someone would do the honest thing, even if it meant helping a Democrat.

This is the sort of understated approach Bliss takes to his achievements. There are no plaques on the wall in his tastefully furnished office reciting his achievements and no pictures showing him rubbing shoulders with great and would-be-great Republicans.

A display of miniature elephants in one corner of the room is the only hint of his partisan preference.

"If I have to put up pictures to convince people of my record and my career," Bliss says, "I'm not interested."

Bliss is not a gregarious backslapper. At first, he seems a bit gruff, but that may be due more to shyness than hostility. He doesn't have a good speaking voice, although he is articulate.

Bliss insists on being himself. He's seen reporters come and go, and he says he's interested in neither a "hatchet job" nor a "pump up." At his age, Bliss says, he needs neither.

Bliss hasn't earned the respect of both Democrats and Republicans by meekness, but he's governed by good manners. Salty language is limited to a few mild expletives when the conversation gets heated.

Also, while Bliss does not delight in revenge, he remembers, which is important in politics. In 1978, for example, he was backing Arshinkoff for county executive committee chairman. Ballard, the former mayor, and former county commissioner Richard Slusser were not.

In the heat of battle, Ballard and Slusser charged that they hadn't received financial help from the party in the past.

"One present officeholder (Ballard still was mayor) and one former officeholder have said the party organization provided them with no money," Bliss said without naming names. "They got thousands of dollars. I want to set the record straight. These careless statements make it difficult to build a party."

These days, he cultivates the image of a successful businessman, which he is. His black shoes are brightly shined and the gray slacks, blue coat, white shirt and dark striped tie help him fit in easily with the bankers, lawyers and corporate leaders at the Portage Country Club, where Bliss likes to lunch.

Such success was hardly assured when Bliss broke into politics in 1931, after being thrown out of The University of Akron in his senior year.

He had gone to college intending to become a lawyer. Bliss graduated from the old South High School in 1927 and said he was "up in my grades." He also attended Miller, Margaret Park and Firestone Park grade schools.

It did not take Bliss long to find something on campus that interested him more than textbooks. Through membership in Sigma Beta Nu, then a local fraternity and now a national affiliate of Phi Kappa Tau, Bliss discovered campus politics.

In those days, campus fraternities and sororities were organized into political combines. The combine to which Bliss' fraternity belonged was not the big power on campus, but Bliss changed that.

He became, according to one newspaper account, the "political czar of the campus."

It was during those years on campus that Bliss developed many of the habits that served him well later. He began working long hours and paying attention to every detail of campus elections and fraternity life.

"I was a perfectionist," Bliss recalls. "I tried to make sure our (fraternity) rush was the best. I don't believe you should get involved in something unless you're going to do a top-flight job."

In a recent article for his fraternity magazine, Bliss described how he made the fraternity and the political combine campus powers.

Bliss and his colleagues kept track of who voted and who didn't. Those who didn't vote were fined.

Appearances weren't ignored. Pledges were required to have tuxedos for campus formals, and they had to know how to dance. Arrangements were made for sorority women to give them lessons at the old East Market Gardens.

Bliss, clearly, did not take the *Animal House* approach to fraternity life.

"It provided me with constructive leadership that served me well in later life," Bliss said in the magazine article. "I've said to people since, campus politics was much faster than downtown politics."

Despite all the good things that happened to Bliss as the result of his involvement in fraternity activities, it also led to his temporary downfall and probably the only blemish on his political record.

He was expelled from the university for allegedly stuffing the ballot box in the May Queen election.

Also disciplined in the incident was Ellen Frances Palmer—she became Mrs. Ray Bliss in 1959—one of the May Queen contestants, who insisted that Bliss was not guilty of the offense, according to a 1931 Beacon Journal story.

The future Mrs. Bliss was given eight credit hours of additional work as a penalty but was able to graduate on time because she already had completed nine extra credit hours of work.

There were reports that ballot box stuffing was not unknown at the
university during Bliss' campus career.

"I was head of the combine," Bliss says. "I took full responsibility for
what happened."

While Bliss is still uncomfortable about discussing the incident, he
clearly doesn't hold a grudge against The University of Akron.

In addition to serving on the university's board of trustees, Bliss and
his wife have established a scholarship in their names to provide $400 a
year to four political science majors.

"What we look for are young people who have a potential interest in
party organizational politics, not in people who are interested in theoretical politics," says Bliss.

———————

Bliss, of course, needed no scholarship to get his start in practical politics.
Shortly after leaving the university in 1931, Bliss showed up at Republican
Party headquarters.

He met James A. Corey, the party boss, whose relationship with Bliss
was not unlike the relationship Arshinkoff has with Bliss today.

A former Beacon Journal reporter wrote that Bliss and Corey became
a "father-son political team."

(Bliss' own father died in an explosion during construction of the
State Office Building in Columbus in 1932. His mother died in 1956.)

"Jim Corey had a natural instinct for politics," says Bliss. "He took
me under his wing."

Corey kept Bliss busy. The party's new operative organized a county
Young Men's Republican Club and then a separate club for young women
Republicans.

"The ERA (supporters) wouldn't have liked that," Bliss chuckles.

Soon Bliss was in the thick of mayoral and gubernatorial campaigns.
Corey died in 1941, and in 1942 Bliss succeeded him as chairman of the
county party's central committee.

———————

His reputation began to grow around the state as he developed the techniques that later would help him succeed in Columbus and Washington.

Bliss made it his policy to always associate himself with the party, never too closely with individual candidates.

"I got into politics because I believe in two strong parties," says Bliss. "I believe that the two-party system provides us the best government. When you're dedicated to that system, you can't say 'you're my candidate' to the exclusion of everyone else."

It also meant Bliss didn't have to spend lots of time soothing the egos of thin-skinned politicians to whom he was beholden. Instead, he could concentrate on developing the grassroots support needed to help the whole Republican ticket.

"No one person does these things alone," Bliss says. "They're really 'we' things. I want to make that clear."

Motivating party volunteers from the precinct level on up cannot be overemphasized, Bliss says.

"If you don't produce in a corporation, you know what happens," says Bliss. "If a volunteer doesn't produce, you just have to go out and recruit additional volunteers."

Bliss at first resisted invitations to share his techniques with the rest of Ohio Republicans by taking over as state chairman. The disastrous 1948 election results, however, made it impossible for him to say no and in 1949, he went to Columbus.

This gave Bliss a larger stage on which to display his skill. Although Bliss became very close to Ohio Sen. Taft and backed him for the 1952 GOP presidential nomination, he eventually came to the attention of Dwight D. Eisenhower, the man who defeated Taft for the 1952 nomination and went on to become president.

Bliss' penchant for organization helped win Eisenhower's respect and friendship. Eisenhower made his first campaign trip to Ohio after being confronted with swarming admirers everywhere he stopped in the previous state.

Bliss gave orders that when the campaign got to Ohio, no one was to leave his or her place. At train stops, only persons assigned to the platform were permitted there.

Bliss is reluctant to rank the politicians with whom he's associated but allows that Taft and Eisenhower are at the top of the list.

"I have a very, very high regard for former President Eisenhower," Bliss says.

––––––––––––

Just as Bliss' success in Summit County attracted attention across Ohio, his success at the state level brought feelers from Republican leaders who wanted him to go to Washington.

Again, Bliss resisted, until Goldwater's disastrous defeat in 1964 made it impossible for him to refuse.

Rep. Rhodes remembers the relief of party leaders when Bliss became national chairman.

"He had everybody's confidence," Rhodes says. "The whole party felt the best qualified man to be chairman was Ray Bliss."

Rhodes soon found out that under Bliss all points of view would be heard. His seat on the Republican Coordinating Committee was right between Richard M. Nixon and the late Nelson Rockefeller, two men who often disagreed.

"That was interesting," says the low-key Rhodes.

Bliss' work resulted in major gains for the party, but it also put Nixon in the White House. In an interview last year, Bliss admitted his reservations about Nixon:

"When I went home at 10 a.m. the day after the (1968) election, my wife congratulated me after I told her Nixon had won. I looked at her and said, 'I don't know whether I've done the country a service or disservice.'"

Nixon made it known that he wanted his own man as national chairman, and Bliss resigned, to the regret of many Republicans.

"If Richard Nixon had kept Ray Bliss, there never would have been a Watergate," says Rep. Regula. "He would have blown the whistle the first day."

Watergate was hard for Bliss to take. During his tenure as national chairman, polls showed a gradual revival of interest in the two-party system.

"Then came Watergate and the bottom fell out," Bliss says. "He (Nixon) nearly destroyed the two-party system in this country."

Instead of working through two parties, voters now tend to give their allegiance to special-interest groups which, Bliss says, are not good for the country.

Elected officials guided by two parties with well-defined agendas provide better government that legislators beholden to a variety of special interests, Bliss says.

"I may sound like a soap box speaker, but that's what I believe," says Bliss.

Back in Akron, Bliss seldom gets up on soap boxes. That doesn't mean, his admirers say, that he has given up working for the party or the community.

His contributions to the area often are overlooked because he makes them quietly, says Regula.

"Without Ray Bliss, there never would have been a Cuyahoga Valley National Park," Regula says.

While acknowledging Akron Democratic Congressman John Seiberling as the driving force behind the national park, Regula says it was Bliss who saved the project from a veto by Gerald Ford when Ford was president.

Rogers C.B. Morton, Ford's interior secretary, had advised the president to veto a major park bill, Regula says. Bliss sent Ford a message, asking the president to give the park consideration.

There was no veto.

Ford says he doesn't remember the specific incident but adds:

"If he did (send a message), I certainly considered Ray's views in deciding whether to veto or not."

Bliss does not take credit for saving the park, but it is clear that he still enjoys the contacts he made over 50 years. Hardly a major Republican politician comes to town without visiting Bliss. Often, a visit with Bliss is the reason they are here.

His pace has slacked off a bit from the seven-day weeks he worked in Columbus and Washington. He goes to work about 8 or 9 each morning and usually goes home by 6. He no longer works Sundays but often spends time at his insurance office on Saturdays.

After a heart attack in 1976, Bliss gave up cigarettes and has cut down on the beer he once enjoyed.

He has been easing out of politics for the last 12 years, but he had much further to ease than most people.

Last year Bliss stepped down from membership on the Republican National Committee after 28 years. Beacon Journal political writer Brian Usher wrote that Republican leader Ray C. Bliss had become "Citizen Bliss."

Bliss likes the title.

"I reserve the right to support anybody I please," says Citizen Bliss. "I may not do anything. I don't know."

The Democrats can only hope.*

---

*   Bliss died in 1981 at 73, shortly after this profile was published.

Eddie Davis: Still Eddie After All These Years

The coal miner's son learned a smoother style,
but the song remains the same

Akron Beacon Journal Beacon Magazine, February 8, 1981
WILLIAM HERSHEY

Tim Davis—no relation to the hero of this story—recalls an occasion a few years ago when Eddie Davis had a role in a play at The University of Akron.

"It was the perfect character for him," says Tim, who is Summit County's elections director.

"Eddie played an aging steel mill worker, trying to hold his family together with pride and dignity. He put his hands in his pocket and threw back his head, just like he does when he's bemoaning the decline of liberal politics."

The sagging jowls, the slight limp and the pleading voice created exactly the effect Davis wanted—just as they had for years in the paneled chambers of Akron City Council.

"Shoot," said Eddie when Tim congratulated him on his performance. "I been doing this all my life."

Eddie Davis, 63, has been performing in Akron since 1939—and in those 41 years he's played many parts. He became the city's first Black councilman in 1957—and the only one until James R. Williams was elected in 1969.

He served six years as council president, and for longer periods as a labor leader, civil rights champion, peace activist, Democratic party loyalist, Americans for Democratic Action officer, smooth political operator and incurable tennis nut.

Early in his career, Davis acquired a reputation in local political circles as an unwelcome liberal agitator; he admits now that on some occasions he talked too loudly and cooperated too little.

But by 1977, he'd become a sufficiently acceptable landmark to have a community center named after him in Perkins Park.

Davis never changed his liberal stripes, however; he simply tempered his style. And if other politicians now talk about Davis as if they were throwing a testimonial dinner, note that he gets equal praise from people who wouldn't be caught dead at the same table.

"Eddie Davis always emphasized the overall interest of the city," says Councilman Ray Kapper, a Democrat-at-large who succeeded Davis as council president in 1976. "Eddie's word was good. If he told you one day he was going to support something, he didn't change the next day."

"He's like a father to me in many ways," says former Democratic councilman and independent mayoral candidate Reggie Brooks, who didn't have a father-son relationship with Kapper. "You can always count on him giving you good advice."

"The important thing is that Ed somehow had an instinct for leadership," says former Democratic councilwoman Elsie Reaven, who was on Brooks' side and not Kapper's during intra-council spats of the late 1970s. "He was a strong leader, and at the same time he involved everybody. He was never rude."

"He always treated me as an equal," says former councilman Harold Neiman, the council's only Republican during part of Davis' tenure as council president.

"He's done so much for the community, generally without recognition," says former councilman Jim Winter, now a judge in Akron

Municipal Court. "He was an expert in his field. His field was helping people."

But don't think this is Eddie Davis' political obituary. He may be old enough to consider retirement from the council clerk's job he's held since stepping down as council president, but Davis says he's made no decision about his future. Even from a rocking chair or a tennis court, he'll probably find a way to get his messages out.

There were a few who prematurely counted Davis out of politics when he left his Third Ward council seat and the council presidency to take the clerk's job.

"It certainly doesn't deprive me of my citizenship," Davis said then of the Civil Service status that goes with being clerk. "There's nothing to stop me from seeing a guy and telling him my position."

Which, of course, he does. How many guys he's seen, and what he's told them, only Davis knows. Until last fall, most of his seeing and talking was behind the scenes.

Then along came State Issue Two, the controversial proposal to reform Ohio taxes, and Davis couldn't resist getting publicly involved.

"It's morally wrong to tax those who have the least ability to pay," says Davis, who felt Issue Two would have made positive changes for working men and women.

Those were the people Davis was trying to help in 1959, when he proposed a 10-member committee to investigate unemployment in Akron. That was 21 years ago, before layoffs and plant closings had become a chronic illness in the Midwest and the Northeast.

Davis wanted to know what effect automation would have on office and factory workers. He wanted to know what new employment prospects might develop for Akron workers, and what could be done to retrain them.

"He really was a visionary in being able to see what was happening to the community's economy," says Tim Davis.

Eddie Davis' proposal to form the study committee was killed two months after he introduced it. And Issue Two went down to a resounding defeat, its proponents outspent by big business and criticized in newspaper editorials as well-meaning but misguided.

"It was a good issue," says Davis, who minimizes his own role in the local campaign by simply saying, "I talked to people. I did a couple of radio shows."

In fact, he was co-chairman of Summit County's "Yes on Two" committee. The cagey veteran had found a new way to get his ideas across to Akron voters. As a civil servant he was prohibited from actively campaigning for candidates, but there were no rules stopping him from stumping for issues.

"He doesn't give the appearance of being that smart," says Akron lawyer Joseph Wheeler, a member of city council when Davis was elected in 1957. "He gives the appearance of having the 'slows.' But don't you believe that. He was as bright a guy as ever served on the council."

If much of the community hasn't caught on to Davis' disarmingly slow—and yet sincere—style, Wheeler has.

Davis recently appeared before the Civil Service Commission to criticize the annual peer evaluation used to determine pay raises for top city managers.

"Maybe you understand it, but I don't understand it," said a perplexed Davis, shuffling papers and looking forlornly through his glasses. "Sometimes I'm a little slow."

Wheeler, a member of the commission, replied: "No you aren't, Mr. Davis. You just want people to believe that."

"When I can't have fun in this job," Davis said later, "I'll quit."

———————

In 1939, Davis wasn't having much fun contemplating a future that appeared pretty limited. Born in Birmingham, Ala., he'd moved north to Pennsylvania with his parents when he was five.

His father, Isiah, now 89, went to work in the coal mines about 40 miles east of Pittsburgh. Although they didn't know it, said Davis, his father and other Black men who were brought north to work in the coal mines were being used by mine operators to try to break the unions.

"They told them they had a job for them up North—the 'land of freedom,'" Davis says with an uncharacteristic touch of sarcasm.

———————

Two things happened in the early years that affected Davis' image: He changed his name—sort of—and got his limp. Named Eddie—not Edward—by his parents, Davis was a sophomore in high school when a teacher declared, "We'll have no nicknames in this classroom."

"I just assumed she was talking about me," Davis remembers. "So I just wrote on my paper 'Edward Davis' and I've been using it ever since." He appeared on ballots as "Edward" but remained "Eddie" to his friends.

The limp developed after Davis took a shortcut home from a baseball game, fell and landed on uneven ground.

"I twisted my ankle, and I didn't have the money or means of getting it taken care of," he says matter-of-factly.

After graduation from high school in 1934, Davis worked in the mines for a few years, took some "open-air excursions" on freight trains and ended up in Akron.

"I didn't like coal mine work," he says of his decision to leave home. "I didn't see much of a future."

Davis' role in Akron was modest at first: He washed cars for 50 cents a day and was innocent of any political opinions when he reached voting age.

Even then, of course, there was more to Davis than anybody who was waiting for a car to be washed suspected. At night, at Hower Vocational High School, he was learning how to read a blueprint and do machine shop work.

After two years of washing cars and studying in night school, he took a job in—of all places—Cuyahoga Falls, a community still burdened with the nickname "Caucasian Falls."

He did construction work and then became the first Black employee in a machine shop, where he made parts for tanks and guns.

His dry verdict on his co-workers: "They weren't very helpful to me."

What upset them most, he adds, was the hiring of a second Black employee: Two white employees made good on their promise to quit if a second Black person was hired.

Davis didn't exactly jump into the mainstream of Cuyahoga Falls social and business life. "I'd get out of the bus, right into the plant," he remembers. He brought his lunch in a paper bag and "didn't really have to patronize any businesses at all."

Davis didn't really accept those conditions; he simply bided his time. "You have to pick your time and place," he says. And through his job, he was moving toward that time and place.

At the machine shop and in later jobs, he got involved in union activity. Eventually he became president of a small United Auto Workers local, at about the time the late Walter Reuther was making a name for himself as a UAW leader.

On the job and outside the shop, Davis began to understand the problems Reuther was talking about. He says Reuther and Dr. Martin Luther King Jr. were the two men who most influenced his development as a political and community leader.

Until he better understood Reuther's emphasis on research and sophisticated bargaining techniques, Davis says he used old-fashioned negotiating:

"You'd talk loud, and you'd talk hard, you'd pound your fist and try to get another half cent out of management."

The interest Davis developed in minority rights and better wages led him toward local and national politics. When an Akron chapter of Americans for Democratic Action formed about 1950, Davis was quick to join.

"We wanted to find a place for liberals who weren't Communists," he says. As one of a few Black labor leaders with connections to liberal politics, Davis frequently was asked to meetings of Communist-leaning groups.

While he didn't disagree with some of their goals—such outlandish ideas as racially integrated public housing—his admiration for Reuther and others, like the late Hubert H. Humphrey, kept him in mainstream politics.

By 1953, local ADA members decided Davis should run for city council. He disagreed. In 1955 they tried again, and Davis still said "no."

But in 1957 he changed his mind. He upset the late Ed Flowers in the Third Ward Democratic primary and went on to win the general election.

Retired Akron lawyer Nicholas Syracopoulos, along with Elsie Reaven and her husband Sidney, were among local ADA members who campaigned for Davis.

"There was really a certain ineptness, as compared to his present style," says Syracopoulos. "Not only in public speaking, but in dealing with people, Eddie would be brusque."

Mrs. Reaven says winning the election wasn't easy: "It was sort of a bolt of lightning that Ed was put on council," says Mrs. Reaven, who now lives in San Francisco with her husband. "It was a very unfavorable climate for Blacks. He was a pioneer."

So Davis won the general election and became the city's first Black councilman. Then what?

"He didn't know how to get things done," Joe Wheeler recalls. "He came in there with a little chip on his shoulder. He came in there with the burden of being a spokesman for all the Blacks."

Davis doesn't complain about that burden, but he concedes he was ineffective at first—partly because the fist-pounding approach he'd used to bargain with hard-nosed factory managers didn't suit his new situation.

"When I started here at City Hall," he says, "you didn't need to come down to hear me. You could hear me from the Beacon Journal."

Other council members weren't hostile, Davis says, but some coolness was evident.

Monthly card parties among council members and their wives were "suddenly stopped" when Davis and his wife Glendalyn came on the scene.

———

As Davis began to notice that other council members weren't paying much attention to his ideas, he also began to realize that Walter Reuther and Martin Luther King Jr. were shouting less and thinking more.

While Davis says it took two or perhaps even four years to change his approach, Wheeler says it didn't take that long.

"Six months, nine months to a year," estimates Wheeler.

Davis didn't stop talking about the issues that mattered to him— integrated public housing, publicly owned mass transportation, better parks and playgrounds. He just quit "shooting from the hip," Wheeler says, and "developed facts and figures" instead.

"Eddie hasn't changed his politics," says Wheeler. "He's still the flaming liberal he always was." Davis, who calls Wheeler "extremely conservative," doesn't disagree with the analysis: "Joe understands me a lot better than a lot of people," Davis says.

(It was typical of Davis' early period, Jim Winter recalls, to suggest that the city pay people to use the local bus system. If people were *given* a dime when they climbed aboard instead of being charged, Davis cheerfully reasoned, there would be more people on the buses.)

Syracopoulos was disappointed with some of the accommodations Davis had to make but says he accepts that they were necessary.

"There was never a sense of betrayal," says Syracopoulos. "There was an understanding of the necessities of the situation. Once you function in the political arena, you can't function alone, or you're frozen out."

"I should have realized," Davis adds, "it took seven votes to get something through council, plus a mayor's signature."

He also began to understand that even when he lost—as he did on the employment study committee and Issue Two—he was at least putting his ideas before the people.

His early suggestion that the city buy out the privately owned and notoriously unreliable Akron Transportation Co. didn't go over at the time, but it helped lay the groundwork for the idea of publicly owned mass transit.

And while Davis took some lumps on the floor of council, his reputation was growing among Black people.

Cazzell Smith Sr., now president of the Akron NAACP and executive director of the East Akron Community House, was Davis' Beacon Journal carrier during some of the early years.

"People would come to his house at all times of night looking for help," Smith says. "Anything that he got passed in council, he had to work his tail off for."

"He was someone who, as a youngster, you really wanted to be like," says Smith. "He was one of my heroes." And besides, he adds, Davis "tipped pretty good at Christmas."

Reggie Brooks, also growing up during Davis' early years on the council, says "He was heaven-sent. I was relieved to have a person of his social consciousness on the scene."

One person who would have preferred that Davis spend less time on the political scene and more on the home scene was his wife Glendalyn.

She'd grown up in the same region of Pennsylvania, meeting Davis through her brother. They were married in 1941.

It seemed to Mrs. Davis that Eddie never had enough time for her, nor for their sons—Keith, 26 and now married, and Robert, 19, who lives at home.

Mrs. Davis said their younger son once told his father that "maybe someday his daddy would have time for his son." But politically, she says, "It seemed he helped everybody on every issue he could."

Politics wasn't the only thing that kept Davis out of the house. There was tennis.

How did the son of a Black coal miner get hooked on tennis—then, even more than now, the province of the wealthy and white?

About the time he came to Akron, Black people began to move into the neighborhoods around Perkins Woods, well furnished with tennis courts. Davis was among those moving in.

"A large number of Blacks were unemployed, and they didn't have anything else to do, so they started playing tennis," Davis remembers.

He played too much to suit his wife, who says he would leave the house—ostensibly on more serious missions—and then grab the tennis racket he'd sneaked out a basement window.

Davis says he resorted to subterfuge because his wife and son Keith would cry when he left home for the courts. "Sure, I felt guilty," he says, "but I didn't want to hear the noise from the boy and her."

Syracopoulos, who still plays with Davis, says Eddie plays tennis the same way he plays politics: "He qualifies as a good and cagey player."

It wasn't tennis, of course, that brought Davis to the public's attention. By 1961 he'd turned down the volume of his rhetoric and fine-tuned some of his proposals.

His fight for integrated public housing raised the ire of at least one official—M.P. Lauer, then head of the Akron Metropolitan Housing Authority.

When Davis complained that Black people were denied access to certain of AMHA's buildings, Lauer branded Davis a "troublemaker."

"He wants colored people anyplace, and that isn't going to work," Lauer fumed. "We can take care of this situation if he keeps his nose out of it."

But it did work, at least eventually, and Davis was one of the reasons it succeeded, along with other local efforts at integration. The evaluation comes from Robert Blakemore, the Akron lawyer who's a former Democratic Party chairman in Summit County.

"I think most white people, once they met Eddie, recognized that he wasn't somebody to be feared—he was not a threat to their security," Blakemore says.

While Davis' manner made people feel comfortable, he didn't discourage protest.

During one of his crusades for more public swimming pools, a group of youngsters showed up in council chambers and started leading cheers of, "We want swimming pools."

Had Davis asked them to come?

"I didn't discourage them," he replies.

The softer voice and smoother delivery didn't mean his tongue was less sharp, either. He was particularly critical of the city's urban renewal programs.

He says now that he asked "the impossible" when he suggested that people who were forced to sell their homes in renewal areas should receive a big enough settlement to build a new house.

Not wanting the relocation of families to continue segregated housing patterns, he voted "no" on much legislation to acquire property, even if his was the only "no" vote.

"I think it got us somewhere," he says, adding that much unnecessary resegregation still occurred. Akron planning director James A. Alkire says Davis' efforts helped.

"His criticism caused the city of Akron to undertake some unique programs that eventually were accepted around the country," says Alkire. "I did feel the sting of his tongue."

As Davis' popularity grew, there were occasional suggestions that he run for a citywide council seat or even for mayor. In 1968 he ran in the primary for Summit County Commissioner, won a spot on the general election ballot, but finished third in a race for two seats.

Some thought he made the race as a favor to Blakemore and other Democrats who wanted him to defeat Democrat John Poda in the primary—a task Davis accomplished.

That's wrong, says Blakemore, at least from his perspective.

"The one criticism I had of him is that he didn't work the county (outside Akron)," says Blakemore. "They would have found out he's a sensible fellow who understands government. I wouldn't have asked him to run in the first place if I hadn't thought he could have won."

Nevertheless, Blakemore says, Davis was a "victim of time and circumstance."

"If he were a young man today, I don't know what his limits would be," Blakemore says.

Davis, adds Blakemore, "would have made a hell of a good mayor, but I don't think he could have been elected."

Such talk is academic, says Davis: He never wanted to be mayor. "It's pretty hard to go after a position when you don't want it," he says.

He doesn't like to be pressed about how he thinks he would have done had he made such a race.

For 20 years, he complains good naturedly, reporters have asked him one particular question: "Are there any rednecks in Akron?"

He doesn't answer. You're left with the assumption that there might indeed be a few, but Davis likes it here anyway.

"Even though we face adversities," he says, "and even though poor and lower-paid Black people have some difficult times, I think we will arrive at the day when we can get the type of total leadership in this community that will address all the problems we face and help convince the total community of what is morally right."

The same year he ran for the County Commissioner's seat, Davis performed the feat that gave him citywide recognition, if not citywide office.

As chairman of the council's Finance Committee, he led the effort to line up council support to give permanent status to Akron's 1% income tax, which had started as a 6-year tax.

Peter G. DeAngelis, an insurance agent who then was Ward Two councilman, was the last Democrat to hold out against the tax. There was no Sunshine Law in those days, and Davis went to work on DeAngelis in the Democrats' private caucus.

DeAngelis recalls: "Eddie told me, 'You're a stubborn son of a gun. I'm not letting you out of the room until you agree.' We were there all night. He just tried to tell me in the long run it was for the good of the city."

DeAngelis gave in.

The income tax wasn't the only issue that put Davis on the spot in 1968. There were racial disturbances along Wooster Avenue that stopped just short of full-fledged rioting.

While calling for calm, Davis maintained his credibility.

"He fully understood the frustration and rage people were feeling," says Reggie Brooks. And Davis didn't want those who were feeling the frustration to get themselves killed, Brooks says.

The 1968 disturbances also brought out Davis' practical side. When he attended a session of Mayor John Ballard's cabinet to discuss a community meeting at South High School, the plan was to put Davis and other officials at tables on a stage.

"There's no way you're going to get me up there," one person at the meeting recalls Davis saying. "We'd make too good a target."

The tables were placed on the floor.

A year later, veteran council president Ralph Turner announced that he wouldn't seek re-election.

———————

Davis, who was next to Turner in seniority, appeared to be the likely successor—except that council members decided they would no longer choose their leader solely on seniority.

Davis, who'd opposed the congressional seniority rule, which automatically gave key committee assignments to segregationist Southerners, supported the local change in rules. And he still won the presidency.

"We told him our reason was to get him of the floor of council so he couldn't speak on every issue" jokes Winter. "In truth, it was because he was the best qualified leader in council."

Also in 1969, James Williams was elected in Ward Four, becoming the second Black council member.

Davis no longer was "the Black councilman." He still tended to ward business and had time for social issues, but he also began to assert himself as a citywide leader.

"There were certain people who didn't respect him as president because he was Black," said Kapper bluntly. "Eddie knew this but that didn't change how he treated them. I've never seen him malicious with anybody."

Davis had not become a defender of the status quo, as he demonstrated with his outspoken local opposition to the Vietnam War.

Tim Davis, who opposed the war after serving in Vietnam as an Army officer and returning home wounded, says Davis and U.S. Rep. John Seiberling legitimized local antiwar efforts.

"It was their participation that kept us from getting our heads bashed," Tim Davis says.

Eddie Davis' opposition to the war wasn't confined to peace marches; it was also brought to the floor of city council to the displeasure of some members.

He introduced a resolution in 1970 calling for an end to the war, but that failed. Showing that he had learned a few political tricks, Davis tried again in 1972 by attaching a plea for an end to the fighting to the traditional Memorial Day resolution mourning the loss of servicemen killed in battle.

The resolution passed.

While Davis occasionally took advantage of his leadership position to press for special projects, Williams says some people considered it a weakness that David didn't do more to challenge Republican Ballard and expose the mayor's weaknesses.

"Ed was the leader of the council, but he always placed the interests of the city ahead of politics," says Williams, who now is the U.S. Attorney for the Northern District of Ohio. "I think he did the right thing."

In retrospect, Davis wishes he'd pushed harder for the economic study in 1959 and against the recycle energy plant in the early 1970s. But he says he has few other regrets.

He predicted the recycle plant would cost much more than the $18.5 million price tag its backers originally estimated, and he questioned whether it would work.

(It appears now that the plant will work after some design changes are carried out, but the final price tag—including some operating deficits that weren't expected—will be about $66 million.)

"Maybe we should have listened," says Winter.

While fighting for civil rights, world peace and more tennis courts kept Davis busy in town, he maintained his contacts with national liberal leaders such as Humphrey. For more than a dozen years, until stepping down in 1980, he was national secretary of ADA.

Davis maintains a lifestyle inconsistent with the usual image of political wheeler-dealers. He doesn't drink or smoke and serves as a trustee of the Wesley Temple AME Zion Church.

He admittedly has a sweet tooth, but a sugar problem has helped him keep his weight down to about 190, much less than the almost 250 pounds he once packed onto his five-foot-ten frame.

"I tried smoking corn silk when I was in the eighth grade," Davis recalls. "The teacher related that incident to my father. He was highly displeased. He related that to me in a manner that was extremely physically uncomfortable for a few weeks."

As for drinking, "I tasted it a couple of times and despised it."

The Rev. Eugene Morgan, Davis' pastor, says Davis is "very effective" in talking with church members about how social justice relates to being a Christian.

Davis worries that his church has too much of an "establishment" image because its members include such community leaders as Jim Williams, former NAACP legal counsel Edwin Parms, Beacon Journal assistant editor Albert Fitzpatrick, Davis himself, and his pastor, who is also an Akron school board member.

"I'm really sorry we got it," says Davis of the church's reputation. "That makes it unattractive to persons of low income."

So Eddie Davis still is crusading—even to make sure poor people know they're welcome at his church.

He isn't allowed, of course, to get publicly involved in partisan politics. But he seems more than casually interested in hearing that his old friend and occasional tennis partner, U.S. Sen. Howard Metzenbaum, a fellow liberal Democrat, considers himself "an endangered species."

"Tell him he'd better see me quick," says Davis.

Why?

Maybe, Davis says, he can do something for the senator.

Hasn't there always been an Eddie Davis?[*]

---

[*] Davis retired as Clerk of Akron City Council in 1988 and died in 1995 at 78.

John Galbreath: Down on the Farm with John Galbreath

…and his jet planes, his zebras and buffaloes, his racetrack and thoroughbreds. Thank God for the Depression.

Akron Beacon Journal Beacon Magazine, January 24, 1982
WILLIAM HERSHEY

John Wilmer Galbreath pulls his black Cadillac Seville off the paved lane and guides it straight across one of the fields on his 4,300-acre Darby Dan farm just 25 minutes west of downtown Columbus.

The slight detour produces less discomfort than a bounce over an Akron chuckhole. Two visitors from the city remark that the car must be well made to handle terrain usually reserved for Jeeps, pickup trucks and tractors.

"I wouldn't own it if it couldn't," the 84-year-old Galbreath replies matter-of-factly.

Galbreath, multimillionaire real estate developer, major league baseball owner and raiser of thoroughbred horses, has not always had a Cadillac to test on country fields.

But he's always known where he was headed and what he had to do to get there. He'll do the driving himself—no chauffeurs, thank you, except maybe in New York City.

"They just don't fit into my way of life," he says. "I never know when I want to go and come."

He runs his real estate business the same way. It is a sole proprietorship, not a corporation. Galbreath and his 53-year-old son Dan, with help from a small group of trusted associates, make all the multimillion-dollar decisions on projects that span the globe.

"I just wanted to be on my own all the way, sink or swim," says Galbreath, who seldom sinks.

A man who neither smokes nor drinks, and who enjoys a bowl of cornflakes as a nightcap, Galbreath has been up since 7 a.m. as usual. After two business appointments in Columbus before, he's returned to the farm to guide his visitors.

The reason for the off-the-road detour is obvious. The car stops on a hilltop, and the sun, shining brightly through the chill, highlights Big Darby Creek, dammed and widened by Galbreath.

Canada geese gather along the shore. They come each year "until it freezes over," says Galbreath.

"Isn't that a beautiful site?" he asks. "It's nature at its best."

Also visible from the hilltop are the Galbreath residence, tucked into a hillside and nearly obscured by large trees, tennis courts, a swimming pool and part of an 18-hole golf course.

The Ewing spread in television's *Dallas* has nothing on Darby Dan, named after the creek and Galbreath's son. Galbreath, however, is no J.R. or Jock. He is a proud but self-effacing tub-thumper for the free-enterprise system who can put at ease both corporate titans and less successful capitalists who must sweat out monthly mortgage payments.

"He's a regular guy. He's no phony," says E.J. Thomas, retired Goodyear chairman who, with the late John S. Knight, helped bring Galbreath to Akron to develop the Cascade Plaza project. "He can talk to the man on the street. He can talk to the man on Wall Street."

Galbreath is short, almost diminutive at 5-foot-7 and 145 pounds. While he may like to think of himself as a farm boy, there are no hayseeds on the three-piece suits he favors.

His black shoes are always well shined, and his hair is neatly parted just left of center. He looks like the high-powered businessman he is.

Galbreath wasn't born on a Darby Dan-type spread. He was second youngest of six children in a farm family that scratched out a living in rural Mt. Sterling, south of Columbus.

The Galbreaths were poor, but "I don't mean we were starving," he says.

To help out, young Johnnie—as he's still called by his longtime friend John Bricker, former Ohio governor and U.S. senator—ground horseradish and sold it for five cents a glass.

In high school too, Galbreath showed signs of his later enterprise. Imported Italian workers were putting a gas line through the county. They wanted pictures to send home. Galbreath, the schoolboy photographer, obliged for a reasonable price.

At Ohio University in Athens, Galbreath continued his photography sideline and played saxophone at dances to help pay his bills. He also washed dishes and waited tables.

After graduation, he chose real estate over law because "I wanted to go to work" and law school would have taken several more years.

(Bricker says Columbus attorneys should be glad he didn't take up law. "He'd have half the business in town," Bricker says.)

Galbreath started with residential real estate, eventually buying whole towns of "company housing" built by corporations near mines and mills. He resold them to the corporations' employees, making capitalists of the employees and money for himself.

"I think the thing I've gotten more joy from that than anything is the towns and selling the houses," he says. "I could make a speech that would last for an hour on the value of home ownership. Homeowners are the best citizens in the world."

Now, of course, he dramatically reshapes city landscapes with projects such as Akron's Cascade Plaza and Hong Kong's Mei Foo Sun Chuen (the beautiful living) with 13,000 apartments and between 70,000 and 90,000 residents. It is believed to be the world's largest privately financed housing development.

Galbreath is relentless but patient. In the 1930s, as a sidelight to an interest in polo, he bought his first horses. He gradually turned from riding polo ponies to raising thoroughbreds.

In 1963, Chateaugay became the first of two Galbreath winners in the Kentucky Derby. In 1972 Roberto—named for the late Pittsburgh Pirate, Roberto Clemente, Galbreath's favorite baseball player—won the Epsom Derby in England and Galbreath became the only person to win derbies on both sides of the Atlantic.

The victory in England was especially sweet for the always-competitive Galbreath. The English had called him and his entourage "good sports" for entering the race but had not expected a Yankee victory.

Sports Illustrated has called Galbreath "one of the most powerful men in racing," but Galbreath demurs. Because he is a steward for the Jockey Club and chairman of the board of Churchill Downs, "they had to write something," he says.

He helped buy the Pittsburgh Pirates in 1946 and, after several youth movements and false starts, the Pirates won a World Series in 1960, followed by two more in 1971 and 1979.

Despite his achievements in real estate, horse racing and baseball, it's just being at the Darby Dan that gives Galbreath the greatest pleasure.

"He'll be in New York, he'll be in Pittsburgh, wherever he happens to be for the day. If it's 8 o'clock he'll come home for dinner," says Jim Justice, a manager at the farm.

Not that Galbreath has to return to the farm for a place to sleep. Also available are an apartment in New York, two homes in Florida, a condominium in Denver and a lodge in Canada.

He also can stop at the 600-acre farm in Lexington, Ky., where his stallions stand at stud and his foals are born.

The yearlings train at Darby Dan, and that is where their owner best likes to unwind.

Just because he arrives at the farm late at night doesn't mean he'll stay put. After eating, says Justice, Galbreath is likely to take off for a two-hour ride in the well-preserved 1959 Chrysler Imperial convertible that is his pride and joy.

––––––––––––

The farm is something to come home to. The 4,300 acres, set off by 58 miles of four-board white fence, include 46 houses and 28 barns. An outsider might have trouble believing such a place exists, as one of farm manager Justice's daughters found out while she was a student at Ohio State University.

Faced with one of those "what-did-you-do-last-summer" English assignments, she wrote about life at Darby Dan. The teacher gave her a C-minus, saying that he hadn't asked for fiction.

He later apologized, after two of the girl's classmates came for a visit and attested to the truth of her report.

Galbreath started with 110 acres in 1935 and gradually added to the spread as other farmers sold out. Most of the houses are original farmhouses.

The farm probably is best known for the thoroughbred yearlings that are trained there. After a thorough education, they're tested on the farm's mile-and-one-eighth track, which comes complete with a starting gate.

But the 50 year-round employees, whose number doubles in the summer, have much more to attend to. There are 260 wild animals, from African zebras to American buffaloes, in three large pens. There also is a hangar and runway for the three Galbreath jets.

One thousand acres of the farm is in Ohio bluegrass, as pretty as its Kentucky namesake. There are cash crops—soybeans, corn and wheat—and orchards full of apples and other fruits.

Galbreath likes nothing better, says farm manager Justice, than to fly in to New York for a meeting with some corporate head, carrying a bagful of fruit from home.

"This is what I raised on my farm," Galbreath will tell the giant of steel, oil or whatever.

There are also 300 head of white-face cattle, enough for a small ranch.

Besides Galbreath's house, there are residences for Dan, his wife and their three children, Galbreath's daughter Joan, her husband James W. Phillips and their four children.

Dan and Joan are from Galbreath's first marriage to the former Helen Mauck, whom Galbreath met at Ohio University. When she died of cancer in 1946, Galbreath gave the Helen Mauck Galbreath Chapel to the university in her memory.

Galbreath has been married since 1951 to the former Dorothy Bryan Firestone, the widow of Russell A. Firestone, a son of the founder of the Akron rubber company.

The second Mrs. Galbreath brought to the marriage an interest in horse racing as avid as her new husband's. Their stables were combined under the Darby Dan colors, fawn and brown.

The Galbreath children and grandchildren are frequent visitors to the farm, but Treetops, Dan's place, and Chateau Gay (named after the first Kentucky Derby winner), the Phillips' house, are for summer and weekends.

————————

Galbreath is the full-time lord of the manor, albeit a benevolent one. In the summer he relaxes by driving through the farm in the convertible with one of his managers, pointing out what needs to be done.

"He hates to see a dead limb in a tree," Justice says. So the offending limbs are removed and rotting boards in buildings are replaced.

Galbreath is no less demanding at the farm than when putting together a real estate deal.

"You don't work by the clock," says Justice. "You work until you're done. If you work until 1 o'clock in the morning, you don't get the next day off."

He marvels at Galbreath, just as does Pittsburgh Pirates slugger Willie Stargell, a loyal subordinate in Galbreath's baseball enterprise.

"I've never met anyone who doesn't have good things to say about Mr. Galbreath; I think if I ever run into anybody, I'd probably get into my first fight," says Stargell, who next to Clemente, is probably Galbreath's favorite Pirate.

Back at the farm, Galbreath shares with the rest of the world the rewards he has reaped from the free-enterprise system.

Darby House is a meeting hall that gives real estate associations and other groups a chance to have their annual banquets in a setting removed from the marketplace.

Displayed at Darby House are large pictures of Galbreath's seven grandchildren, as well as countless trophies from racing and baseball.

Just inside the entranceway is a stuffed tiger, 10½ feet long, which Galbreath shot on a 1961 hunting trip in India.

Galbreath's hasn't forgotten his hometown of Mt. Sterling. Once a year, he hires women from Mt. Sterling's United Church to put on a dinner for the farm employees.

You don't turn your back on your origins, he says: "I grew up there and a lot of people were nice to me."

"Roots. That's the word I would use. John's proud of his heritage," says Dean Jeffers, retired head of Nationwide Insurance in Columbus and a longtime Galbreath friend.

There are more stories about the farm than Galbreath has time to tell. It's been the site for wooing Ohio State basketball and football recruits.

Although he's been generous to his own alma mater, Ohio University in Athens, Galbreath now considers Columbus his hometown and follows the Buckeyes closely. He tries to make sure home-state talent doesn't go fishing for scholarships elsewhere.

Former All-American basketball player Jerry Lucas of Middletown, for example, decided to play for the Buckeyes after Galbreath promised him he could fish at the well-stocked farm.

––––––––––––

But the farm is only part of the Galbreath story. Real estate came first. It produced the revenue that made the farm, the racehorses and the Pittsburgh Pirates possible.

Galbreath says he was an unlikely prospect for real estate greatness when he left the Ohio University campus in 1920 for Columbus, where he was to join a friend in the real estate business.

"I didn't even know what the word equity meant," he recalls.

But he learned quickly, and not even the Depression could slow him down.

"The Depression was the best thing that could have happened to me," he said; it forced him to think of new ways of making money, ways that required all his considerable talents of persuasion and imagination.

What Galbreath found were banks, insurance companies and savings and loan associations flooded with foreclosed property for which they had no use.

Galbreath found a way to help them unload it, for a fee.

He went to people who owned property free and clear, persuaded them to use it as collateral to buy large amounts of the foreclosed property, and convinced the banks to accept the deals.

The first such big deal Galbreath put together was right in Akron, where he arranged for the sale of 297 properties from a savings and loan company to a real estate firm.

That got Galbreath off and running, but it was the company town idea that convinced him he was in the right race.

Galbreath has estimated that over 25 years he purchased and rehabilitated 30,000 houses. He never had to foreclose on the new owners, many of whom he still remembers.

There was, for example, the "gray-haired lady" who came in and announced that she was in the "twilight of life." She asked if it was true that she really could buy her own home. When Galbreath said she could, she counted out $4,200 in old, gold certificates.

"We've made capitalists out of a lot of people," says Galbreath with pride.

By the 1960s Galbreath began shifting his attention from residential real estate to downtowns, specifically dying downtowns in major cities.

Twenty years later, that still is where much of his business is done.

In real estate, Galbreath says, "timing is everything." But he adds a patriotic note:

"It all gets back to a very simple philosophy. Do you believe in the future of your country?"

Galbreath did and does. He helped get real estate moving during the Depression, turned residents of company towns into good citizen-homeowners, and determined that the nation's deteriorating central cities weren't dying—only dormant.

Such reasoning may not make cynics stand up and salute the flag, but it keeps John W. Galbreath moving and making money.

When he came downtown, Galbreath knew it would take more than patriotic intentions to bring investors with him.

When a company shows interest in a new building, Galbreath takes care of all the details. He works out the tax advantages with local government, assists with financing, helps find tenants, builds and manages the building. It's one-stop shopping on a multimillion-dollar scale.

Such package deals have transformed the skylines of every major Ohio city and also made their mark on New York, Pittsburgh, Chicago, Los Angeles and San Francisco. A major project is under way in Denver.

Galbreath is such a charming and persuasive salesman that it's easy to forget he isn't just a benevolent knight in shining armor. He likes putting together downtown projects, but only those that make good business sense.

"We're not going to take any risks beyond normal business judgments or entrepreneurial sense," Dan Galbreath says.

John Galbreath can be as competitive and hard-nosed as he is patriotic and nostalgic.

"He's one of the greatest competitors I've ever run into," says his friend Dean Jeffers. "He likes to win."

Galbreath, as the cliché goes, plays hardball, and he wants the field to be suitable for his game, as Jeffers recalls.

A few years ago, Galbreath and Jeffers were negotiating details for a new Nationwide building. Their meeting took place in Jeffers' old office, which had a wood-burning fireplace. The glow from the fire provided a cheery atmosphere, which Galbreath found unsuitable for tough bargaining.

"Damn you, Dean," he told Jeffers, "this fireplace puts a whole new dimension into doing business with you."

Because he pioneered downtown projects 20 years ago and proved they could work, Galbreath is now greatly in demand. And he has the luxury of taking fewer risks than others who buy into a project.

For example, he may be guaranteed a fee for managing the construction of a development and serving as leasing agent. The company that puts up the building, however, may have to lease space it doesn't need just to get long-term financing.

The company is gambling that it will eventually be able to sublet the space, because Galbreath is doing the project and it will succeed.

The city may be taking a chance, too, betting that the tax breaks it grants will bring jobs and people and tax dollars downtown.

The Galbreath approach doesn't sit well with everyone, although admirers far outnumber detractors.

A redevelopment official in one Ohio city feels Galbreath and his aides were arbitrary and unwilling to compromise with their redevelopment plans.

Some architects have knocked Galbreath's buildings as unimaginative.

Dayton's city manager, Earl E. Sterzer, agrees that Galbreath and his crew are "tough negotiators," but says that's understandable.

"Why should they compromise when they're in demand?" asks Sterzer, who worked with Galbreath on Dayton's Courthouse Square project. "All I can say is that he's a quality developer."

Galbreath is still doing business with architects, so he doesn't want to quarrel with them. He says he builds buildings the way people want them built and lets the critique go at that.

To understand Galbreath, says James E. Kunde, a former Dayton city manager who also took part in the Courthouse Square project, one must consider what many downtowns were like 20 years ago.

"Look at the environment he walked into," says Kunde, now urban affairs director for the Charles F. Kettering Foundation outside Dayton. "Cities decaying, downtowns really beginning to look shabby. In walked Galbreath saying, 'You know, I think I can rebuild.'"

Then, Kunde adds, Galbreath proved he could do it.

He not only built new buildings, he built them on time. And by making his buildings energy-efficient and redesigning them for the computer age, he allowed his tenants to justify the expense in the long run.

It's more than punctuality and cost-effectiveness, however, that attracted business leaders such as John S. Knight and E.J. Thomas of Akron and Mead Corp. chairman James McSwiney of Dayton to Galbreath, says Kunde:

"A lot of the business is conducted in clubs, in small groups where people feel they can trust each other."

The executives who make those decisions need to let their hair down, he adds.

"Galbreath is the kind of guy who fits right into this. He's so comfortable. He's like an old shoe. When you talk to him, you feel he's as sound as the dollar. He's your grandfather."

Galbreath is a real grandfather and twice a great-grandfather, even if his life and business—they seem inseparable—don't move at a grandfatherly pace.

He says he's gradually pulling out of the real estate business, with Dan taking more and more control. They keep adjoining offices in a downtown Columbus building that Galbreath built for the Borden Co.

"He's done a magnificent job," Galbreath says of his son. "I'm so proud of him because he's been everything I always wanted him to be and more."

There he goes again, sounding corny, like an advertisement for the American way, the proud father passing on the torch to a hardworking and deserving son.

But it's classic Galbreath. It's hard not to believe him. He's even optimistic about real estate—no matter that mortgage rates are soaring and home sales are stagnating.

"Don't worry a bit about it," says Galbreath, adding that somebody will figure a way out.

Who knows? Maybe Galbreath still has time. His gait is steady, he wears glasses only occasionally, and his hearing seems unimpaired.

As new technologies appear, there are more opportunities now than when he put down his saxophone and started selling real estate. He said wistfully: "I wish I were 25 or 30 years younger."

But Galbreath, the Ohio country boy, knows that even he grows older, not younger. He likes to philosophize about that with one of the many poems he's memorized:

> *When the burdens of life I am called to lay down,*
> *I hope I may die in Ohio.*
> *I can't think of a more glorious crown*
> *Than one of the sod of Ohio.*
> *And when the last trumpet wakes the land and the sea.*
> *And the tomb of the earth sets its prisoners free*
> *You may all go aloft if you choose, but for me*
> *I think I'll just stay in Ohio.**

---

*   Galbreath died in 1988 at the age of 90.

Johnny Apple: The Life and Times of Akron's Apple

Akron Beacon Journal Beacon Magazine, October 18, 1992
WILLIAM HERSHEY

Shaw's Crab House in downtown Chicago is overflowing with noise and people, but Akron's R.W. "Johnny" Apple Jr. barely has time to order a martini at the bar before his table is ready.

At 57, Apple is what one friend calls a "legend that's still active" in American journalism.

A detractor calls him a "bit of a blowhard," but more on that later.

Senators, prime ministers, and maybe even presidents want to answer Apple's questions. Headwaiters from New York to San Francisco—not to mention Tokyo. London, and Nairobi—make sure he's taken care of.

He is the chief Washington correspondent and deputy Washington editor for the New York Times. And that's just his current assignment. He's been the Times' bureau chief in London, Saigon, and Africa, and tracked presidential candidates from Barry Goldwater to Bill Clinton.

Journalism has changed in the nearly 30 years since Johnny Apple began reporting for the Times. Larry King and Arsenio Hall have become almost as important as Walter Cronkite and Edward R. Murrow used to be. C-SPAN and CNN have made newspaper "Extras"—and even maybe the network news—almost obsolete.

But the New York Times abides. What the Times puts on page one sets the tone for the rest of the business. And as often as anyone—and too often for some—the byline "R.W. Apple Jr." appears on page one among "All the News That's Fit to Print."

He is one of the last great cowboy journalists. In a business now dominated by specialists—some papers have a political writer for campaign finance and one for political ethics—Apple's willing and able to rope in any story.

Need a story to explain the effect of the European currency crisis on the presidential race?

Apple had come to Chicago to report on another story when the calamity struck. But it was his byline that appeared above the fold on page one of the Times under the headline "Crisis There, but Not Here."

———————————

Johnny Apple's career did not start with the New York Times. It began as a copyboy at the Beacon Journal, when Apple was 19.

"He was a brassy little upstart—cocky," says retired Beacon Journal reporter Polly Paffilas. "He filled the paste pot when you asked him, not with grace and pleasure."

Even then Apple was pursuing the news.

"He was always looking over your shoulder," Miss Paffilas says. "When he was carrying one piece of copy from one place to another, he was always reading it."

Copy boys were supposed to take orders, be seen and not heard. Not Apple.

"His eyes, ears and mouth were always open all the time," Miss Paffilas recalls.

And modesty was not an Apple virtue.

"He swaggered, but in a likable way," Miss Paffilas says. "He had dreams and I think he knew he was going to pursue them."

Apple grew up on Storer Avenue and went to Rankin School before attending Western Reserve Academy in Hudson.

On Storer Avenue, incidentally, he had his first brush with a political giant. He shoveled snow for the late Ray C. Bliss, who went on to become chairman of the Ohio and National Republican parties.

"Out, Out! I wanted out," Apple recalls amid the pleasant chatter at Shaw's Crab House. "Like most teen-age kids, I wanted to see if I could make it in the big time."

But Apple's dreams weren't the same dreams his family had for him. His great-grandfather, Fred W. Albrecht, had founded the century-old grocery company that operates the Acme, Click and Y-Mart stores.

Apple's mother, Julia, was the daughter of Hurl Albrecht, one of Fred W.'s two sons. Hurl and brother Ivan followed Fred W. in running the company.

Julia's husband, R.W. Apple Sr., who's also known as "Johnny," became a company executive. The senior Apple still lives in Akron.

At Western Reserve Academy, where he was sports editor of the newspaper and editor of the yearbook, Apple's interests were turned forever from fresh fruits and vegetables to putting sentences and stories together. Franklyn Reardon, who taught honors English, did it.

"It was he who made me a writer," Apple says. "My grandfather was of course enraged with the idea that I should become a newspaperman and not go into the family business."

Apple's first trip away from Ohio didn't last long. After graduation from Western Reserve Academy, Apple headed for Princeton.

"I had gotten bounced out after my first term," Apple says. "I was chasing a girl at Vassar. I was doing splendidly academically on the days that I went to class, but on the weekend, I was in Poughkeepsie and not in class. What did I know?"

Back in Akron, the family realized that young Johnny needed to work, and that's how he became a copyboy at the Beacon Journal. His father knew the late Ben Maidenburg, then executive editor of the Beacon Journal. Apple's grandfather was a good friend of the late John S. Knight, then Beacon Journal editor. "So I think he said a word to Mr. Knight," Apple says of his appointment as a copy boy.

If Franklyn Reardon had whetted Apple's interest in writing, the Beacon Journal steered that interest forever toward newspapers.

"I was awed by the Beacon Journal," Apple says, "It was a real newspaper."

He can still see Maidenburg stalking through the city room, amid the clatter of typewriters and wire machines and the haze of cigar and cigarette smoke.

"The first really tough, cynical, street-wise person I'd ever really known was Maidenburg, this tall man with this hawk-like face who would scowl," Apple recalls.

Maidenburg taught Apple a lesson that he says still dominates his approach to reporting today.

"He made a huge impression on me on the importance of getting it right," says Apple, who believes that the payoff is not in getting a story first, but in getting it right.

John S. Knight also made an impression. Every Thursday, the day Knight wrote his "Editor's Notebook" column for the Sunday paper, Apple delivered Knight's lunch on a plastic tray with a starched white napkin on top from a nearby restaurant.

"There was Mr. Knight," Apple says, "who was, as far as I was concerned in my lowly position, akin to a Greek god."

Knight made it acceptable for Apple to become a journalist instead of a grocery executive.

"The thing that saved me being cast into outer darkness was that my grandfather thought so much of Mr. Knight," he says. "God knows what it would have been like if the local paper had been a scandal sheet."

Apple also remembers the late Murray Powers, then managing editor, who wore a fedora, "which I thought was very cool."

In 1953, when the Russian leader Joseph Stalin was very ill, Powers told Apple to keep an eye on the wire machine for word that he was dead. The story clattered in, and Apple handed the copy to Powers.

"He yelled, 'Stop the presses!'—the only time I ever heard it," Apple says.

Johnny Apple made it back to Princeton and almost graduated. The second time around he got in trouble while editor of the of the campus newspaper and chairman of the undergraduate council.

"Essentially, I was a terrible troublemaker," Apple says.

There was plenty for Apple to write and rage about. Anti-Semitism on campus made it hard for Jewish students to join clubs that provided dining and social life for upperclassmen. The Army-McCarthy hearings in Washington had made some journalists and some professors at Princeton suspect of being communists.

"The university was operating under the old social rules and Johnny was not," says Hodding Carter III, a Princeton classmate who was President Jimmy Carter's State Department spokesman and now is a freelance journalist and the owner of a television production company in Washington.

Apple's raging, to say the least, caught the attention of the people running the school. "The dean, who was quite a good friend of mine, said 'You are functioning as a journalist, you ought to go and be a journalist. Go be a journalist,'" Apple recalls.

So Apple left Princeton and landed a job at the Wall Street Journal before serving in the peace time Army. (He did eventually get his degrees—a bachelor's and master's in history from Columbia University.)

While in the Army, Apple worked part time for a local newspaper, covering the cops, zoning disputes and other news far removed from the presidents, wars, and prime ministers that would become Apple's beat.

"That was very important to me in a way," Apple says. "I never had been a local reporter. I'd had a screwy career."

After the Army, it was back to the Wall Street Journal and then on to NBC News, where he covered the most important story of his career.

"I spent most of a year covering the civil rights movement," he says. "That's the most important story. That's the story that will be remembered as the great transforming event of the 20th Century in this country and to some degree in the world."

By 1963, the New York Times had a new metropolitan editor, an aggressive former foreign correspondent, named A.M. Rosenthal, who was to become the newspaper's executive editor and lead it, along with Apple, to some of its greatest triumphs.

Johnny Apple was the first reporter Rosenthal hired.

Other applicants told Rosenthal all the great stories they'd write if they had the chance. Apple, while working for NBC, had also been free-lancing magazine articles on a variety of subjects.

"Here was a guy who writes about cancer, politics...not saying 'I could do it,'" recalls Rosenthal, now a New York Times columnist. "I thought this guy was very impressive."

The first day on the job Apple impressed Rosenthal more. Rosenthal was handed an important story to work on—he can't remember exactly what it was.

"I looked around," Rosenthal says, "I walked up to Apple, 'Hey, Johnny, do you happen to know anything about this?'"

"Yes, I do," replied the eager rookie. "I once wrote an article about it."

Apple's first story for the New York Times ended up on page one.

"I was very impressed with him," says Rosenthal.

As Apple kept on impressing Rosenthal, the importance of his assignments grew.

He worked in Vietnam from 1965 to 1968, becoming the paper's bureau chief there. A story he wrote shortly before returning to the United States, headlined "Vietnam: Signs of a Stalemate," won both the Overseas Press Club and George Polk Memorial awards for foreign analytical reporting.

The job was hard and dangerous. Apple took a bullet in the seat of his pants. But he says the job was worth it.

"'The most professionally satisfying (assignment) was the war in Vietnam because I was able to play some, I think relatively significant, role in driving home not the morality or immorality of the war the war, but the fact that we were not doing very well.

"It was I who first used the word 'stalemate' to describe the war."

After Vietnam came a year in Africa.

"I was the New York Times in Black Africa," Apple says. "In many of those places there never had been a New York Times or American reporter."

New York called, however, and it was back home, where Apple took the job of national political correspondent.

It was that assignment, which lasted until 1976, that gave Apple the reputation of being as full of himself as he was full of enthusiasm for his assignments.

In his book on the 1972 presidential campaign, *The Boys on the Bus,* author Timothy Crouse described Apple as both hard-working and self-promoting. Also, Crouse wrote, Apple was a reporter who knew how to enjoy an expense account. Crouse described how Apple and he shared poached eggs and caviar for breakfast.

"In a business populated largely by shy egomaniacs," Crouse wrote, "Apple stuck out like a drunk at a funeral."

Yet, Crouse also wrote that Apple, just like Ben Maidenburg had taught him, got it right, even when nobody else did.

When the Iowa caucuses were held in January of 1972 to select delegates, there were no handouts to guide reporters, and only one of them could make sense of the hour-by hour returns as they came into Des Moines, Crouse wrote.

That guru was Apple. Other reporters peered over Apple's shoulder, just as copy boy Apple had done at the Beacon Journal—to take their lead from the New York Times man.

The combination of careful reporting, clear writing and preening became an Apple trademark, says a longtime friend from the New York Times Washington bureau.

She recalls how Apple acted when he and others were dispatched from Washington to New York for election-night coverage one year.

Apple believed that he really should have been back in Washington, where he had been invited to spend the evening with Ambassador Averill Harriman and his wife, Pamela, one of Washington's top power couples. Harriman is now dead, but his wife remains a formidable Washington hostess.

"He would talk about the fact that he really should be with the Harrimans," the colleague says. "He was kind of insufferable."

Apple loved to mix with what this colleague calls the "swells," and his next assignment, as London Bureau chief, gave him plenty of opportunities.

"He was in his element with the Brits," the colleague says.

Another Washington bureau colleague, now retired, agrees.

"Johnny had gotten very comfortable over there" he says. "In a bon vivant sense, his waistline had gone up. He had a cellar of wine… He used to chuckle 'How can they move me? They can't move all my wine.'"

Apple loved the European assignment.

"By all odds," he says, "It was the richest (assignment) because for 10 years I wandered all over Europe and wrote about everything from architecture to music to politics to economics to diplomacy to food and drink."

At the New York Times no assignment is forever, and by 1985 Rosenthal had decided it was time for Apple to come back. There were suggestions that Apple had gone soft, shunning a diet of hard news for stories about wine, restaurants and the good life.

A 1985 story in the Washington Journalism Review, heralding Apple's return to Washington, asked, "Has Johnny Apple written one restaurant review too many for the taste of his boss, Times executive editor A.M. Rosenthal?"

"I really needed him," Rosenthal says, citing changes he wanted to make to the Washington bureau. "I thought he'd done a wonderful job in England. I thought it was time he came back. I had planned to do it a year earlier."

But had Apple gone soft?

"He did write about cooking," Rosenthal replies. "But he also wrote about politics and kings."

Back in Washington, Apple and his wife Betsey settled into Georgetown, and he settled in at the Washington bureau with his own office and dual titles as chief Washington correspondent and deputy Washington editor.

Apple no longer swaggered like he did in the old days back in Akron. He now moves with what might be called a jaunty waddle. His huge appetite for news—still intact—is matched by an appetite for food and wine.

"I have no idea how much I weigh," he says.

Apple is as likely to be in Colorado or Illinois or Ohio as he is in the office.

"What they made it possible for me to do," he says, "is what is very hard to do around here, which is to have one toe in the structural hierarchy—that is to be a manager, but still to be a writer. That's what I've always wanted to do."

No longer does Apple pursue the breaking news story—what Bill Clinton or President Bush did or said today. Instead, he writes news analysis from a historical perspective of covering previous presidential races that occurred before some of the boys—and girls—on today's campaign buses were even born.

Instead of writing about what the candidates did, Apple tries to figure out—with the benefit of as much reporting as he did for breaking news stories—"why did these people do what they did."

This year's election, as Apple sees it, has become Bill Clinton's to lose.

"In modern times, there never has been a president re-elected with the economy in a shape like this," he says.

Clinton, however, has not handled the problem of his draft record well, letting negative stories drip out one at a time, Apple says. "I don't think there are a lot of hard, fast rules in politics. One of them is you get the negative stuff out, and you get it over with."

Not everyone is enamored with Apple's writing and reporting these days.

An article in the September issues of Campaigns & Elections by James Ledbetter, media critic for the Village Voice, savaged both Apple and David Broder of the Washington Post as among the worst reporters on this year's presidential campaign.

"Reading Apple's copy, you can almost hear the bones creak as he strains to turn out his cliché-ridden, centrist bilge," Ledbetter wrote.

Rosenthal takes offense. Reporters are not supposed to be leftists, rightists, or identifiable anywhere on the political spectrum, he says.

"One of the best things about Johnny Apple is that I cannot tell you about his politics. He writes with flesh and blood; he's a square writer. He doesn't cook his stories."

Apple doesn't mind sticking up for himself.

"Oh, be snotty, why not?" he says. "The Washington Post thinks that David Broder is a pretty good political reporter. The New York Times obviously finds some small virtues in me or I presume they would have put me on the bench."

He certainly is not on the bench, but where he will play the rest of his career at the New York Times is unclear.

A series of management change has left open the job of Washington bureau chief—one of the most prestigious at the paper. In the past, Apple had been mentioned as a candidate for the job, but it has always gone to someone else. Again, he's being mentioned as a front-runner.

"He is very desirous of becoming bureau chief," says the former colleague who is now retired. "He feels as if he has been bounced around a little. He sort of regards it as his due."

Apple concedes that he would like the job but denies that he thinks the Times owes it to him.

"I've been pretty well rewarded," says Apple, who declines to say how well he's paid except that his income is in six figures. "I don't think you're owed anything in this world."

He wanted to travel the country and the world and write about it; the New York Times has given him that opportunity.

Not that he's finished. He has won prizes, met presidents and tasted great wine. He still has an edge. There' s something he hasn't done. Never, on his own, has he won the Pulitzer Prize, journalism's highest honor, although he has been a finalist.

"Damn right I'd like to win a Pulitzer Prize," he says, finishing up a meal and two bottles of wine at Shaw's Crab House. "Wouldn't you?"*

---

*   Apple was the New York Times Washington Bureau Chief from 1993 to 1997. He died in 2006 at 71.

Jim Williams: "Rare Jurist" Will be Missed

James R. Williams, first Black judge on Summit County court, retiring

Akron Beacon Journal, December 21, 2004
CARL CHANCELLOR

If life had gone in another direction, James R. Williams might have made a name for himself legging out ground balls and snagging one-hoppers.

Fortunately for the folks of Summit County, it was the gavel and not the bat that Williams ultimately decided to swing.

Nonetheless, in January, after 16 years on the Summit County Common Pleas Court bench, Williams, the first African American to serve on the county court, will take off his black robe and retire from what has been a distinguished judicial career.

"I am looking forward to retiring. I have no apprehensions whatso-ever," said Williams, who turned 70 in September and by Ohio law was barred by age from seeking re-election.

However, retiring does not quite mean retiring for Williams.

"I plan to accept assignments as a visiting judge," he said. So it's almost a sure bet that the august, silver-haired jurist will continue to be a familiar figure at the Summit County Courthouse.

Akron attorney Ed Gilbert certainly hopes that is the case.

"He is a rare, rare jurist who will be very much missed. I hope he will agree to come back on a visiting basis," said Gilbert. "We relied on him. He was a levelheaded jurist with a sensitive heart to all who came before him."

Assistant Summit County Prosecutor Michael Carroll agreed.

"Those are some tremendous shoes to fill," Carroll said of the position that will be filled by Elinore Marsh Stormer, elected Nov. 2.

Carroll said he truly appreciated the way Williams ran his court—both before and during trials.

Beforehand, Carroll said, the judge had a particular talent of being able to dissect a case from both sides, analyzing the strengths and weaknesses facing both the prosecution and the defense.

"Then he pointed us toward a resolution," Carroll said. When both sides failed at reaching agreement, the trial would go forward.

Williams was a "middle of the road" judge, Carroll said.

"Some judges have a way of leaning towards their feelings, but Judge Williams applied the rule of evidence."

Carroll, who has been with the prosecutor's office since 1981, said even when he wasn't pleased with a ruling by Williams, he still respected the decision.

"Trust me. He made some very serious rulings not all in my favor, some I even disagreed with, but I understood his ruling because it was always based in fact, in law," Carroll said.

U.S. District Judge John Adams, who served on the common pleas bench with Williams, calls the retiring judge an "outstanding jurist" and "wonderful" human being.

"I admired that fatherly way he dealt with individuals. He was understanding and at times stern without being harsh...He was always a gentleman who treated me with kindness and respect, and I will never forget that," Adams said.

Growing up in the South

It is notable that Williams, who is considered a thoughtful, evenhanded jurist of unquestioned integrity and fairness, grew up in the deep South—Lowndes County, Miss., to be exact—where Jim Crow and the doctrine of separate but equal held sway.

"Mississippi could be a very dangerous place at that time for African Americans," Williams observed. "At the same time, I had a wonderful childhood."

Born into a family of modest means, Williams was the oldest of three boys. It was a happy family, one in which value was placed on family and community and the importance of education and hard work was emphasized.

Excellent Education

As a teenager, Williams worked as a hotel bellhop while attending Union Academy High School.

"It was a segregated school system, but they really encouraged education," said Williams, calling his years at Union Academy an extremely "positive and rich" experience.

"Well, not in terms of brick and mortar, but in terms of other kind of materials, the faculty and administration, which were just outstanding and very tremendous," Williams said of his all-Black high school.

"They took a deep interest in the students and took pains to instill pride in us by teaching us African American history."

It was during his time at Union Academy that he first became interested in the law and, more important, Catherine Douglas.

"I was talkative and argumentative," Williams said. Those characteristics served him well at his high school graduation, where the class staged a mock trial of the school.

"I was the prosecutor, and the chief witness for the school was my future wife Cathy, the class valedictorian," said Williams, who took his role as prosecutor seriously and made some harsh statements about the school.

"One school official asked me if I meant the things I said about the school," said Williams, adding that he lost the case.

Speaking his mind

Speaking his mind and taking a stand have never been a problem for Williams, professionally or personally.

"He thinks he is all-knowledgeable about all topics," quipped Akron City Councilman Michael Williams about his father.

Michael's sister, Jacqueline Williams Walton, a social worker in Toledo, said her father always believed in people saying what was on their minds.

"As kids he taught us to always express yourself and take a stand," she said.

Michael Williams recalled that his childhood home was a place where open debate was encouraged.

"He always allowed us a chance to engage in dialogue. But it usually didn't make much of a difference because you got what you deserved."

Both Michael and Jacqueline were born in Akron, shortly after Judge Williams and his wife, whom he married in 1955, settled on the near north side of the city.

"After Cathy graduated from school, she came to Akron to live with her father, and I followed her," said Williams, who first completed a two-year stint in the Army.

"We moved into Elizabeth Park Homes, and that was a very positive experience. That's where I met a lot of good people like Helen Arnold and her family," recalled Williams, speaking of the late civil right activist and Akron school board member.

Williams said the Elizabeth Park public housing project was "ideal" for a young family like his because housing options were limited for Black people in the Akron of the 1950s.

"There was no chance of finding an apartment. We (Black people) couldn't rent an apartment. We could rent out rooms in a house but not an apartment," he said.

Working for the future

While living at Elizabeth Park, Williams worked part time and attended The University of Akron on the GI bill. He also played baseball, a love that was inspired by a childhood mentor.

"Oscar Morgan loved baseball, and we talked about it all the time. Mr. Morgan was a bellhop at the same hotel I worked at as a kid in high school. I remember he was such a dignified man, the way he carried himself. He was such an excellent example for a teen."

Although Williams was considered a good ballplayer, he said he was advised at one of the several training camps he attended to go to college.

While attending college, he joined the Alpha Phi Alpha fraternity. It was while pledging that he met one of the great influencers on his life, the Rev. Eugene E. Morgan.

"He was a great spiritual leader," Williams said of Morgan, who was the first African American member of the Akron Board of Education.

After graduating with a bachelor's degree in 1960, Williams taught in the Akron schools for four years while earning his degree from Akron's law school. He became an attorney in 1965 and went into private practice with Ed Parms.

"I remember Judge Joseph Roulhac (who would later become Akron's first Black municipal judge) opened his law office to Ed Parms in 1965," Williams said. "Judge Roulhac simply said to him, 'Come on in.' Ed did the same for me."

During his early years in Akron, Williams also met Atha and Muriel Walker, who were, with Ed Davis, among the deans of Akron's Black political movement.

"They helped to instill in me the whole idea of politics and the importance of politics," he said.

Active in politics

It didn't take long for those political seeds to take root. In 1969, Williams was elected to Akron City Council in Ward 4. He later served as an at-large councilman.

Michael Williams, who would later follow in his father's footsteps in the city council, remembers shadowing his father as a youngster.

"I think I went to more meetings with him as a kid than I do now. He was very active in the community... He always stressed to Jackie and myself that we had a responsibility to give back to the community."

The Rev. Curtis Walker, pastor of the Wesley Temple AME Zion Church, where the judge has been a member for more than 40 years, said Williams has a passion for community activism and service.

"It's his calling...He has always been mindful of those in need and how to reach those in need," said Walker.

Walker points to Williams' key involvement with the building of the Alpha homes, which provide housing to Akron seniors and those of modest means.

Williams said his experience with trying to find housing when he first moved to Akron sparked his involvement with home building. In the 1960s, when the federal government passed legislation allowing private groups to build housing as part of the urban renewal initiative, he approached his fraternity with a proposal.

"The first one we built was Channelwood. Now we have 2,000 units of housing," he said. Those units include the James R. Williams senior citizen apartment tower.

In 1978, President Jimmy Carter appointed Williams U.S. attorney for northern Ohio.

"It was a challenging position being the chief federal prosecutor," said Williams, pointing out that he was responsible for investigating and prosecuting major crime, organized crime and political corruption.

Williams said in addition to the work, he is most proud of the attorneys he hired to staff the office.

"I put a lot of emphasis on quality appointments...Out of just under 40 lawyers on my staff, nine are now judges and five of those are federal judges," he said.

In 1983, Williams was appointed to an open seat on Akron Municipal Court. In 1989, he was chosen to become a judge on the Summit County bench.

"I've had many fascinating cases over the years," Williams said. One of the most notable came in 1992 when serial killer Jeffrey Dahmer appeared in his court to plead guilty to killing his first victim.

More time for family

Williams said retiring will give him the opportunity to travel and spend much more time with his four grandchildren.

Flashing a smile, the judge said: "Leaving the bench is eased by the fact there is still a Williams on the bench," referring to his daughter-in-law, Annalisa, an Akron municipal judge.

Williams' main regret is that he won't be sharing his retirement with Catherine, his best friend and wife of 46 years. She died of cancer in 2002.

The judge said that he took the opportunity three years ago, when he was awarded the Sir Thomas More Award from the Cleveland Catholic

Diocese and the Akron Bar Association, to acknowledge his wife's contribution and sacrifice.

"I had Cathy stand next to me and I dedicated the award to her," he said, his eyes welling with tears.

"She was the valedictorian of our high school class, yet she stayed at home to raise our children before she pursued her education. And then she went on to her own outstanding career as a teacher…That was the kind of dedication she had to family.

"I couldn't have achieved what I did without her support and understanding. I've been blessed tremendously.

"The biggest challenge of my life has been rallying myself after my Cathy passed two years ago. It's the most difficult thing I have had to face," he said, his voice choking.

"As I look at my career, the people of Akron and Summit County have been great to me. They have given me great support over the years, and I only hope that I earned that support."*

---

* Williams died at the age of 88 on November 6, 2020.

Maureen O'Connor: The Most Powerful Woman in Summit County

Akron Beacon Journal Beacon Magazine, July 12, 1998
STEVE HOFFMAN

Maureen O'Connor was navigating her dark, late-model Buick sedan down Interstate 71 toward the Taft-O'Connor campaign headquarters in Columbus—and a possible future as Ohio's next lieutenant governor—as she considered whether she is the most powerful woman in Summit County.

O'Connor, county prosecutor since 1995, laughed briefly.

"I think that the prosecutor's job is one of the most powerful positions in county government," she said. "Certainly, I think, the most exciting.

"I'm mindful of that, and respectful of the position," she continued. "I always say, take your position seriously, but not yourself."

Nevertheless, early this year, Ohio Secretary of State Bob Taft, the Republican candidate for governor, began to take O'Connor and her political career very seriously. Taft asked O'Connor to be his running mate on the GOP ticket, citing her crime-fighting credentials as a judge and prosecutor and her take-charge, hands-on style.

In an ambitious move characteristic of her quick rise in local politics since 1993, when she was named to fill a vacancy on the Summit County Common Pleas Court bench, O'Connor accepted, plunging herself into

Ohio's tumultuous brand of statewide politics. It is a world of rushed flights in small planes, bus and van trips to all corners of the state, hurried press conferences and interviews—and tremendous political potential.

No one is predicting an easy race this fall against Democrat Lee Fisher, the former Ohio attorney general, and his running mate, Columbus City Council President Michael Coleman, but the Taft-O'Connor ticket has held a lead in statewide polls and has moved aggressively.

Although the job of lieutenant governor would carry a lower salary, much smaller staff and fewer defined duties for O'Connor, it would provide an opportunity to influence policy on criminal justice for all 88 counties, as well as a platform for launching a future in statewide politics.

O'Connor refused to speculate beyond November, but, in just a few short months, she could become one of the most powerful women in the state. Much work lies ahead, however, not to mention the ongoing tasks of being a single mother of two college-age sons, mastering the details of the high-profile public corruption investigations swirling around her Democratic nemesis, Summit County Executive Tim Davis, and keeping on top of local murder cases such as the one proceeding against former Akron Police Captain Douglas Prade.

"This campaign is like having a second full-time job," O'Connor said as she began a recent two-day, eight-city bus tour across Ohio with Taft and his wife, Hope.

"A Means to an End"

What keeps her going?

"I enjoy it," O'Connor said during a campaign trip from Cleveland to Youngstown shortly after joining the Taft ticket. "Isn't that obvious?"

There is a bit more to it than that, however. O'Connor, 46, was raised in a large Irish-Catholic family with a strong sense of duty and responsibility. Her upbringing included a heavy dose of community service, administered by her maternal grandmother, a social worker, who routinely rounded up O'Connor and her seven siblings, piled them into a station wagon and organized cleaning details at women's shelters in Cleveland.

"You are taught that you have a responsibility, and if you are blessed with some talents in some particular area, it's your duty to use those talents," O'Connor said.

She characterizes politics as a means to an end, not an end in itself. Rather than talking about putting bad guys in jail or dwelling on her practice sessions with a .45-caliber pistol, she emphasizes her eight years of experience as a referee in Summit County Probate Court, where she helped families struggle with issues of guardianship, adoptions and mental health.

"A lot of problem-solving goes on in Probate Court," she said. "It's important to know the human element. I've seen that and it gives you more of a sense of compassion that's important to the top of the ticket."

As a more recent accomplishment, she points to her tight management of the troubled Child Support Enforcement Agency, part of the prosecutor's office. When O'Connor took over, the collection rate was 9%, one of the worst in the state. By the end of the first quarter of 1998, the collection rate had risen to 44%.

Sticking to the issues

When she is campaigning, O'Connor tends to be dark-suited and serious, as does Taft. After more than a decade in politics she is practiced in the art of the quick meet-and-greet—smiling, extending her hand, making an introduction and moving on down the line. O'Connor takes an active part in discussions at PTA meetings, county court houses, schools and day care centers, especially when it comes to issues of discipline and values.

Stops at frozen-custard stands, such as Strickland's in Akron, are the exception, not the rule, as the Taft-O'Connor ticket crisscrosses the state in the kind of grinding, retail-level campaigning voters have come to demand. O'Connor is expected to spend a lot of time in her home county of Summit and in Cuyahoga County, where she grew up and where she remains well connected through her extended family, complementing Taft's strengths in the Cincinnati area.

"If there was a different way to do it (hold public office), and you didn't have to run for office...God bless it, I'd go for it. But the truth of it is that you've got to campaign to get where you need to be in order to do what you need to do."

She has, in past campaigns, scorched her opponents with fiery criticism. But with Taft, O'Connor has stuck to the issues, and expects to continue to do so. "Ohio voters want to know, from the top down, what are the solutions," she said.

In Summit County, O'Connor's public image has been forged by the tough political campaigns, a no-nonsense stance on juvenile crime and repeated clashes with Davis. In the most recent skirmish, the County Council voted to dump O'Connor from a multi-agency taskforce probing Davis' former top aide on charges of public corruption. The council also stripped her of authority to represent the Davis administration in civil matters.

O'Connor maintains the council had no authority to do either and is refusing to budge. Enemies call her "Queen Maureen"; critics regard her as cold, imperious and calculating. She has been known to tape bullet-pocked silhouette targets on the back of her office door in the Ohio Building.

"I've seen her invoke some policies that are harsh," said Dean Carro, director of the Legal Clinic at The University of Akron School of Law, which represents indigents and prisoners.

Strong, but Sensitive

But colleagues and supporters find a good deal to admire in O'Connor. Assistant Summit County prosecutor Allison McCarty, who has known O'Connor since 1989, when both worked in Summit County Probate Court, calls her "fearless."

"She walks into a room and she has command presence," McCarty said. "Other people might be intimidated. She doesn't back down. I think she is a very strong woman."

"Maureen is thought of by the press, politicians and opponents as a hard-nosed political player," said a friend, former campaign manager and current Summit County Probate Court administrator Joe Masich. "The side people don't know is that she is a caring, sensitive person."

As prosecutor, O'Connor has taken an active role in the courtroom, something her predecessor, Lynn Slaby, rarely did before he took a seat on the 9th District Court of Appeals bench. O'Connor is well known for going after David Bellomy, the "Goodyear Heights rapist," and for binding over violent juvenile offenders into the adult criminal-justice system. She has lately dropped direct involvement in the courtroom, a practice she found too time-consuming, and instead acts as her own civil and criminal division chief.

O'Connor took up target practice with a .45-caliber automatic to familiarize herself with firearms, often the subject of confusing courtroom testimony. She said she practices, not regularly, and sometimes takes her pistol in the car when heading to a crime scene.

Tough on kid criminals

In legal circles, there are concerns that O'Connor overcharges; critics focus specifically on the juvenile bind-overs. Last year, O'Connor prosecuted 14-year-old Donzell Lewis as an adult for his role in the murder of Rolishia M. Shepard, 16, and two armed robberies. Lewis was sentenced to 22 years in prison, becoming the youngest person tried and convicted as an adult in Summit County. Shirley Thompson, Lewis' mother, said through her attorney that the subject is too painful to discuss.

Amber Eckert was a 15-year-old juvenile involved in planning a drive-by shooting of her estranged father in 1995. The shot missed the father, but severely injured a friend sitting in the living room. Eckert's attorney, Larry Whitney, said she may be the youngest ever to be sent to the Ohio Reformatory for Women in Marysville. She was sentenced in 1996 to 9½ years to 18 years in prison.

Eddie Ware, 15, pleaded guilty in 1997 to voluntary manslaughter in the stabbing death of an 18-year-old. He was sentenced to seven years in prison.

"Little sociopaths," O'Connor calls the violent juvenile offenders.

Some attorneys feel that a case-by-case approach, with consideration for age and past record, has been tossed out in favor of a blanket policy.

"People aren't always receptive to a juvenile being bound over," said O'Connor. "I can certainly take the criticism."

Carro agrees that being tough on crime comes with O'Connor's turf. "She is reflecting a problem, a serious problem. The divergence (of opinion) comes with how you deal with it."

O'Connor has supported alternative programs for youthful offenders, such as the Phoenix Program in Akron, but has drawn a line in the sand with violent juveniles. Carro acknowledges O'Connor's position is in tune with a society that has concluded "we can't solve every problem."

A "Slap on the Wrist"

Former Summit County Democratic Party Chairman Jim Frost is one of O'Connor's more outspoken critics. In 1996, he publicly questioned O'Connor's request for more funds for the Child Support Enforcement Agency. "Her whole career is suspect as far as I'm concerned," he said recently.

Frost also recalled how O'Connor solicited contributions for the local Republican Party from employees while she was running for prosecutor. O'Connor defeated former Barberton Law Director Marty Bodnar with 57% of the vote in the middle of the controversy but was eventually fined $50. She promptly termed the penalty "a slap on the wrist."

Others who have tangled with O'Connor, both in the political and legal arenas, were unwilling or reluctant to talk. They will either have to deal with the next lieutenant governor or continue to deal with O'Connor as prosecutor, at least until her current term expires Jan. 5, 2001.

Bodnar said circumspectly that the law department in Barberton now works closely with O'Connor's office on a program that bypasses probable-cause hearings on felony cases, moving them directly to the grand jury. "Since the campaign of 1996, we've established a solid working relationship on the direct-indictment program," he said.

Friends, family and longtime associates say that beneath O'Connor's stern public persona lies a busy, disciplined person, one who is fiercely guarded about her privacy and sons Alex, 18, and Ed, 17. As a result, she can be very direct, to the point of being blunt.

"She's an organized person," said O'Connor's mother, Mary Elizabeth, who at 71 still runs an antique business in Strongsville. "She doesn't spin her wheels. She's always been a leader. She's not quick to judge, but she doesn't run around the barn looking for a solution either."

No lack of role models

Maureen O'Connor has managed virtually her entire political life as a single mother. "I don't think it is ever easy being a parent, let alone throwing in a campaign and the responsibilities of public office," O'Connor said.

There is not much time for other things, but O'Connor occasionally golfs and goes fly fishing, though not "often enough to get good" at either one. She attends her sons' lacrosse games, but has pretty much given up on downhill skiing, which she took up with her boys and pursued to a memorable winter vacation in the Italian Alps. Sometimes, she relaxes by watching a video.

She dates but has not remarried since a divorce from Akron attorney Jerald B. Kipp 10 years ago. She attends Republican Party social and fund-raising events, is a member of St. Vincent's Catholic Church, and stops for an occasional drink with her staff at a local watering hole on Fridays.

O'Connor has no lack of role models when it comes to educated, independent men and women in her life. She unhesitatingly pointed to her mother and late father, Patrick O'Connor, a dentist, as the biggest influences in her life. The family continues to gather regularly at her mother's home in Strongsville, where campfires on the banks of a pond often last well past midnight.

All of the O'Connor children have forged successful, independent careers in the professions or in business, said brother Patrick O'Connor, 42, a funeral director in Parma. "We were all raised...tell it like it is, don't sugarcoat it."

Setting priorities and getting things done were a regular part of that upbringing. For example, Maureen O'Connor, the second of the eight children, often found herself weeding in the family's large vegetable garden. "Man, did I hate to weed beans," she remembered. "We all hated to weed the garden. It didn't matter; we did it.

"I could not imagine saying to my dad, 'You know, Dad, I really don't want to do that task today,'" she said. "There was absolutely no discussion on that."

O'Connor's mother doled out jobs and responsibilities for all the children, starting at age 2 with emptying bathroom waste baskets. Mary O'Connor also provided an early model for an independent career, starting her antique business as soon as her last child was out of diapers.

Getting through Law School

Educated in Catholic schools, Maureen O'Connor grew up in Parma and Strongsville, was active in student government, edited the yearbook and was a member of the National Honor Society. In the summers, she was a lifeguard at local pools.

O'Connor attended Seton Hill College, in Greensburg, Pa., the alma mater of her mother and an older sister, and was elected class president. She graduated from the small, top-ranked liberal arts college in the Laurel Highlands in 1973.

After college, O'Connor started a master's degree in teaching, at S.U.N.Y. in Binghamton, N.Y. She did not do a thesis, although she did substitute teaching in Catholic schools in Strongsville, at the same time working as a waitress at a Brown Derby.

But law school had always been a dream. O'Connor enrolled at Cleveland Marshall College of Law and in 1979 married Kipp, whose family is from the Akron area. The Hopkins & Kipp Auto Parts business has long operated on West Bowery Street in Akron.

"Getting through law school was just getting through law school," O'Connor recalled, contrasting her years at Cleveland Marshall with outside activities in college and high school days. "I was pretty busy." Her younger son was born the day after O'Connor got her law degree in 1980.

The couple settled in Copley, and O'Connor opened a law practice. Some of her work brought her into Summit County Probate Court, where Judge Willard Spicer asked her to consider an assignment as a referee. She started there in 1981, which brought her into increasing contact with local Republican Party politics.

By 1988, her marriage with Kipp was over. "It was a dissolution," O'Connor said. Legal documents refer only to "unfortunate differences." Friends said they doubt O'Connor will remarry.

Weathering defeat

After the divorce, O'Connor purchased a two-story, two-bedroom brick colonial in the King Elementary School District, now valued at $106,810, continued her work in Summit County Probate Court—and hammered away in local politics. Starting in 1987, she ran four times for local judgeships, losing each time.

Her unsuccessful 1989 effort to unseat Democrat Akron Municipal Court Judge Jane Bond, now a Common Pleas Court judge, still rankles Bond so badly that she refused to speak about it. In that campaign, O'Connor slammed Bond as a "low-bond Jane Bond" for continuing a $2,500 cash bond set by another judge for an accused rapist.

If that loss, or any of her other defeats, ranks as a major disappointment O'Connor doesn't admit it.

"My attitude on that is, look where I am today," she said. "In a way, things happen for a reason; I believe that. I was never devastated by a loss. I always entered a race with my eyes open, knowing what the potential was for success."

"She is ambitious; she is aggressive," said Masich, noting that in an early race, O'Connor got sick from the fresh ink on yard signs but continued working for hours until all the signs were planted.

O'Connor was introduced early in her political career to Summit County Republican Party Chairman Alex Arshinkoff and then-Cleveland Mayor George Voinovich by her uncle, Cuyahoga County Engineer Thomas Neff. Arshinkoff and Voinovich are longtime allies (Arshinkoff headed Voinovich's 1994 gubernatorial re-election campaign), and the introduction proved useful to O'Connor's political ascension. In 1993, after her repeated tries for local judicial office, a vacancy occurred on the Summit County Common Pleas Court bench. A local screening committee named by Arshinkoff recommended O'Connor to Voinovich, by then in his first term as governor, and he gave her the appointment.

Onward and upward

O'Connor won election to a full term as judge in 1994 with 68% of the vote. In 1995, she got her next break. Slaby took a seat on the appellate bench before his term as prosecutor expired, leaving Arshinkoff's local party organization to fill the position by direct appointment.

Arshinkoff took the opportunity to push another agenda. He forced his top pick, Kim Hoover, now a Cuyahoga Falls Municipal Court judge, to dump chief criminal prosecutor Fred Zuch for the way he had handled several big cases involving GOP contributors. When Arshinkoff and Hoover quarreled publicly over Zuch's future, O'Connor asked for the prosecutor's job and got it.

"She was much more ambitious than what the judgeship held for her," said Masich.

In 1996, she ran for a full term, clobbering Bodnar despite being embroiled in charges of improper political fund-raising.

Zuch continued to head the criminal division until April 1997, when he retired, but said he feared for his job when O'Connor first arrived. She told him, however, "You've got a job as long as you want it."

O'Connor did reorganize the department, however. She encouraged assistants to talk with her directly, even while Zuch was still in charge of the criminal division. Zuch said that move "tightened up accountability" and was a relief because O'Connor asked so many questions.

Zuch and McCarty both said O'Connor is forceful but willing to listen and that she has been effective in building ties with local law-enforcement personnel and emergency-room doctors, whose testimony is invaluable in court. O'Connor also has made herself available for difficult negotiations with the families of victims, said McCarty. "She was willing to take those tough calls. She will support you."

Against the odds

With both sons headed for college this fall, O'Connor said, the timing was right for a statewide race, even though, as she told Ed, life seemed easier when the boys were in primary school.

"Mom, if it were back then, you couldn't run statewide," her son responded. "Think about that."

By some measures, O'Connor's run appears curious. The odds aren't great for a Republican gubernatorial candidate to succeed a two-termer of his own party. The last time that happened, according to Taft's own research, was 1903.

If the GOP ticket prevails, O'Connor would take a reduction in responsibility and pay. With 270 employees, O'Connor's office in Summit County handles 3,800 criminal cases a year, provides legal advice to all branches of county government and oversees the Child Support Enforcement Agency. Her total budget for all these activities is approximately $14.8 million. Her salary is $90,315.

In contrast, Ohio's lieutenant governor has a staff of about a dozen, operates on an annual budget of $450,000 and gets paid about $60,000. The only statutory responsibility is oversight of the State and Local Government Commission, a body charged with the relationships between the different levels of government.

But several recent occupants of the office, chief among them Mike DeWine, have been successful in redefining the role of Ohio's lieutenant governor and, in turn, in seeking higher office.

DeWine ran with Voinovich in 1990, then launched an unsuccessful bid for the U.S. Senate in 1992. He tried again in 1994, that time defeating Democrat Joel Hyatt.

DeWine's successor, former Marietta Mayor Nancy Hollister, the state's first woman lieutenant governor, opted to run for Congress this year instead of pursuing statewide office, and won a three-way GOP primary in the 6th District.

As the campaign bus rolls on toward Election Day 1998, O'Connor appears utterly unfazed by the clutter, controlled chaos and nagging fatigue associated with statewide campaigns in one of the most politically diverse states in the nation.

Then again, she didn't get into her first statewide race by following an easy, or necessarily predictable, political path.

"I could see her going anywhere," said McCarty.

"She can do it," said O'Connor's uncle Neff. "She's got the mindset."*

---

* O'Connor was elected the 61st Lieutenant Governor of Ohio and served from 1999 to 2003. In 2002, she was elected Associate Justice of the Ohio Supreme Court. In 2010, she was elected Chief Justice of the Ohio Supreme Court and re-elected in 2016.

Mary Taylor: Legislator Eyes Race for Auditor

GOP Rep. Mary Taylor of Green looks statewide

Akron Beacon Journal, January 20, 2005
DENNIS J. WILLARD AND DOUG OPLINGER

State Rep. Mary Taylor, the twice-elected Republican legislator from Green, is setting her sights on higher office. Taylor is in the early stages of making a run for state auditor in 2006.

She confirmed this week that she has hired a staff person to help her lay the groundwork for a statewide campaign next year. She said she has been traveling the state to meet with GOP county chairmen, central committeemen, businesspeople and others to build support for her candidacy.

"The response has been very favorable. It has gone very well," Taylor said.

Taylor said she has thought about running for state auditor in the past—she is a certified public accountant—but she did not think the opportunity would present itself so soon.

The auditor's seat is expected to be an open race next year. Current officeholder Betty Montgomery has indicated she will be a candidate for governor.

Should Montgomery carry through on her intention, each party would invest sizable resources in trying to win the auditor's race, because the auditor is one of three statewide officeholders on the state apportionment board.

Every 10 years, following the U.S. census, the apportionment board redraws Ohio's legislative district lines. The party that holds the pen historically controls the legislature.

The other two seats on the apportionment board—for the governor and secretary of state—also will be open races next year. Although statewide elections will be held in 2010, prior to the completion of that year's census, next year's races will seat three officeholders who would be considered more difficult to unseat as incumbents four years later.

The auditor's office also employs about 1,000 people in Columbus and throughout the state, contracts with private auditors and reviews the financial books of all state agencies, cities, counties, townships, villages, schools and public universities.

Taylor's career in public office began in August 2001 when she was appointed to fill a vacancy on the Green City Council. Five months later, she formally declared her candidacy for the state legislature to replace Twyla Roman, who faced a term limit. Taylor was elected to her first term in November 2002, then re-elected last November.

Taylor said she is not ready to formally announce she is running, and she has not formed a campaign committee for the office. Instead, she is using her state representative campaign committee and paying Christina Haddad, who worked on her first legislative campaign in 2002, to be her campaign manager. Haddad most recently worked on President Bush's campaign in Ohio, Taylor said.

The campaign does not have an office. Haddad is working out of her home, Taylor said.

Taylor said she told Ohio GOP Chairman Bob Bennett about her plans, and he was "supportive and encouraging."

Jason Mauk, spokesman for Bennett, said that Taylor has a "promising future in the Republican Party. She is one of several Republicans considering a statewide run, and we are encouraging all of them in their exploratory efforts."

Taylor said she also let House Speaker Jon Husted, R-Kettering, know she is considering the run. Last week, when Husted handed out committee assignments, Taylor was one of five Republicans who was not named as either a chairman or vice chairman of a standing committee. Scott Borgemenke, Husted's chief of staff, told the Beacon Journal that Taylor's plan to run for statewide office was a factor in the speaker's decision.

Taylor said she talked to Husted about the issues she wants to focus on in the legislature, and they agreed to place her on three committees: Education, Ways and Means, and Economic Development and Environment.

In Ways and Means, Taylor said, she will pursue tax reform and she will be a strong voice to rid Northeast Ohio of the unpopular auto emissions program known as E-Check.

Taylor said her statewide intentions will not divert her attention from serving her Ohio House constituents.*

---

* Taylor defeated Barbara Sykes for state auditor in 2006. In 2010, she was elected the 65th Lt. Governor of Ohio and re-elected in 2014. She unsuccessfully sought the Republican gubernatorial nomination in 2018. In 2021, she was an executive with the Welty Building Company.

Barbara Sykes: Rep. Sykes to Run for Ohio Auditor

Local Democrat delays exit from state politics

Akron Beacon Journal, January 24, 2006
DENNIS J. WILLARD AND DOUG OPLINGER

Two months after saying she planned to retire from state politics, Akron-area legislator Barbara Sykes confirmed Monday she will run for Ohio auditor.

She formally will announce her candidacy today.

The auditor's race will be one of three state offices in Ohio that will attract national attention—and money—as Democrats try to wrest 12 years of Republican rule in Columbus while establishing a foundation to help elect the next president in 2008.

The auditor, governor and secretary of state sit on a board that controls how state legislative districts are drawn every 10 years, following the U.S. census.

Each party is expected to commit considerable resources to those races this year so that an incumbent could run for re-election at the time of the 2010 census.

State Rep. Mary Taylor, R-Green, is expected to run for auditor in the Republican primary.

Sykes, 50, has been a state representative since 2000, when she filled the seat vacated by husband Vernon Sykes, who faced term limits after 17 years in the House.

Barbara Sykes most recently served as president of the Ohio Legislative Black Caucus.

In the 1980s she was a member of Akron City Council and later worked as an executive in the Summit County Auditor's Office.

She ran unsuccessfully for state treasurer in 1994. Republicans that year mounted expensive campaigns to take control of the legislature and win seats on the Ohio Supreme Court, ushering in 12 years of GOP political domination.

Sykes' announcement represents an about-face from November. She said then she would forgo a possible fourth term representing Akron in the Ohio House of Representatives and retire from state politics.

Vernon Sykes, an assistant professor of political science at Kent State University and director of the school's Columbus program, has taken out petitions to run for her seat.

Barbara Sykes said she made the decision to run in recent days after meeting with Howard Dean, the National Democratic chairman. He came to Columbus last Wednesday to coordinate state and federal initiatives to address ethics violations in Ohio, other states and Washington, D.C.

She said she "won't deny" that she met privately with Dean and has been courted by key union and Democratic Party leaders.

John Reardon, Mahoning County treasurer, announced last year he also is interested in the Democratic nomination for state auditor.

Sykes would bring racial diversity to the Democratic ticket. To date, the Republican statewide ticket is more racially diverse than the Democrats with two African American candidates: Ohio Secretary of State J. Kenneth Blackwell, who is running for governor, and Treasurer Jennette B. Bradley, who was appointed to her seat in December 2004 and will ask voters to elect her in November.*

---

* Sykes lost the 2006 Ohio auditor's race to Mary Taylor. Sykes then served as president and CEO of Ohio United Way, and in 2016, became the state director of AARP Ohio. In 2020, she left that position and became president and CEO of the Ohio Legislative Black Caucus Foundation.

Roy Ray: It's Half a Year of Sweet Music for Akron Mayor

Akron Beacon Journal, June 29, 1980
WILLIAM HERSHEY

"Beautiful music," the kind you hear in elevators and doctors' waiting rooms, purrs from the radio as Akron Mayor Roy L. Ray guides his black Chevrolet Caprice Classic down Merriman Road.

It is a sunny, warm June morning, the sort of day an occasional visitor to Akron might never see.

The Republican mayor is headed for City Hall and he is smiling. His six-month-old administration, like the "beautiful music," is purring along.

Dubbed "his shortness" by one sarcastic observer, Ray seems to be everywhere these days. He is short—5 feet, 6 inches—but he is hardly keeping former Mayor John Ballard's low profile.

Two and three nights a week he shows up at neighborhood meetings, the sort of gatherings Ballard avoided during the last part of his 14-year tenure as mayor.

"I believe it's important that people get a chance to see who's running their city," said the 41-year-old Ray.

He is spending so much time meeting people and organizations that his working day frequently is 12 to 14 hours long, leaving him little time for his wife, Frances, and their two sons, Christopher, 10, and Brian, 9. But that's part of the price Ray is paying for the image change he has achieved.

———————

There have also been other breakthroughs—for example, in the strained relationships between the mayor's office and Akron's Black Community. Ballard stoutly resisted the federal lawsuit filed to force the city to hire more Black police officers and firefighters. He railed against federal judges who, he said, had no business interfering in the city's affairs.

Ray, shortly after taking office, decided against further appeals of a court order requiring the city to consider hiring one Black police officer and firefighter for every two whites hired on each force.

———————

The new mayor, on the heels of the Miami race riots, also met privately with Black leaders, disclosing for the first time the names of the police officers involved in last year's shooting of John Woods, a 16-year-old Black robbery suspect.

The mayor has even turned potential embarrassment to his advantage. When it was disclosed that he would be eligible for a second pay raise this year—pushing his $58,302 salary above $60,000—Ray said he would refuse to take it, even though it meant violating a charter provision that he be the city's highest-paid employee.

———————

If the often-seen Ray has benefited from the contrast with the almost reclusive Ballard, he also has gained from projects the former mayor set in motion.

The recent announcement that O'Neil's would cooperate with the city in developing an enclosed downtown shopping mall, with the O'Neil's store as the anchor, resulted from downtown redevelopment plans set in motion by Ballard.

———————

Plans for rejuvenating downtown received another boost last week when nine leading Akron businessmen, including the heads of four Akron-based rubber companies, agreed to spearhead formation of a multi-million-dollar private corporation to finance development projects.

No specific financial pledges have been made, but Ray said he has asked the corporation to come up with from $5 to $8 million in private funds.

None of this will get Ray's picture on the cover of Time magazine or cast him as a dark-horse contender for the Republican vice presidential nomination. In fact, most of it probably will be forgotten by 1983, the year Ray will have to decide whether to seek re-election.

But they are talking about him downtown.

"I think he's done an excellent job," exudes Alex Arshinkoff, the beefy, easily excitable Republican chairman.

Edwin Parms, the outspoken Black lawyer who formerly served as the local NAACP's legal redress chairman is more objective. Based on his chilly, sometimes hostile relationship with Ballard, Ray's political mentor, you might expect Parms to be antagonistic. But he isn't.

"There's no question that at this point Mayor Roy Ray represents a positive change from the past mayoral administration, keeping in mind my remarks are made from a Black perspective," says Parms, president of the Akron Frontiers, a Black service organization.

_____

Parms isn't nominating Ray for political sainthood. He laments that no Black people are in what he considers Cabinet-level positions and that among the secretaries on City Hall's second floor—where Ray and most of his top aides work—there are no Black faces.

Still, Parms ungrudgingly rates the mayor "between a C+ and B-," not bad considering the C- Parms handed out to Police Chief Robert Prease earlier this year.

The mayor also is off to a good start with the Democrat-dominated city council.

"He likes his job and is really working at it," says Robert J. Otterman, the Democratic council president who could be a 1983 mayoral candidate.

_____

It is a quarter to 8 in the morning when Ray drives the wire-wheeled Caprice Classic, which the city leases for him at $249.99 a month, into the City Hall garage.

He walks the two flights of stairs from the basement to his office virtually unnoticed by the handful of city workers who actually have arrived before the 8 a.m. starting time.

The mayor's office looks much as it did during Ballard's tenure. Green derbies from a St. Patrick's Day parade have replaced ceremonial footballs on a display stand, but the mood still is tastefully conservative—a very Republican office.

Ray himself would fit in as comfortably in a corporate board room as he does at City Hall. His thinning red hair is neatly trimmed and there is no hint of the mustache he once sprouted as city finance director. The tan, pin-striped suit, white shirt and dark tie exude the success ethic.

"I'm going to do what I normally do," the mayor says, as he scans the stock market report in the Wall Street Journal.

David A. Pagnard, Ray's administrative assistant, is one of the first visitors to the mayor's office.

Pagnard is proof that not all of Ray's aides are cut from the same bolt of conservative Republican cloth. He is bright, 35 and a one-time liberal Democrat who used to work for Hustler magazine.

Pagnard—now a registered Republican—and the mayor briefly discuss the city's Human Relations Council, a voluntary, advisory group set up to improve race relations. It became dormant in Ballard's last years. Ray has promised to fill vacancies and to appoint a paid, full-time director.

After Pagnard leaves, Ron Soberay arrives. Soberay is a local business executive who paid $400 at the Akron Symphony Orchestra Ball auction to be "mayor for a day." This is his day to spend with the mayor.

Next is a meeting from which Ray excludes a reporter. Present are Service Director William Sigel, deputy service director David Chapman and Planning Director James A. Alkire.

The subject of the brief, private session is the city's floundering, $55 million recycle energy plant. It is not working as planned and the bonds used to build the plant and put it in operation are nearly exhausted.

The plant is designed to burn garbage and trash and to convert it to steam for sale to businesses and institutions in and near downtown.

At a press conference the day before, Ray downplayed the plant's troubles.

"We're confident the financial feasibility will be confirmed," he said.

Privately, however, the mayor and his aides indicate that they very badly want to see results to justify such confidence.

The recycle session delays the start of Ray's 9 a.m. Thursday Cabinet meeting by 15 minutes. He and his top aides will discuss not only next week's plans for running the city, but also long-range concerns such as how to best allocate the scarce funds available for bridges, buildings and other capital improvements.

The mayor, who had a reputation for occasional temper tantrums when he was a finance director, is upset by what is not happening at Cascade Plaza, downtown's $17 million urban renewal showcase.

Despite an additional $3.5 million spent recently to reconstruct the water-damaged plaza, the fountain isn't working, and nobody has installed the sun umbrellas.

"Is that fountain ever going to work in Cascade Plaza?" asks an impatient Ray, who is not smiling.

Sigel, who as service director is in charge of maintaining the plaza—as well as everything from garbage and snow removal to street repairs—says it takes a lot of money to run the fountain. Alkire, who regularly disagrees with service directors, says it should be working.

Ray sides with Alkire.

"I want the fountain to work and the umbrellas up," he declares. (The fountain still isn't operating, but the umbrellas have gone up.)

During the cabinet meeting, Ray impatiently asks why Law Director Robert Pritt isn't there. Pritt, unknown to the public before his appointment, has been the surprise hit of the Ray administration.

A veteran City Hall worker, who requested anonymity, says Pritt is respected because he listens as much as he talks. "He doesn't hesitate to ask people who've been around how to do things," the city worker says.

During the meeting, Ray notices that his hands are dirty. Pagnard quickly shows up with paper towels to wipe away the dirt and Ray's frown.

Ray is scheduled to speak at noon at an insurance company luncheon at the Fairlawn Country Club. After the cabinet meeting, he reads aloud the speech Pagnard and he have worked out on escalating health care costs.

Then Ray, Soberay and his wife Joni and a reporter pile into the mayor's car for the trip to the country club. Pagnard follows in his own car.

Unlike Ballard, who usually was chauffeured by former deputy mayor Jack Fitzgibbons, Ray often drives himself.

Ray, the candidate who once told reporters that he wanted to "expose himself"—he meant be more visible publicly—seems at ease making small talk with the Soberays, who live in the Portage Lakes area.

The luncheon goes smoothly. Ray's weight is up to 155, five pounds more than he weighed during the 1979 campaign, so he passes on the cheesecake with strawberries.

His speech is brief but well received. Ray has learned to react to his own text with a humorous ad lib. After including health care professionals among the villains in the drama of rising health care costs, he adds:

"That would include my wife, who's a nurse."

On the way back to City Hall, the mayor is temporarily stymied by a sign prohibiting left turns onto always-busy West Market Street.

"Close your eyes," orders Ray, who as mayor also serves as safety director. When the eyes are opened, the mayoral car is traveling east on West Market Street, the no-left-turn sign notwithstanding.

Two meeting are scheduled for the afternoon. The first is with officials of Warner Cable of Akron, which has the city's cable television franchise.

Next, Ray meets with Sister M. Brigid, executive director of St. Thomas Hospital, and William H. Considine, administrator of Akron

Children's Hospital. Ray has invited them to discuss the city's emergency medical service.

The meeting is instructive not so much for the subject matter but for how Ray handles himself. "I just want to get your thoughts and ideas," Ray says. He listens more than he talks, the same approach he will take later with a neighborhood group.

This approach seems to be winning friends for the mayor. It eventually could backfire, however, if his sympathetic ear is mistakenly interpreted as a pledge to take some specific action or finance a particular program.

Councilman-at-large Ray Kapper, the Democrat whom Ray defeated last November, says Ray should remember this.

"You can't be all things to all people," says Kapper. "That's the thing Ray needs to be very careful about."

By 4:10, the City Hall meetings are over, and Ray prepares to go home before heading out for an evening meeting.

"I'm very impressed with you," says Soberay, who ends his mayoral tenure without taking in the evening meeting.

On the way home, Ray explains the difference between being mayor and finance director, a job in which he probably was Ballard's closest adviser.

"Everything you do (as mayor) is totally visible," he says. "You can't spend a lot of time on one particular subject."

John E. Holcomb, former law director under Ballard, likes the approach Ray has taken.

"I think he surprised a lot of people," says Holcomb, now in private law practice. "A lot of people thought he was going to be a smaller version of John Ballard."

Ray, who as finance director was "more reserved" and content to work behind the scenes, now is "much more open, much more willing to talk to people," Holcomb says. Ray says he knows that events beyond his control could abruptly end the era of good feeling he's enjoying.

The current recession, for example, appears to be slowly having an effect on city income tax receipts, the mayor says. "We try to do the best job we can on a day-to-day basis," he says. "We can't take counsel with our fears."

————————

Unpopular decisions can quickly wipe out the good will generated by a sympathetic ear, Ray is learning. When he recently ordered the fire station at Canton Road and Triplett Boulevard in Ellet closed, councilman Floyd Sypherd, who represents the area, was beside himself.

Sypherd, chairman of council's powerful Finance Committee, said the mayor and Fire Chief Carl Best apparently aren't concerned about fire protection in the Ellet area. Sypherd said his constituents may have to depend on suburban communities for fire-fighting help.

Problems like this turn up daily, no matter the hour.

————————

Ray usually arrives home about 5:30. On some days the dinner hour is the only time the mayor has with his wife and sons.

The Ray home on Malvern Road is tucked in a West Akron neighborhood of well-kept houses. Dandelions are unwelcome on the well-manicured lawns. It is a neighborhood favored by young executives and professionals and their families.

Mrs. Ray agrees that the 12- and 14-hour days require sacrificing family time, and so far, she's willing to pay the price.

"I think people have a right to meet with their mayor and talk with him," she says.

By 7 o'clock, Ray is back on the road, heading for a meeting of the board of directors of the Firestone Park Citizens' Council. He has changed the pin-striped suit for a more casual ensemble—blue blazer but still with a white shirt and dark tie.

————————

As the Ray car passes Ray Kapper's home on Firestone Boulevard, two boys are playing catch in the yard. The ball flies out of control, narrowly missing Ray's car. It is not a planned attack—last year's election is over—and Ray enjoys a laugh.

John Cochrane, citizens' council president, greets Ray at the Firestone Park shelter house. Dave Bryant, councilman for the area, is there.

Cochrane shows slides indicating the council's work and neighborhood problems.

Ray makes no promises but sympathizes with efforts to improve the Aster Avenue business district and rehabilitate Firestone Park.

"I'm here to listen," says Ray.

Someone asks if efforts to renew downtown will be at the expense of the neighborhoods.

"We have to do both," Ray says. "I'm not here to tell you it's simple."

―――――――――

By 8:50, nearly 13 hours after his day started, Ray is ready to leave the meeting and go home.

The mayor is asked if he felt uncomfortable away from West Akron, meeting with the Firestone Park group in Kapper country.

He shrugs. "It's my city," says the mayor.*

―――――――――

* Ray lost his bid for re-election as Akron mayor in 1983. He was elected to the Ohio Senate in 1986 and served until 2001.

Tom Sawyer: Coming Home to Capitol Hill, Washington

Akron Beacon Journal, February 8, 1987
WILLIAM HERSHEY

Tom Sawyer talked like a man who wanted to smack his lips. Akron's new congressman wouldn't do that, of course. He carefully choreographs every political word and movement. He even tells photographers where to stand when they take his picture. Lip-smacking is not in the script.

But here in Washington last December for the new member orientation, Democrat Sawyer clearly was a happy man. He talked enthusiastically about the "enormous menu" of committee assignments possible for a House member.

He wouldn't say what he ordered, but the "range of options"—from Agriculture to Ways and Means—seemed to appeal to him. The "institutional depth" of the House—with a tradition of more than 200 years—is "enormous," he said admiringly.

Tom Sawyer, who's officially been a member of the U.S. House for a month, has come home, even though he's never been a congressman before.

He started his elected career as a state representative in Columbus and relished the legislative process and the relative anonymity in which he worked. Then, he became Akron's mayor, and after three years in the job, he adjusted to the bright spotlight that always shines on a city's chief executive and said he actually enjoyed the job. But in discussing his new assignment as the successor to Rep. John Seiberling, Sawyer seemed happy to be back in the business of making laws, not administering them.

"I'm more comfortable making this transition than I was from the legislature to the mayor's office," Sawyer said. "That was an extremely difficult and very intense effort."

Sawyer took over the mayor's office in 1984 after a hard-fought and occasionally nasty campaign against Republican incumbent Roy L. Ray. It was the first time since 1966 that the mayor's job passed from one party to another. That year, Republican John S. Ballard took over from Democrat Edward Erickson.

In the House, Sawyer took over from a political ally, Seiberling, who had handpicked him as his successor. Members of Seiberling's congressional staff, many eager to stay on with Sawyer, did all they could to make the transition smooth.

Besides, "I've been a freshman before," said Sawyer, referring to 1977, the first of his seven years in the state legislature.

Fourteen of Ohio's 23-member congressional delegation, including Sen. Howard Metzenbaum, served in the state legislature before arriving here. Reps. Dennis Eckart, D-Mentor, and Bob McEwen, R-Hillsboro, both former members of the Ohio House, said there isn't a better training school.

"The ones who were the most successful were the ones who came out of a legislative background," Eckart said of the newly elected members who came to Congress with him in 1980. "They knew how to find votes. They knew how to get committee assignments. They knew how to make deals."

"The skills used in a state legislative contest are the same skills used in a congressional contest," said McEwen, who also came in 1980. "There is no more sophisticated politics than that which exists in the Ohio House of Representatives."

During his orientation, Sawyer called on senior Democrats who play key roles in making committee assignments. These included chairmen and members of committees on which Sawyer hoped to sit and, perhaps most important, members of the Democratic Steering and Policy Committee. This 31-member group assigns Democrats to committees.

Rep. Louis Stokes, D-Warrensville Heights, represents the Ohio-Pennsylvania region on the committee. Rep. Mary Rose Oakar, D-Cleveland, holds a seat because she is vice chairwoman of the Democratic Caucus. A third Ohioan, Rep. Marcy Kaptur, D-Toledo, was picked by Speaker Jim Wright, D-Texas, as one of his eight personal Steering and Policy appointees.

Sawyer touched as many bases as he could. He was so intent on speaking privately with Stokes that he huffed at a Beacon Journal photographer in Stokes' office taking pictures for this article. The photographer, after a little huffing of his own, left.

"You do more listening than talking," Sawyer said of the private meetings with senior members. It's important, however, for a freshman to let the big-shots know what job he wants.

Seiberling, for example, said that in his first term he ended up on the Science Committee because then-Speaker Carl Albert, D-Okla., thought that's where Seiberling wanted to be. He had wanted a seat on the Interior Committee and got it in his second term.

The key to success is to be eager, but not too eager.

"You've got to be very careful about running for something and losing," Eckart said. "You don't want to look like a loser when you go for something."

Being careful, of course, is part of Sawyer's style. During orientation week, he wouldn't even publicly state what assignments he wanted. But last month, after the Steering and Policy Committee picked him to serve on the Education and Labor and the Government Operations committees, he said that those committees had been his first choices.

While a first-year House member has some control over what committee he or she gets on, chance determines where his or her office will be. Sawyer didn't do very well in the office lottery. He got the 44th pick out of 46 new members competing in the drawing.

In drawing poorly, Sawyer was in famous company. Massachusetts Rep. Joseph P. Kennedy II, son of the late Sen. Robert Kennedy, picked 45th.

Sawyer ended up on the third floor of the Longworth House Office Building in a small suite, one floor up from where Seiberling's office was. He was assigned an "annex" on the fifth floor to house some of his staff.

That outcome, so far, has been an improvement over what happened to Rep. Edward Feighan, D-Lakewood, when he arrived in Washington in 1982 fresh from a seat on the Cuyahoga County Commission.

"When I was a county commissioner—Oh, for those glorious days!—we had large spacious offices with conference tables and couches and offices to conduct a lot of work in comfortably," Feighan recalled.

Few, if any, of the other offices here match the accommodations most other locally elected officials have. But Feighan had a special problem at first. New members are last on the list when it comes to painting and cleaning up old offices. His simply wasn't ready.

"My first office was a closet off the staff room of Dennis Eckart's office," he said. "That was for three or four weeks."

Sawyer and other new members have more control over filling their offices than they do in picking them. They can hire up to 18 staff members to help them analyze legislation, study issues and field constituent complaints.

To help him in his new position, Sawyer has hired James M. Dolan Jr., 40, as his administrative assistant, one of two top jobs in a congressional office. Dolan, who worked as a consultant and fundraiser in Sawyer's successful election campaign against Republican Lynn Slaby, is a former newspaper reporter and previously was administrative assistant to Rep. Barney Frank, D-Mass., and press secretary to former Rep. Margaret Heckler, now U.S. ambassador to Ireland.

Dolan's appointment drew applause from one veteran House staffer familiar with the Ohio delegation.

"Dolan will help Sawyer hit the ground running," said the staffer. "Jimmy's very well plugged in around here."

Sawyer also indicated that he would keep a half-dozen or more of Seiberling's top aides on his staff. Another House staffer, who asked to be nameless, questioned the wisdom of this. Questions could arise, the staffer said, about loyalties—whether they were to Sawyer or to the departed Seiberling.

Sawyer brushed aside such questions. Strong, experienced people generally do better work, he said.

"If I were concerned about strong people, I'd never have hired Ray Kapper (as Akron service director), a very strong man, but he is a man who I know can look you in the eye, and give you his word, and that's the end of it," Sawyer said.

Seiberling's aides were too valuable a resource to waste, he added. In addition, he got to know many of them when he was mayor.

"What's important is that they are a group of people who both know the (Capitol) Hill and the 14th Congressional District," Sawyer said. "That's unusual."

Eckart applauded Sawyer's decision to go with experience.

"It's essential. You pay a premium for that," Eckart said. "The worst mistake is to bring in the campaign manager from south somewhere who never has seen Washington before."

McEwen, however, said that bringing in some fresh faces has advantages. "People that go to work for new members generally are more energetic and committed than some of the more seasoned employees."

While House members have long hours, they also need a place to live, and that also posed a challenge to Sawyer.

The basic choice was: Should his family—wife Joyce and daughter Amanda, 11—move to Washington or should he get a place here for himself and commute home on the weekends?

There really wasn't much of a debate. The Sawyers chose the second option.

"Joyce (a school teacher) has a career," Sawyer said. "It's a 20-year career to this point. She enjoys it and she's good at it."

Finding an apartment in Washington can be a headache, but Sawyer had assistants scout out the possibilities, and he looked at just two places before deciding on a one-bedroom apartment within walking distance of the Capitol.

Commuting is nothing new to Sawyer. During his seven years as a state representative, he became very well acquainted with Interstate 71 and the 2 ½-hour drive from Akron to Columbus.

He and his family knew when he'd be home, and they made the most of their time together. Actually, Sawyer said, he saw his family more when he was a legislator than when he was mayor.

"The kind of arrangement I envision, at least in the near term, is they're home...I'm gone three or four or five days a week, from time to time, but then when we're home, we're doing things together and even those things that involve meetings…we've done that our whole lives."

Sawyer said it's important for him, for his family and for his constituents that he preserve a "sense of home," as embodied by his house on Akron's North Hill.

Not everybody does it the same, of course. Eckart's wife and son live with him in Washington, while Feighan's wife and three children live in Lakewood. Feighan commutes on the weekends and during recesses. Feighan's family tried living in Washington for a while but preferred living in Ohio. "We simply feel more comfortable as a family," Feighan said.

Back in December, Sawyer already was feeling comfortable enough to begin thinking about what resources he would need in two years to keep the $77,400-a-year job he's just been elected to. A House member generally is considered most vulnerable after his first term, and Sawyer knows the Republicans will come gunning for him in 1988.

That's as good a reason as any why he made time on his schedule for a dinner meeting with a representative of the National Association of Realtors. Sawyer's record as a mayor and state legislator generally had the approval of realtors, but the Akron Area Board of Realtors supported Slaby last November. It would be nice to have support—translate that into money—from the realtors next time.

"It was just a way for them to say we understood what you were doing and for me to say I understood what you were doing, and I didn't have to agree with it, but it was not a problem," Sawyer said.

The lobbyists won't start banging hard on Sawyer's doors until he's settled into his committee assignments and has cast a few votes. By then, he'll be further along on his "action items" agenda, which covers everything from conducting workshops back home on federal aid to establishing a political program of fundraising and, if necessary, fence-raising.

The pace will be hectic and, according to others who have made the "freshman passage," Sawyer may occasionally have second thoughts about coming to Washington. There'll be frustrations, and the commutes home may seem endless. The exterminators won't show up to do battle with the cockroaches who somehow survive in the House office buildings.

But there will be plenty of rewards.

Eckart recalls the thrill of walking across Independence Avenue and "seeing the (Capitol) dome illuminated for your first State of the Union speech."

Feighan remembers having dinner with former Speaker Thomas P. "Tip" O'Neill and spending an evening with Rep. Dan Rostenkowski, D-Ill., powerful chairman of the Ways and Means Committee.

"It is your first introduction to the greatest seat of power in the world and the individuals who, in some instances, have taken on mythic proportion," Feighan recalled.

It's all on that "enormous menu" that Sawyer is just beginning to know.*

---

* Sawyer was elected to eight terms in the U.S. House. He tried for a ninth in 2002 but lost in the Democratic primary after the district lines were redrawn. He was appointed to the Ohio Senate in 2007 and elected to two terms in 2008 and 2012.

Don Plusquellic: A Kid from Kenmore

Don Plusquellic blooms right where he's planted

Akron Beacon Journal Beacon Magazine, September 17, 2000
BOB DYER

It's a comfortable choice. Very Akron. Very familiar. Don's kind of dish.

And Don, without a doubt, is Akron's kind of dish. How else to explain the incredible political success of a man who has broken every rule in the political science book?

You can't be the mayor of a modern American city and tell people exactly what you think. Not if you want to win any more elections. You can't take things personally. You can't lash out and burn bridges. You can't enjoy a brew or two or three with the guys, swear like a longshoreman and still win the hearts of little old ladies from Ellet to North Hill to Wooster Avenue.

Oh, yes you can. You can if your name is Don Plusquellic. In his case, you can come roaring onto the political scene as a 24-year-old Democratic councilman, spend the next three decades sounding off more than Don King, and—as of Jan. 1, 2001—become the longest-serving mayor in Akron's 175-year history.

When Don Plusquellic thinks people are lying to him, Don Plusquellic calls them liars. And he doesn't much care who's listening. If

Don Plusquellic thinks the local newspaper is doing him wrong, Don Plusquellic will fire back with gusto, even though the conventional wisdom says you don't get into fights with people who buy ink by the barrel. This guy simply doesn't follow the plays. He wings it. He scrambles. He goes with his gut.

But he keeps getting re-elected. Four straight times. As many times as he wants, probably. The votes aren't even close. His approval rating continues to hover around 80%. Eighty percent! That kind of number nearly *requires* you to run for higher office. But Don Plusquellic doesn't want to run for higher office. He's happy doing exactly what he's doing.

To paraphrase Butch Cassidy, who *is* this guy?!

The answer is remarkably well hidden, given the fact that Plusquellic has become a household name—and not just in Greater Akron. He is increasingly known in the households of national reporters and political leaders. The Wall Street Journal praises him on Page 1. The National Conference of Mayors asks him for hints on Joint Economic Development Districts. He has visited the Clinton White House so many times he has lost count.

This year alone, the Akron Beacon Journal has printed 298 stories containing the name Don Plusquellic. Over the last 15 years, that number is 4,671. But when you subtract the stories about civil celebrations and city projects and major news developments and personnel conflicts, what remains? Peel away those very public activities and the person who is seemingly omnipresent is barely even there.

So…who *is* this guy?!

Well, he's not terribly complicated. Most people think he is, which doesn't bother him a bit. In fact, he kind of likes it. But to fully understand Don Plusquellic, you only need to know three things:

- His favorite song is *The House of the Rising Sun*.
- He makes $119,925 a year but still lives in a small house in Kenmore, right next door to his mother-in-law, two doors down from his sister and one block from his mother.
- He hated Woody Hayes.

Now, this will take a bit of amplification. Bear with us, though, because getting to know the personal side of Don Plusquellic is a lot like spending a couple of days with him: There's a lot of verbiage to wade through, but the end result is worth it.

Along the way, we will also solve such long-running mysteries as:

- Did he really pinch that woman's posterior in 1986 on a boozy chartered bus trip home from a Browns-Steelers game?
- When did he quit stealing souvenirs from the White House?
- Why was he as white as a ghost at his own wedding?
- Who was that stout guy sitting with Sophia Loren?
- Was he really a football superstar, or is that just political hype fueled by the passing of the decades?

Well, let's start at the bottom. After all, that's where Plusquellic believes the media always starts.

Quite a sport

Once and for all: This guy could *play.* As a quarterback for the Kenmore Cardinals, he was all-city, all-district and all-state. First team all-state, as a matter of fact.

That accomplishment is even more amazing when you peer into the archives and learn that he hardly even played as a junior. He had the misfortune to be one year younger than schoolmate Keith Gross, an all-district quarterback. When he finally got his chance, Plusquellic broke the school passing record in only half a season. By the end, he had thrown 20 touchdown passes and led Kenmore into the city championship game.

That spring, the Akron Beacon Journal ran a four-column headline announcing his college choice: "Plusquellic Picks Pitt." He had visited seven other schools—Ohio State, Purdue, Iowa, Northwestern, Cincinnati, Vanderbilt and Columbia—but chose a school whose football program was in the dumps. He didn't want to sit around, waiting for somebody else to graduate. He wanted to play. Right now.

That wasn't the only reason he turned down Ohio State. When Plusquellic sat down with the legendary Woody Hayes, his worst fears were confirmed. It wasn't just that Plusquellic found Woody to be "the most arrogant son of a gun I'd ever met." It was more Woody's style of football. Woody had absolutely no intention of moving away from his play-it-safe, 3 yards-and-a-cloud-of-dust offense. When you throw the ball, Woody believed, bad things can happen.

Plusquellic knows throwing the ball is more risky. But he thinks you won't make the big plays if you don't take chances. The analogy is obvious: As a mayor, if you keep on running straight ahead, helmet down, doing the same things everybody else has done, you're not going to transform a downtown that by 1985 had become a corpse.

But we were talking football.

In the 1960s, freshmen were ineligible for the varsity. No. 10 won the starting job on the freshman team and went to war against schools such as Penn State. Then he suffered the first of a series of physical setbacks, blowing out a knee in practice. It still wasn't fully healed by the time the varsity started practicing in the spring, and he was edged out for the starting job as a sophomore. With Pitt losing 49–0, he was sent into a game against UCLA, got no blocking and was beaten to a pulp. Soon, the Beacon Journal ran a headline that spanned the top of an entire page: "Plusquellic Quits Pitt Grid Varsity."

Pitt's football program was in disarray and the coach would soon be fired. Plusquellic transferred to Bowling Green and, after sitting out a year, found himself the backup again. As a junior, playing behind a senior, he completed 21 of 48 passes, according to the Bowling Green sports information office, with no touchdowns and five interceptions. But his teammates thought so highly of him that they voted him a captain for the following season—an amazing honor for a transfer student.

One week before the opening game of his senior year, he was clobbered during a scrimmage and suffered a separated shoulder, which ended his career.

Today you ask whether he thinks, without the injuries and in the right program, he could have gone on to play professionally. He smiles. For once, this man with the gift of gab—this fellow who, in the words of a college friend, "could talk a penguin off an ice cube"—hesitates before answering. He gazes out the window of his second-floor office. He is weighing his options, which are two: He can downplay his talent to avoid the possibility of coming across as a braggart, or he can tell his version of the truth. The truth wins out. "I could throw 75 yards," he responds.

"People would say, 'Hit me right here in the eyes,' and I'd say, 'Which eye?' I had great accuracy."

One of his teammates at Bowling Green was Tony Kijanko, a 6-foot-6 offensive tackle who played one year with the Cleveland Browns before going on to become a celebrated coach at Tallmadge, Stow and Cuyahoga Valley Christian Academy. "We had four of five guys who went on to the NFL, and there was certainly no reason he couldn't have," says Kijanko. "Donny had a great arm. He was amazing. He would put on a show. I would have to throw the ball three times to match his one."

Even today Plusquellic's hand-eye coordination is so good that four months ago he jacked a batting-practice pitch over the wall at Jacobs Field. And he didn't just squeak it over; he drove it about a third of the way onto the home-run porch in left field. He has a video to prove it. And he doesn't mind showing it to you. As many times as you'd like.

Plusquellic's athletic prowess seems ironic, given the fact that the man is a walking physical disaster. You may not realize this, but Akron's mayor appears to be well on his way to establishing the Guinness World Record for Most Food Poisonings.

Casualty List

First, there was that day on the beach when he ate a peach seed because he didn't know it was poisonous. Then there was the Florida vacation in the mid-1980s when he ate a contaminated raw oyster and on the drive back to Ohio had to check into a West Virginia hospital. And, of course, early this year, he returned home from the Bahamas with such a horrendous case of food poisoning that he was hospitalized for four days. (All of which makes you wonder why anyone would ever go on vacation with this man.)

That's just his stomach. We also have the football injuries to his knees (two surgeries) and the perpetually bad back (three surgeries). And then there was the bodysurfing episode. On vacation—naturally—at Rehoboth Beach, Del., he attempted to ride an 8-foot wave and was pile-driven into the ocean floor, which scraped half the skin off his face, pinched a nerve in his neck and left him temporarily paralyzed.

We also have the scare of 1989, when he was hospitalized for severe head pains twice within the same week. (The doctors, suspecting neck injuries, put him in traction.) And the scare of 1998, when he was hospitalized with chest pains. (No surgery, but he takes medication.)

If you're a tough guy from Kenmore, though, you don't whine about a little pain. You're accustomed to it. You remember how you felt after a football game. You remember how people feel after a day of manual labor, like that miserable winter you spent loading lumber at Brown-Graves after quitting Pitt. You remember your dad working six days a week in the rubber shop, hands gnarled from years of abuse. Most of all, you remember that your dad died at age 49, and that his brother died at 33, and that not one other male member of the Plusquellic clan lived past 50. You're never totally certain today won't be your last. So you shrug off the aches and carry on.

You do more than that, actually. You wear your blue-collar background as a badge of honor. You love the concept of toughing it out, of overcoming long odds, of being a regular guy who can hold his own with the hotshot Ivy Leaguers in their fancy suits. You pride yourself on facing off with the nastiest opponents and simply outlasting 'em.

Your favorite song is *The House of the Rising Sun*, the 1964 remake by the Animals, a soul- and blues-influenced rock band that turned the tune into a primal scream of pride in a hardscrabble existence. You love that song so much that you sing it everywhere, from your bachelor party to your daughter's wedding reception to the rotating stage at a Florida karaoke bar during a gathering of the nation's mayors. You love the song so much that you've customized the lyrics to refer to the mayor of a certain Midwestern city.

Not the song that is autobiographical. Your father was the polar opposite of the lowlife in the song. Your own pop was a hardworking, straight-ahead guy, a man who gave his employer a solid day's work for a solid day's pay, a guy from the generation that wasn't afraid of hard work, that wasn't afraid of much of anything—except, of course, of revealing its true feelings. Guys from that era didn't do much of that.

Your dad never told you or your sisters that he loved you. But you knew, even as a youngster. You knew it instinctively. Later, you would come to know it intellectually as well. But only after Dad was gone. Only when it was too late to hang out with him, to sit around talking like a couple of grown-ups, talking man-to-man. Bleep.

But they knew, the children of David Plusquellic, the three girls and the athletic boy. They knew by his actions. They knew love was the reason that, after joining the Navy, he moved from western Pennsylvania, where the coal mines had nearly run dry, to the Rubber Capital of the World, following the woman who would become his wife, moving to a place where a man could find honest work and support a family.

Don Plusquellic will tell you all about this stuff. But he'll tell it to you more slowly than he tells most stories. That's because he has to make sure the moisture in his eyes doesn't build up so much that it trickles down his face, messing up his tough-guy image. He's not as tough as his dad, you see. The son gets emotional. And the son has no qualms about telling his kids he loves them.

But Don Plusquellic is tough enough. Too tough, some say. Critics call him a bully, a man who perceives any disagreement as a personal affront. His supporters admit he is opinionated, but say he works hard to build a consensus on issues and agonizes over important decisions.

Motoring mouth

Ask Plusquellic about this and he'll talk your ear off. Ask him *anything* and he'll talk your ear off. If the subject is politics, he'll talk *both* your ears off. If the subject is sports, he'll talk the ears off you and your spouse and your kids and your dog and the horse you rode in on.

But the stories are great. And it doesn't take long to figure out that a significant part of Don Plusquellic's success can be attributed to his pure personal magnetism. When you talk to him, he makes you feel important. He remembers things about you and drops them into the conversation. The blue eyes pop. The wit crackles. The perpetually tanned face and the silver hair give him the look of an aging movie star. And, for a 51-year-old fossil, he's reasonably fit. Well, *almost* fit. OK, *potentially* fit.

The Wall Street Journal, in an otherwise flattering profile, identified him as "stout." Which wounded hizzoner to the core.

"I knew it had more than one meaning. I just didn't know how he meant it," says the man who weighed 185 in college and currently carries a driver's license that reads 225. During a breakfast meeting the day of the article, a woman pointed out that *stout* also can mean "courageous" and "strong of heart." Another woman said it means "virile."

Responded Plusquellic: "Damn! Why didn't he just use the word virile?"

That's typical Plusquellic. Brash and funny and always talking.

His friends are the same way. They simply can't keep their mouths shut, even when they know they should. Call up Bill "Pete" Pietrantonio, Plusquellic's roommate at Pitt, tell him you're looking for some dirt to use in a newspaper article, and he eagerly complies.

A lieutenant in the fire department in Everett, Mass., near Boston, Pietrantonio regales you with old war stories. Like the time during their sophomore year when Plusquellic was invited to the Pietrantonio house for the weekend.

Pietrantonio's grandparents lived next door and, despite being in their 80s, could party with the best of 'em. So when Plusquellic and Pietrantonio came home after an evening on the town, they headed next door for a nightcap. Plusquellic was about to discover what Pietrantonio already knew: Don't try to keep up with Granny when she's knocking back her Seven-and-Sevens.

Plusquellic gave it the old college try but came up short. Just about everything else came up, too, if you catch the drift. The future mayor spent the entire weekend in bed. "He was so sick my parents wanted to take him to the hospital," Pietrantonio says, cackling. "He stayed in bed for two days. That's how he spent the weekend at my house—throwing up and sleeping."

Plusquellic almost pulled an encore at his own wedding. Pete was the best man, you see, and Pete saw to it that his buddy had the traditional bachelor party send-off the night before. Had a merry old time, they did. But the morning of the wedding, things did not go as smoothly.

"He couldn't get out of bed," says Pete, howling again. "His mother was petrified. They wouldn't tell Mary (his fiancée) because she would have gone ballistic. They were feeding him coffee and trying to make him get sick…His parents were screaming and yelling at him."

But Plusquellic rallied and made it to the church on time. "He's still white as a ghost," Pietrantonio continues. "Don's not Catholic but Mary is, and it's a Catholic wedding, and they have to sip the wine…He's breaking out in a sweat. He couldn't even look. He was dying. He was sick as a dog. It was terrible. It was funny."

Loose lips

Just before hanging up the phone, Pietrantonio says, "I shouldn't be giving you all this." Probably not. But this time, Plusquellic can't blame the media. Can we help it if everybody in this story acts like Jim Carrey in the film *Liar, Liar?*

"He's horrible at managing his time," says another alleged ally. The speaker would be none other than his wife, the former Mary Goffee. The woman who grew up in the house next door, where her mom still lives. The one who sent Don a Valentine's Day card in fifth grade that said, "I Love You." The one who sent him a get-well card after hearing about his knee injury at Pitt. The one who didn't get a real date with him until years later.

She is smiling. She is sitting on the sofa of their small but beautifully decorated home near Nesmith Lake, the place they bought 15 years ago for $48,500. Don is away, dropping off his 1-year-old granddaughter after an early morning visit, and now his wife is alone with an arsenal of potentially damning stories built up over 28 years of marriage.

She confirms the complaints of his longtime colleagues at City Hall, who say the guy is great to be around but manages his time about as well as his granddaughter does. He's always late. He's always going off on some tangent. He is so horrid at time management, says Mary, that she has simply given up. "He's too old to change."

He doesn't pay the bills either. She does. He doesn't cut the grass. They hire somebody.

Her brown eyes sparkle under thick hair. Her manner is easy and pleasant. She had worried about the interview earlier, insisting that her husband ask her some practice questions before the reporter showed up. But now she seems to be relishing the chance to drop a little dust onto the gloss of Mr. 80% Approval Rating.

Later, though, she'll call you up and ask if you noticed the roses on the kitchen table. Don grew those, she says. She wants to reinforce her earlier comments that Don has a sensitive side. She wants to make sure you know about the guy who comes home after a tough day and needs a hug.

That side of the mayor is the reason the marriage was able to survive some rocky moments. Things got particularly shaky in 1980, when he was going to law school at Akron and she was working outside the home and the kids were young and nobody had any time and nobody was doing what they pictured themselves doing when they both said "I do." But they worked it out. Just like they worked things out after the infamous butt-pinching incident in 1986.

It was all over the newspaper. During a beer-sodden bus ride home from a Browns-Steelers football game, a woman who had gone to the rear of the bus to use the restroom was pinched in the posterior on her way back. She initially thought the pincher was Plusquellic. It was not. Given the position he was in, to pinch her on the spot she was pinched would have required the flexibility of a contortionist, as she later conceded. But the PR damage was done.

"I took that very personal because, you know, whenever there is a sexual connotation there, yeah, that bothers me," says Mary. "But I felt that I knew the whole story, and we got through it."

They work at the marriage. And it gets easier. The memories pile up. The fondness grows.

For Mary, the union has also delivered totally unexpected fringe benefits. Hanging just inside her front door are color photographs from the White House. Mary and Don with Bill and Hillary. Mary and Don with Tipper and Al. Tuxedos and formal gowns and big smiles. Some of the photos include her kids and her mother.

"Here I am, the daughter of a truck driver, and Don the son of a rubber worker, and we are standing in the White House. I was in awe. I am every time I go. It's amazing to me."

Neither of them knows exactly how many times they have attended White House functions—so often, Don jokes, that he has stopped stealing stuff to prove he was actually there. He goes to a drawer and pulls out evidence of petty theft, some paper napkins with the presidential seal in gold.

Magic moment

The mayor's biggest White House heist, though, was aided and abetted by a White House staffer who apparently figured Plusquellic would fit right in at a state dinner for the president of Italy. When Plusquellic heard the other names on the guest list—most of which ended in a vowel—he informed the White House that his roots are actually French, not Italian, and offered to surrender his spot. When the White House lamely insisted it had not made an error, he gladly accepted—and found himself seated with Sophia Loren.

Jokes Plusquellic: "We had a great conversation going, but the president kept butting in."

For the first few decades of his life, Plusquellic didn't know much about his heritage, either, because so many of his ancestors had died prematurely. Through a series of coincidences, he eventually tracked his lineage to a tiny village named Plusquellic in Brittany. On a visit to a cemetery there, he and his wife spotted a 450-year-old tombstone shared by a husband Plusquellic and a wife named Goffe. Which prompted Don to intone: "I made this same mistake 450 years ago."

Although Don didn't set foot out of North America until 1988, he now routinely jets around the globe. Mary has branched out as well. With the kids now gone—Michelle, 25, is teaching and Dave, almost 27, is in new business development at FirstEnergy—she has embarked on a new career. She is (excuse the expression) an intern, working as a chemical-dependency counselor at Oriana House, where she hopes to land a permanent job after graduating from The University of Akron.

Given Don's prominence, the couple did a remarkable job of keeping the public spotlight off of the kids while they were growing up. The parents were determined to give their children a normal life. It's not easy being in a fishbowl, even when it's a small bowl.

The mayor insists that the media—particularly the Beacon Journal—almost made him quit before the last election because of its misleading stories. He insists the newspaper temporarily chased his son out of town while he was job-hunting because nobody wanted to hire him for fear it would trigger a front-page story implying somebody was playing favorites. The offers eventually came, but much later than they would have, Plusquellic maintains.

He seems to forget all the praise, like a 1975 editorial that called the young newcomer "one of the brighter lights on the council," praise that expanded into a degree of prolonged editorial-page support that, by his own admission, was almost embarrassing. He forgets the news stories and columns that credited him with almost single-handedly bringing downtown Akron back from oblivion. He focuses on the digs, the times he thought somebody was trying to boost circulation at his expense. He sincerely believes one reason politics is such a mess is that the press will hop all over an innocent slip of the tongue—see Quayle, Dan—and turn it into perpetual ridicule.

Plusquellic will remember every dig in this story. He will try to exact retribution on his old buddy Pietrantonio, who offered up the long-ago tales of debauchery. He won't remember that Pietrantonio, in a serious moment, also offered the ultimate praise: "If you had a son, Don is who you'd want him to be modeled after."

Don's own father died 28 years ago this very day, Sept. 17. And Don Plusquellic—who once won awards for perfect attendance at Bible school and Sunday school—hasn't been to church since. Truth be told, he's holding a bit of a grudge.

It just wasn't fair what God did. When Don was working as a beer delivery man, he would go into the neighborhood bars and see guys drunk at 9 in the morning. He'd see the drug dealers on the street. And he'd say to himself, "Why not have lightening hit and scatter 16 times and kill 16 of those SOBs and leave my dad alone?"

How could God snuff out a guy who, during his last four years, didn't take a single week of vacation? A guy stuck on the overnight shift at age 43? A guy who in three more weeks was finally going to fulfill a longtime promise to take his wife to Hawaii, where he had served in World War II, to show her how beautiful it was?

Instead, the man is zapped by a heart attack at work in a filthy old rubber shop. A lifetime of labor and this is how it ends. Before the big vacation. Before the father and son can sit down and talk like adults. Before either one of them could tell the other he loved him.

Don Plusquellic was determined not to make the same mistakes, even if his father's mistakes were simply a product of the prevailing culture. Don wouldn't make his own kids wait so long to discover how much their accomplishments meant to him. They didn't have to learn years after the fact, like he did, that the day after he led his football team to a 42–38 win over powerful Barberton in 1966, his dad took great pride in marching into Barberton's Seiberling Rubber and strutting past the co-workers who had taunted him about Kenmore's allegedly inferior team. Don's football accomplishments meant a lot to his dad. A lot more than he ever let on.

So Akron's mayor can accept the fading eyes and the creaky bones and the endless days and the late-night phone calls. He can even roll with the ongoing punches from the evil beings in the media. Because— bleep!—he wasn't even supposed to live this long. All of this is a bonus. The family. The job. This place. A place where he doesn't have to sit on the sidelines and watch other people get things done. A place where he belongs. A place where 80% of the people say they like him. A place where family members says they love him.

And the grandkid—well, the grandkid looks just awesome through any old set of eyes.*

---

* Plusquellic resigned as Akron mayor on May 31, 2015 after more than 27 years in office, making him Akron's longest-serving mayor.

George Voinovich: A Voice of Tranquility on Road to "Normalcy"

Akron Beacon Journal, August 17, 1980
WILLIAM HERSHEY

The dull but honest mayor, known for his low profile, was talking about what most citizens want from City Hall.

"I think," said the mayor with gee-whiz, gosh-darn sincerity, "that people are just basically interested in getting good service."

If you're from Akron, it's easy to recognize the speaker: Republican John S. Ballard, the non-cheerleader who for 14 years used his low profile to keep the Democrats at bay, the business community happy and the garbage trucks running on time.

But you're wrong. Ballard has retired.

The city is Cleveland. The mayor is another Republican, George V. Voinovich, who has taken this town of chicken paprikash and sauerkraut by yawn with a style as spicy as a McDonald's hamburger—with salt and pepper.

"Let's accentuate the positive," says Voinovich, 44. "Let's disagree without being disagreeable."

He really talks that way.

For the nine months he has been mayor, Voinovich has been an uncommon voice of calm in an urban caldron where mayors regularly bubble over.

Ralph Perk's antics ranged from igniting his hair with a welding torch to ordering garbage crews to conduct pornography surveys. Dennis Kucinich, Voinovich's immediate predecessor, kept Cleveland in the headlines with a loud, two-year holy war against banks and big business.

———————

Recognition of any similarities between him and Ballard, Voinovich and his aides make clear, will be taken as a compliment.

Phillip C. Allen, Akron budget director under Ballard, was recruited by Voinovich to serve as director of budget and management.

"Their approach is pretty much the same—let's get the job done and the hell with politics," Allen says of his old and new bosses.

It's not by accident that Voinovich's name seldom is in the headlines and his face only infrequently shows up on the local newscasts.

"We're not out to make stories," says Allen. "We're out there to get the job done."

Allen's new boss, Mayor Voinovich, said that "people will never realize how lucky they were to have a guy like Ballard, a bread and butter guy," gee-whizzing again.

———————

George Forbes, the 6-foot, 3-inch Democratic city council president who doesn't try to keep a low profile, says Voinovich has "restored (Cleveland) to normalcy."

Confrontation is out. Cooperation is in. Forbes couldn't be happier.

"At this particular time George Voinovich is what the city needs," says Forbes, who once turned off Kucinich's microphone when that mayor was addressing the council.

"After the storm, somebody has to clean up. We don't need anybody to take chances. We need somebody to restore confidence in ourselves."

"He (Voinovich) seems to go about this without making a big splash," says Larry A. Retallick, executive vice president of the Urban League of Greater Cleveland. "It's kind of refreshing not to see somebody with a big toothy smile at every little thing."

The Voinovich profile, Retallick adds, isn't as low as it seems. This summer, Retallick learned from his wife who learned from a friend, Voinovich was taking unannounced walks through city neighborhoods, listening to the residents, examining the problems.

Edric Weld Jr., a professor of urban studies at Cleveland State University, is slightly amazed that what Voinovich is doing could happen in Cleveland.

"The key point is that Mr. Voinovich has people back working together," says Weld. "I mean the whole community."

Timothy F. Hagan, Cuyahoga County Democratic chairman, pays grudging tribute.

"I think he has lowered the rhetoric," Hagan concedes. "The decibels are down. There seems to be rational discussion. In fairness to him, he doesn't look at people who oppose him as enemies but as adversaries."

Not everyone is in love with Voinovich and "normalcy."

To councilman Jay Westbrook, "normalcy" hasn't changed much since Warren Harding and Calvin Coolidge returned the country to it in 1920.

It means, Westbrook says, government controlled by big business and the banks, with the citizens ignored and on the sidelines.

Voinovich, by moving to pull the city out of default and pay overdue bills, has pleased the bankers and the business leaders (most of whom don't live in Cleveland), but generally has ignored the citizens, Westbrook accuses.

This is the same "cooperation" that existed under Perk and other mayors until Kucinich, a populist Democrat, tried to change things, adds Westbrook.

"What the people have gotten out of it," Westbrook says of the Voinovich tenure, "is nothing but declining service, increased rates (for city services) and a proposed tax increase."

So far, Westbrook is in the minority. Voinovich, a Cleveland native of Serbian-Slovenian descent, has brought at least temporary relief to residents tired of hearing their city called the "mistake on the lake."

And, after a decade and a half of seeking and holding various offices, Voinovich, a lawyer, appears to have found the one he really wants.

The 1979 mayoral race was his ninth campaign in 14 years. He ran successfully for state representative in 1966, 1968, and 1970. He lost to Perk in the 1971 mayoral primary but was elected county auditor in 1972 and 1974. In 1976, he won a county commission seat and, as Gov. Rhodes running mate, was elected lieutenant governor in 1978.

The problems he inherited in his new job, Voinovich concedes, were worse than even he anticipated.

They started at least as far back as Mayor Carl Stokes (1967–1971), continued under Perk (1971–1977), and culminated with Kucinich (1977–1979), Weld says.

Faced with a declining population, a stagnant property tax and increasingly expensive city services—and generally bound by their own pledges of "no new taxes"—the mayors muddled through.

For example, the city's sewers were sold to a regional authority and the money from the sale, while it lasted, was used for day-to-day operating expenses.

Millions of federal revenue-sharing dollars, which are appropriated at the whim of Congress, were spent to pay police salaries.

(In contrast, Ballard and the Akron City Council put aside most of the revenue-sharing money sent there for capital expenditures. The theory was that the money was nice while it lasted, but that what Congress gives, Congress also can take away.)

Borrowing increased, without anticipated revenues to handle the debt.

Making problems worse, Weld says, was the voters' perception that "inflation only hits them." In fact, adds Weld, the labor-intensive city machine of police officers, firefighters and garbage collectors was getting increasingly expensive to run as resources continued to dwindle.

Cleveland, Weld says, was a "time bomb ticking away."

It went off Dec. 15, 1978 when the city defaulted on $10.5 million in notes.

Voinovich and eight Cleveland banks have worked out a tentative agreement for refinancing $36 million in city notes, including the $10.5 million from the default. In addition, the state has agreed to lend the city $15 million to pay off overdue bills.

"Something is going on in Cleveland that is right," says Weld.

Weld's optimism is relative. Default may soon end but the city's staggering problems will be far from solved.

"This is a great big hospital for all the people who can't make it," Weld despairs.

He rattles off statistics backing up his claim. Two examples: One-fifth of the mothers in the state receiving Aid to Dependent Children benefits live in Cleveland; in 1970 only 37% of the city's adults were high school graduates and it's likely to be worse when this year's census figures are released.

"We are a city of old people, poor people and Black people," echoes Forbes.

For the young people that are left, Forbes and Weld agree, the immediate future isn't bright.

"Our public education system is probably the worst in the state," Forbes says. "The crucial problem we don't have solved is the Cleveland school board," Weld says. "Until somebody can mobilize somebody to do something there…"

The board's most recent setback came earlier last month when U.S. District Judge Frank J. Battisti found the board in contempt and took over control of desegregation.

Whether Voinovich can reverse Cleveland's slide into a welfare center and provide leadership to help with the schools remains to be seen.

His hands are full just trying to give organization and direction to city government. Cleveland, it seems, simply doesn't work.

Upon taking office last year, the mayor temporarily forgot to emphasize the positive.

"This whole city is so screwed up…I've never seen such a God-awful mess in my entire life and it just seems to go from one department to another," he said.

Until Voinovich began making changes, Weld says, the city's accounting system was like the kind used by "mom and pop grocery stores." Until the end of the year, nobody knew if revenues matched debts.

When the books get too far out of balance, "mom and pop" stores close. Cleveland just kept getting further in debt.

Creditors, Allen says, know about the city's problems and aren't eager to do business. "If we get one bidder to bid (on supplies or construction), we're lucky," Allen says.

The billing procedure used for the Northeast Ohio Regional Sewer District, which serves Cleveland and some suburbs, reflects accounting problems, Allen found. The city handles billings for the whole district and forwards to the district an amount of money based on the billings.

Each year an adjustment is to be made to the city, equal to the difference between the amount billed and the amount actually paid.

The adjustments haven't been made, Allen says, because city records don't show whether bills have been collected. From $2 million to $13 million could be due the city, he adds.

The city council has noticed this blunder. Until it's solved, some councilmen say, they won't agree to put Voinovich's proposed one-half of one percent income tax increase on the Nov. 4 ballot. It would increase the tax from 1.5 to 2%.

There are other problems.

"When people put out their trash in Akron on Thursday, it's collected," Allen says. Here it might be Thursday, it might be next Thursday, or it might be a month from now."

Cleveland police officers are so used to worn-out equipment that they replace their own cruiser lights, he adds.

Nobody even knows for sure how many cruisers the city has, but many are 1974 models, Allen says. In Akron, Allen remembers, the fleet was replaced every two years.

These are the sorts of problems, says banker John McCarter, that make comparing Cleveland and Akron like comparing apples and oranges.

McCarter, who until May was chairman and chief executive officer of Akron's Centran Bank, now is in Cleveland as senior vice president and senior loan administrator of the Central Bank of Cleveland.

Ballard and Voinovich, McCarter says, share a "quietness" and "lack of flamboyance." Ballard, however, was able to emphasize economic development and increasing the city's tax base.

"Voinovich has got some things to do before he gets to that place," says McCarter, who was president of the Downtown Akron Association and a member of the mayor's Akron Action Committee.

"He (Voinovich) has got to get the tires inflated and the motor tuned before he drives the car," McCarter adds.

If the tires ever are inflated, McCarter says, Voinovich will have more trouble than Ballard mobilizing community resources.

"In Akron we could pull together 25 people and have representation from the primary private sector elements," he says. "In Cleveland, to get that kind of representation, you'd have to pull together 100."

Mobilizing such a large group, McCarter says, will be tough. To just get the fine tuning done, Voinovich must continue the fragile political calm he has helped achieve.

A threat, Voinovich believes, is a petition drive calling for the city-wide election of the council president. Forbes, as council presidents before him, was elected by members of the council.

"It would be like electing a second mayor of the city," says Voinovich. "It would set the stage for more confrontation."

———————

Forbes, who is Black, says the drive is directed against him and is racist.

"That's ridiculous," says Councilwoman Barbara Pringle, the white petition drive leader. "I don't think he has a comeback for the issue, so he uses race."

Council presidents historically have had "too much power and no accountability," says Mrs. Pringle.

Mrs. Pringle and Forbes both celebrate birthdays April 4 and, she recalls, "we did share a piece of cake once." Life with Forbes as council president, however, has not been a party, she adds.

Although Mrs. Pringle turned in more than enough signatures, Forbes so far has avoided taking the council action necessary to put the issue on the Nov. 4 ballot.

"We have an option to go to court," retorts Mrs. Pringle.

And so life and politics in Cleveland goes on.

Voinovich's two-year term as mayor is nearly half over. He says he'll run for re-election and categorically denies he'll be a gubernatorial candidate in 1982.

(He also categorically denied he'd run for Cleveland mayor in 1979 while serving as lieutenant governor.)

His greatest allies next year will be the feuding Democrats.

Kucinich is expected to make a political comeback of some sort. Maybe he'll run for mayor again or, if Mrs. Pringle's amendment passes, for council president.

———————

The former mayor is mum about his plans and is not "ready to make public my assessment" of Voinovich.

Hagan, the country Democratic chairman, didn't support Kucinich against Voinovich and is scorned by Kucinich backers. Westbrook calls Hagan and his pal Cuyahoga County commissioner Edward Feighan "schizophrenic Democrats." They try unsuccessfully, Westbrook says, to be loyal both to big business and citizens' needs.

"We don't know who, but we'll have a candidate," Hagan says, speaking for the party organization.

"It's not going to do any good," says Forbes. "He's not going to win." Cleveland, believes Forbes, is ready for at least one more term of "normalcy."*

---

* Voinovich served as Cleveland mayor from 1980–1989. He was elected to two terms as Ohio governor in 1990 and 1994 and to two terms in the U.S. Senate in 1998 and 2004. He died at the age of 79 in 2016.

Jim Rhodes: Is This *Really* the End of His Era?

Akron Beacon Journal, January 2, 1983
BRIAN USHER

He was a millionaire governor who loved to golf at his favorite country clubs in Columbus and Ft. Lauderdale. But he was born into poverty in a coal town near Jackson, earning money as a teenager to support his mother and sisters.

He was not well educated, spending less than a year at Ohio State University. But he was the shrewdest and most successful of Ohio politicians, serving 16 years as governor—a national record.

With his southern hills accent, he said "commeeshun" instead of "commission" and "feesh" instead of "fish," and he called the vice president George "Boosh." But he became a master communicator with modern political techniques—polls and television ads.

He loved to tell off-color stories to cronies in private, but he prayed often in public, including the prayer his mother taught him: "Dear God, permit me to become somebody in this world."

James A. Rhodes became somebody. At 73, he will be leaving the governor's office Jan. 10 as a wealthy man with his very own statute on the Statehouse lawn.

At times, he seemed a simple man, even a buffoon. But he was a complex man of many careers.

He was a four-term governor, but along the way he suffered and survived three major statewide defeats, controversies and the inglorious massacre on the Kent State University campus in 1970. As the state's chief executive, he remade the face of Ohio in 20 years, building highways, universities and other public projects with bonds.

But as a private businessman, he made most of his wealth outside of Ohio. He built motels in Florida, Georgia, Indiana and Illinois and sold hamburgers in New York.

He bossed the Ohio Republican Party but stumbled in national politics.

He was a merry huckster, peddling Ohio and himself—a master of half-truths who baffled the press and made them love it.

Disdaining to live in the governor's mansion, he moved out for his last two terms. But in his final year, he didn't mind sleeping in a cow barn at the Ohio State Fair.

What was Rhodes' Secret of Success? "It's all in the timing"

Richard F. Celeste, the Democrat who finally would succeed Republican Jim Rhodes as governor, first coined the phrase in the opening debate of his 1982 fall campaign.

"Jim Rhodes is the all-time, grand champion of Ohio politics," Celeste told the Columbus lobbyists and political junkies jammed into the Ohio Press Club hall on Sept. 8. They laughed and clapped. But the story of how Rhodes did it is more amazing than amusing.

He preached "jobs and progress," but after his 16 years as governor, Ohio has the worst unemployment since the Great Depression.

He advocated "no new taxes," but raised nearly every state tax and created a few new local ones, too.

He wanted "no hostility" in politics, but he won two of the roughest campaigns in Ohio history, ousting incumbent Democratic Govs. Michael DiSalle in 1962 and John J. Gilligan in 1974.

He was a business-oriented Republican from rural, southern Ohio who got Clevelanders, union members and Blacks to vote for him in greater numbers than Republicans usually get.

In the 1950s, he failed twice in campaigns for governor. After that he never lost another primary or general election for governor (although he lost a GOP primary for U.S. senator in 1970).

Clearly, he had a knack for political survival. Governor-elect Celeste, who will succeed Rhodes Jan. 10, often has said he learned more as a "Rhodes scholar in Ohio"—losing to Rhodes in 1978—than as a Rhodes scholar at Oxford University. In 1982, Celeste borrowed from Rhodes his techniques of TV advertising and issue handling. "Celeste thinks he's a Rhodes scholar," snorted Cuyahoga County GOP chairman Robert Hughes, longtime Rhodes confidant. "He ought to sit in on one of Rhodes' sessions at the country club in Ft. Lauderdale. He talks about what the price is on this guy or how to get to that one. Celeste would really learn something then."

As a politician, Rhodes negotiated the price of people just as he negotiated the price of property as a developer. But timing, television and temperament were also secrets to Rhodes' success, especially in his comeback in the 1970s, according to many Rhodes scholars. Less charitable critics contend he was also lucky and the best half-truth artist in the business.

"It's all in the timing," Rhodes counseled his aides through the years. Like a street brawler in the clinch, Rhodes would wait for an opening in campaigns. "Tax-hike Mike," he would jeer at DiSalle in 1962, possibly the nastiest campaign for governor in modern times. Rhodes was a 53-year-old state auditor and DiSalle was governor. Each managed to use his office to get a grand jury investigation going on the other's turf—DiSalle's liquor control department and the rental of adding machines in Rhodes' office. Nothing came out of the charges, but Rhodes beat DiSalle into oblivion at the ballot box.

In 1978, Celeste fell victim to Rhodes' timing after he launched a summer assault on the 69-year-old governor for "lack of leadership" and for ignoring school-funding problems. Rhodes' aides wanted to reply immediately, but he cautioned them: "You don't try to bash the rabbit the first time he sticks his head out of the hole. Ignore him awhile and let him get out away from it."

While Celeste boasted he would "have the guts to tell the truth" about raising taxes, Rhodes saw his opening and countered with his usual "no new taxes" position.

Finally, Celeste backed away from endorsing a specific tax program and announced he would appoint a task force to make recommendations. Rhodes had him. "We don't need a new sales tax. We don't need a new income tax, and we don't need a governor who says we do...or perhaps... or maybe!" Rhodes crowed. Of course, Rhodes and the legislature had to increase taxes several times in Rhodes' fourth term. But the issue here is Rhodes' skill in seizing power, not exercising it.

In 1974, Rhodes launched a comeback with Gilligan leading in the polls. Gilligan gave Rhodes plenty of openings by joking at the State Fair sheep barn, "I shear taxpayers, not sheep." Also, Gilligan's budget advisers suddenly found an $80 million surplus in the state budget during the campaign. Rhodes responded with a fall TV ad blitz. One TV ad showed a lamb being shorn like a taxpayer. Another blasted Gilligan for his "$80 million shell game" with taxpayers' money.

Rhodes, who had once been nervous around TV cameras in the 1960s, became the Ohio master of the new campaign technology with help from his media wizard John Deardourff, a Washington consultant.

Then in 1978, Rhodes and Deardourff showed they could produce positive as well as negative TV ads. In one flag-waving, emotion-laden ad, Rhodes directed the cherub-faced Ohio Youth Choir in a stirring rendition of "The Battle Hymn of the Republic." "The message was: Rhodes is Ohio," said Tom Dudgeon, longtime Rhodes ally. "Jim really knows Ohio. If you ever fly with him, he can look down and pick out the county lines and tell you who owns the farms down there."

But Rhodes was also lucky in his comeback years of the 1970s, said Warren Smith, secretary-treasurer of the Ohio AFL-CIO and a longtime Rhodes foe.

"Jim happened to be in the right place at the right time," Smith said, noting Rhodes beat Gilligan by fewer than 11,000 votes and Celeste by fewer than 48,000. Winning Democratic votes (or having them stay home) in Democratic strongholds like Cleveland was part of the Rhodes' knack for survival in the close races of 1974 and 1978. His "jobs" pitch and bond issues helped him win union votes and newspaper endorsements in major cities.

He also made a special appeal to Black voters. Rhodes appointed Black people to several offices, including the Ohio Supreme Court. In addition, he cultivated powerful allies in the Black community of Cleveland like the late W.O. Walker, publisher of the Call and Post in Cleveland. Walker served in Rhodes' cabinet in the 1960s and used his newspapers to aid Rhodes in 1974 and 1978. Another Rhodes favorite was Cleveland City Council President George Forbes, a Black Democratic leader, who said publicly about Rhodes' retirement from politics this year: "I'm going to lose my meal ticket."

The real key to Rhodes' success, the governor believes, lay in his motto: "We have no open hostility." Although this suggests he might harbor a little covert hostility, Rhodes often added, "Never get so mad at someone that you cannot sit down the next morning at breakfast." In a Dec. 10 interview with the Beacon Journal, he said, "If there's a secret to success, it's: Don't look back; somebody may be following you."

When it comes to huckstering for Ohio, Rhodes has no peers

Within a few hours of landing in Peking, Jim Rhodes and his Raiders (a group of Ohio business owners and officials) were standing on the 11th floor of the Peking Hotel banging at the door of Bob Hope's suite. The comedian, a golfing buddy of the governor, opened the door and then shut it playfully in Rhodes' face. Opening it again, Hope said, "What are you hustling now?" Rhodes barged into the suite, barking, "Ohio! Trade! Industry!"

The next day, Hope began filming his TV special from China, as Rhodes and his Raiders began selling Ohio to Chinese top brass. "Ohio is No. 1 in rubber, No. 1 in glass, No. 1 in machine tools, No. 1 in auto parts!" Rhodes exclaimed, waving his index finger under the nose of his host, Xian Fan, vice chairman of the Chinese Council for the Promotion of International Trade.

Rhodes pulled out a dollar bill and told his hosts, "We're here to make China green." The vice chairman looked puzzled. Then Rhodes bragged through interpreters about the exploits of Ohio-born aviators and astronauts. "Wright brothers," Rhodes croaked and flapped his arms at Xiao.

It was the ultimate Rhodes Raiders trade mission on that hot July day in 1979. Six months after the U.S. officially recognized China, Rhodes was in Peking trying to make capitalists out of the Communists. He told them they should build a Disney World at the Peking Airport and an escalator up the Great Wall of China.

Ever since he sponsored turtle races at his campus restaurant in the 1930s near Ohio State, Rhodes has been the master of perpetual promotions.

In his first two terms as governor, he hawked tomato juice, a bridge over Lake Erie, the Ohio State Fair. As he leaves office, he talks of developing an electric car.

Rhodes has always been the wizard of jobs. Like presidential candidates and Dorothy's friend from Oz, he seems at times to do it with mirrors and blue smoke.

Drink up, he told Ohioans in 1965. Tomato juice, that is. "If every Ohioan would drink an extra 16-ounce can of tomato juice a year, 2,000 jobs would be created in Ohio," Rhodes said. That would mean $13 million more in personal income, enough to support 6,240 persons, pay the rent on 2,320 homes and educate 1,020 children, Rhodes figured.

To get the program rolling, Rhodes installed a merry-go-round in the Statehouse rotunda and loaded it with tomato juice cans. At a banquet in the Cabinet Room, he gave reporters and Cabinet members 66 ounces of tomato juice each.

So it was, too, later with sauerkraut and rutabaga juice to make Wapakoneta "the rutabaga juice capital of the world." And snow tires. And ceramics. Each meant jobs. "That's what elects me more than anything else, jobs," Rhodes said in a Dec. 10 interview. He even led a Rhodes Raiders mission to New York City on March 25, 1966, to invite the New York Stock Exchange to move to Ohio. But that brush fire, like many others set by the irrepressible governor, burned itself out quickly.

But Rhodes' flashiest promotion was the bridge over Lake Erie that would have cost $250 million to $600 million in 1967, depending on where the span was built. Rhodes preferred to see it built from the east side of Cleveland to the Ontario shore town of Rondeau Harbour 50 miles away. It would have been the longest overwater structure in the world and would have opened a northeast passage to Canadian trade.

A.G. Lancione, Democratic House minority leader at the time, condemned it as "a haphazard highway program by press release." Canadian officials were cool, but receptive to a study if they didn't have to pay for it.

The study cost about $300,000 and was shelved as Rhodes left office in 1971. Adamant to the end, Rhodes insisted, "I believe traffic congestion eventually will force something across Lake Erie."

During his four years out of the governor's office, he turned his sales and promotion talent toward making money in hotels, discount houses, other real estate ventures and Wendy's International hamburgers.

Even when he returned as governor, he kept promoting Wendy's hamburgers. Wherever he went, Rhodes shamelessly pushed hamburgers and fries from the restaurant chain he owned stock in. "Eat! Eat! Eat!" he hollered at five governors visiting from Japan who dined at the first Wendy's store in Columbus.

Annually he served Wendy's food at a pre-Christmas news conference, prompting some reporters to question the ethics of his commercialism. On one occasion, Rhodes shocked them by waving their questions away with an exasperated malaprop: "We have no ethics."

But the governor's hardest sell and biggest flop came in 1975 when he tried to sell the Ohio voters $4.5 billion in bonding programs. Rhodes raised and spent more than $1 million for the four statewide "jobs and progress" issues to "make Ohio depression-proof." But voters buried them by a 3-to-1 margin in 1975, the first year of Rhodes' third term.

Shrugging off the ballot defeats, Rhodes resurrected Rhodes Raiders for missions to Michigan, Pennsylvania, California, Europe, Japan and China. His critics viewed the overseas trips as junkets and doubted that the hard-to-measure results were worth the state money and hoopla.

Exceptions to that rule were the Honda Motor Co. plants near Marysville north of Columbus and the Ford plant east of Cincinnati. Rhodes gave the impression he would do anything to get those plants—provide state roads and water systems, get his friends to give away land. He even gave away strokes on the golf course.

Soichiro Honda, whom Rhodes called "the Henry Ford of Japan," told some Rhodes Raiders in Tokyo: "I feel Ohio is a strange place because every time I play a round of golf with your governor keeping score, I come in with a par. With assistance from your governor, I think next year I will take part in the world championship."

That was in July of 1979. Eighteen months later, Honda announced plans for a $5 million auto parts plant for Marysville.

Rhodes' last bit of self-promotion as governor was unveiled Dec. 5—his own statute on the northeast corner of the Statehouse lawn. On this bronze monument to his brass, these words are immortalized for archeologists of the future: "Profit is not a dirty word in Ohio."

He may be a top politician, but as for his leadership...

James A. Rhodes has a favorite homily at campaign time: "When you elect a governor, you elect management."

But, his critics insist, you can hire management; you elect leadership. And despite Rhodes' success as a politician, his leadership has been sorely lacking in his last two terms, according to many in both political parties.

"Rhodes was a terrible governor," said Warren Smith, secretary-treasurer of the Ohio AFL-CIO. "I don't think he was a leader at all. He didn't confront problems and try to solve them. He leaves the state a terrible wreck."

Many Rhodes critics do not go quite that far, but there is a general consensus among legislators, reporters, lobbyists and other Statehouse watchers that Rhodes was productive in his first two terms, building highways, campuses and public facilities. But in the last eight years, he became a crisis manager reeling from one disaster to the next—deadly blizzards, natural gas shortages, school-funding problems and budget deficits.

Rhodes' personal style of management was unusual. "He ran his office like a message center," said Tom Dudgeon, Columbus lobbyist and long-time Rhodes' ally. "Some governors run their offices like throne rooms with aides isolating them. Rhodes constantly picks up the phone. He listens to everybody."

Rhodes prided himself on having relatively few aides as governor and candidate. He also delegated a lot of authority to his Cabinet members and department heads.

There were three Rhodes commandments for Cabinet members and other administrators: "Keep your hands off the secretaries, keep your hands out of the till, and don't be seen drunk in bars."

Rhodes was Columbus city auditor, mayor and then state auditor before becoming governor in 1963. "He knows more about state and local government than almost anyone else," said Howard Collier, Rhodes' veteran budget director. "He's the sum of the most organized learning process we've ever had with an elected official."

Rhodes said recently of his years in office: "I knew where all the bodies were buried. It's different, the things that come up here. You don't get them out of the book."

In a Dec. 10 Beacon Journal interview, Rhodes acknowledged that his job was easier in the boom times of the 1960s than it has been in the recent years of budget deficits and high unemployment: "There's nothing the matter with Ohio that 500,000 jobs wouldn't cure overnight." Rhodes said there is one measurement for his management: "We had the lowest number of state employees of any state. We were always one or two in that."

That was relatively easy in the booming 1960s. Rhodes kept the payroll small and state taxes relatively low. He staved off attempts to create a state income tax while he built buildings with bonds at low interest rates all over Ohio.

Even in those days, there were budget crunches and school aid shortages. Resisting the creation of an income tax because he had pledged "no new taxes" in his campaigns, he had the GOP-controlled legislature raise the rates of some old ones such as the cigarette, sales, liquor and inheritance taxes. Rhodes once charged Gov. John J. Gilligan with taxing "everything that walks, crawls or flies." That brought a retort from Gilligan aides that Rhodes taxed everything that "smokes, drinks, buys or dies."

But by the time Rhodes left office after his second term, the state budget was in such bad shape that the debate in the 1970 governor's race between Gilligan and Republican Roger Cloud was not whether to create an income tax, but how it should be collected and spent.

Gilligan and a GOP-controlled legislature passed the state personal income and corporate franchise (profits) taxes in 1971. That cleared the way for a Rhodes comeback in 1974 on the old "no new taxes" pledge.

It worked. Rhodes beat Gilligan but bombed when he tried a return to his 1960s-style leadership. Voters clobbered his massive $4.5 billion bond proposals on the 1975 ballot by 3 to 1.

Rhodes then resorted to Rhodes Raiders' missions, caretaker government and crisis management the rest of his years in office. The crises included natural gas shortages in the winter of 1977, the "killer blizzard looking for victims" of 1978 and budget problems nearly every year.

Rhodes set up his office like a war room with charts on the wall and Cabinet members on hand for media interviews.

In 1977, Beacon Journal associate editor David B. Cooper interviewed Rhodes for his first time and got a lecture on the governor's problems in selling his ideas to solve the natural gas problem. "When I talk about this, I ain't E.F. Hutton—nobody listens," Rhodes complained. "We have plenty of brains and know-how. You have to refinance the utilities. They don't like how we talk. We're trying to save them, but they don't know it."

Natural gas and blizzard crises passed, but the budget problems remain. Rhodes vowed "no new taxes" again in 1978 and pushed through a school-loan program to keep schools from closing during his campaign against Richard Celeste.

Finally, as unemployment rose, Rhodes pushed through an emergency sales tax increase in December of 1980, threatening to close mental institutions and prisons if legislators didn't do it. After again proposing "no new taxes" in his 1981 budget message, Rhodes reversed field once again and backed more tax increases on sales, gasoline and income.

Collier defended Rhodes: "Everybody talks about him and no new taxes, but in my experience, he's supported whatever taxes necessary to support an acceptable level of government services."

But others viewed it differently. "He's shown no leadership," said Smith of the AFL-CIO. "Jim's very passive about government."

Governor-elect Richard Celeste, for his own political reasons, refused to criticize Rhodes' performance in the 1982 campaign, but many of his top aides agree with the assessment by one Celeste adviser who described Rhodes as a "do-nothing governor who waited until crisis time to act."

Rhodes still Ohio GOP boss after 20 years

"I don't tell the state chairman how to run the party, and he doesn't tell me how to run state government."

That is what Jim Rhodes always would say about the Ohio Republican Party whether the state chairman was the late GOP patriarch Ray Bliss of Akron or its current young chairman, Michael Colley of Columbus.

Rhodes was half right. No state chairman, including Bliss, ever told him how to run the Statehouse. But Rhodes dominated the state party for nearly two decades.

That meant picking a state chairman loyal to him personally. It meant collecting money for his campaigns first over other candidates. It meant keeping a whole generation or two of Republican candidates at bay—and mostly out of office—while he piled up his record 16 years as governor.

Rhodes' influence over the party greatly troubled Bliss in his later years while he still remained active through the 1980 national convention.

———

Bliss usually confided in only his closest friends, but in 1979 he told a UPI reporter: "We Republicans won in the 1950s and 1960s because we built up a stable of candidates and put on aggressive campaigns. But nobody's willing to do that anymore. There's been no leadership in Ohio to get a stable of candidates or to find people to finance campaigns."

Then Bliss added the stinger: "To have a strong party organization, you have to have a strong chairman. He can't be the lackey of the governor. John Andrews and Earl Barnes (former state chairmen) had different ideas than I did. They thought the party ought to work closely with the governor. But Jim Rhodes never did anything unless it was to benefit Jim Rhodes."

Sour grapes of an aging leader? Maybe. But the record speaks for itself. When Bliss left Ohio in 1965 to become national GOP chairman, Republicans controlled everything in state government. Now as Rhodes retires, the only thing Republicans hold is one statewide office—a seat on the Supreme Court.

After Democrats swept all statewide offices last Nov. 2, state GOP chairman Colley said, "We need to return to the spirit and the nuts and bolts politics of Ray Bliss."

Conservatives and rural county chairmen often fought to unseat Rhodes' handpicked state chairmen at GOP headquarters (including Colley) in Columbus during the 1970s and 1980s but lost every time.

In party matters, Rhodes imitated former Democratic Gov. Frank Lausche, said Charles F. Kurfess, the former House speaker who lost to Rhodes in the 1978 primary.

"Lausche did nothing for the Democratic Party. He did it for Frank Lausche," Kurfess said, adding about Rhodes' stewardship of the party: "One or two generations of Republican leadership in this state never blossomed."

A veteran Democratic leader recalled, "When Rhodes became governor in 1962, he took the party right away from Ray Bliss. Rhodes became the party...and they have never been able to build statewide personalities."

The Bliss-Rhodes relationship was always strained. "Bliss was suspicious of Rhodes' independence and Rhodes was jealous of Bliss' power and respect," said one GOP leader. Columbus was hardly big enough for both of them when Rhodes first became governor in 1963, and Bliss was a veteran state chairman at party headquarters a block from the Statehouse.

Bliss said in later years he believed Rhodes released the Ohio delegation to Barry Goldwater at the 1964 GOP national convention to show Bliss and the nation that Rhodes "was the real boss of Ohio."

After Bliss went to Washington as national chairman in 1965, he and Rhodes shared influence on state chairman John Andrews and the Ohio GOP throughout the 1960s. The state party split in 1970 when Rhodes lost to U.S. Rep. Robert Taft Jr., son of "Mr. Republican" Robert Taft, in the GOP primary for U.S. Senate. Taft won the Senate seat and Rhodes forged a comeback four years later to defeat incumbent Democratic Gov. John J. Gilligan.

Then Rhodes began installing a series of handpicked state chairmen with backing on the state GOP executive committee from a coalition of key big-city chairmen, including Robert Hughes of Cleveland and Earl Barnes of Cincinnati.

———————

Rhodes dominated the state party since the early 1970s through chairman Kent B. McGough of Lima, Barnes of Cincinnati and finally Colley of Rhodes' hometown Columbus organization. Rhodes helped each one defend against challenges from the conservative and rural party elements.

Meanwhile, Republican state officeholders fell to Democrats throughout the 1970s. To survive, Rhodes needed to control the money flowing into GOP coffers to make sure he kept the governor's office whether or not anyone else lower on the GOP ticket survived. With the defeat of 28-year Secretary of State Ted W. Brown in 1978, Rhodes was left as the lone GOP statewide officeholder.

When some Republicans grumbled later that Rhodes had grabbed the lion's share of GOP campaign funds, he said, "They all have to have an excuse why they lose."

Even the winners were not happy. Rhodes' 1978 handpicked Lt. Gov. George Voinovich gave up after Rhodes gave him nothing to do in 1979. Voinovich returned to Cleveland to run successfully for mayor.

The latest would-be GOP successor to Rhodes was 1982 Republican nominee for governor Clarence J. Brown Jr., who suffered from Rhodes' lukewarm support. Indeed, Rhodes upstaged Brown last fall with a series of Rhodes Roasts all over Ohio raising money for the state GOP.

"It was like a deathbed conversion, the first time he ever did anything for the state party," said one GOP headquarters aide. "Actually," said Cuyahoga County GOP chairman Robert E. Hughes, "the Rhodes Roasts gave Rhodes a way to run for governor in 1982 without really running." Rhodes shrugged off the criticism, saying he had helped raise money for the state party, often, even personally co-signing loans to help GOP headquarters out of fiscal binds.

Despite persistent rumors that Rhodes is planning a comeback for governor in 1986, Rhodes told the Beacon Journal in a Dec. 10 interview he would not. "Why should I come back?" he said, noting satisfaction with his record number of terms as governor—recorded 100 yards away on his Statehouse lawn statute.

At GOP conventions, he was no kingmaker

Flashback to California Aug. 13, 1968 in Sacramento. Gov. Ronald Reagan had left behind the 1968 Republican National Convention in Miami Beach one week and 3,000 miles ago.

The "new" Richard Nixon had won the GOP nomination for president. Reagan returned to California a loser, but he offered a startling revelation to the California press corps.

If he had been nominated, Reagan would have asked Ohio Gov. James Rhodes to be his vice presidential running mate. "Frankly, in my mind, Jim Rhodes is as good a man as we could have," Reagan said. "I had no second choice."

A week earlier in Miami Beach, Ohioans placed the name of favorite-son Rhodes in nomination for president. In the balloting, Rhodes held on to his 55 favorite-son delegates while Nixon captured the nomination over Reagan and Rhodes' first choice—New York Gov. Nelson Rockefeller.

Ohio's champion politician has often played—usually badly—at being convention kingmaker, but those 55 delegates and Reagan's disclosure were the closest he ever got to being king—or vice king. On the national scene, he usually stumbled around.

"Nationally, Rhodes drove them all nutty," recalled Cuyahoga County GOP chairman Robert E. Hughes, Rhodes' Cleveland confidant. "He told Reagan not to debate Carter in 1980. Ford always used to say, 'Isn't he a piece of work?'"

The national press corps more or less tolerated him as an after-hours conversation piece.

But did Rhodes ever nurse real presidential ambitions beyond favorite-son status?

"I never had a great desire to go to Washington," Rhodes said in a Dec. 10 interview. "The glory road never did anything for my ego."

But there were some indications in 1967 that the glory road beckoned. Rhodes hit the out-of-state Republican dinner circuit in 1967, making forays into Indiana and Illinois and drawing the usual media speculation.

In the fall of 1967, Texas millionaire H.L. Hunt offered to back Rhodes for president and gave him this advice in a letter:

"You could take a few lessons in speech, as Ike did, and make some speeches for practice."

But Rhodes quit the glory road and never declared his candidacy for the White House. He stuck to kingmaking—or tried to. He was often clumsy in national convention arenas. Here is his record, in brief:

1964—At his first national convention as governor, Rhodes was supposed to lead an uncommitted "favorite-son" delegation to San Francisco. Rhodes and Ray Bliss, then Ohio state chairman, had given their word of "favorite-son" neutrality on the first ballot to GOP moderates opposing conservative Sen. Barry Goldwater for president.

Bliss and the moderates were outraged when Rhodes released the 58 delegates to Goldwater before the convention started without notifying Bliss before the media.

Rhodes was showing his career penchant for "going with a winner," but Bliss said later he thought freshman Governor Rhodes was trying to show the national leaders "who the real boss of Ohio was" in 1964.

In *The Making of the President* (1964), Theodore H. White described Rhodes as a "courthouse politician whose promises and commitments are now held at general discount among high-level Republican politicians."

1968—At the Miami Beach convention, Rhodes learned his lesson of 1964 too well and sat on his favorite-son delegation too long. Nixon won without him.

1972—Rhodes, out of office, supported incumbent Nixon for nomination at Miami Beach but prematurely announced that his presidential preference for 1976 was then-Vice President Spiro T. Agnew. Neither Nixon nor Agnew make it to 1976 in office.

1976—Rhodes backed President Gerald Ford, his golfing buddy, for nomination at the Kansas City convention but missed on his first two choices for Ford's vice president—Rockefeller and John Connally.

1980—Rhodes backed Reagan at the Detroit convention and boasted about advising Reagan to make the dream ticket of Reagan-Ford. Reagan picked George Bush for No. 2.

Rhodes' favorite would-be president was Nelson Rockefeller. The Rhodes-Rockefeller relationship went back to 1962, when they met at West Virginia's Greenbriar resort, according to Chan Cochran, former Rhodes' press secretary.

Rhodes was sitting at a table drinking and eating with others when the check for about $200 came. Spying Rockefeller across the room, the brash governor-to-be told the waiter to give the New Yorker the check.

"Rhodes impressed Rocky because Rhodes is such a free spirit," said Clevelander Hughes, who observed the relationship firsthand for years. "It's like the rich kid getting infatuated with the poor kid across the tracks. Rhodes talked up to Rocky, and he liked it." On one occasion, several Rhodes aides recalled, Rockefeller asked Rhodes advice on divorcing his first wife and marrying Happy, his second wife.

It's bad politics, Rhodes advised him: "Rocky, if I had your money, I'd build a castle, fill it full of naked women and sit around with a whip."

Although they were allies, Rhodes and Nixon were never close personally. Long after Watergate, Nixon re-emerged publicly in Ohio at a 1981 GOP fundraiser in Columbus. Rhodes skipped it.

"That's the night I have to stay home and pay the paper boy," Rhodes said.

For years, Rhodes had backed Rockefeller and Ford against Reagan in national politics, but in 1980, Rhodes was not shy about telling the Californian how to campaign after the Detroit convention.

"Ronnie, you're fouling up," Rhodes told Reagan (only in stronger language) during Reagan's August visit to Ohio. Rhodes then helped Reagan aides rewrite a speech to the Ohio Teamsters, inserting the word "depression" instead of "recession."

Rhodes told Reagan he had to stick with pocketbook issues in Ohio and "forget the two-China policy" and other foreign affairs.

The president with possibly the most interesting relationship with Rhodes was Democrat Lyndon B. Johnson. In 1967, Johnson called Rhodes "one of my best friends" and gave Rhodes a personally guided tour of the White House.

Why? Rhodes was a staunch defender of Johnson's Vietnam policy. When opposition arose in Congress in 1966, Rhodes pushed through the National Governors Association a resolution backing Johnson's policy. It won unanimous approval.

A year later, Republican leaders, including then-national GOP chairman Ray Bliss, began to regard Johnson as vulnerable in 1968. But in a White House meeting with governors, Rhodes offered a toast of fractured syntax in support of LBJ:

"We only have one president and one commander-in-chief. In beating the breasts of 200 million Americans tonight from coast to coast and from the Gulf to the Great Lakes, they want victory. They want to stand with a leader.

"Mr. President, I propose a toast. The annals of this great country are placed indeed for those who stood up—stood up for the American boy."

Republicans of that era wondered why Rhodes would butter up a president whom Bliss wanted to unseat. However, latter-day GOP leaders have learned this about Rhodes: The party is secondary to political survival—Jim Rhodes' survival.

Gilligan's criticism restored Rhodes as winner

Jim Rhodes may be the "all-time grand champion of Ohio politics," as Governor-elect Richard Celeste said. But in 1970, after two terms as governor, Jim Rhodes went out a loser.

"We have been a very provocative governor," Rhodes told a Medina country club crowd in 1970. "We have been controversial. We have even been hung in effigy." He entered 1970 reeling from Life magazine charges that he had gotten in trouble with the Internal Revenue Service by tapping campaign funds and that he may have been bribed to commute the sentence of convicted mobster Thomas "Yonnie" Licavoli.

Then he sent the Ohio National Guard to Kent State University and four persons were killed and nine wounded May 4. The next day, he lost the Republican primary for U.S. Senator to Robert Taft Jr.

But Rhodes figured he would weather all of that. What really angered him was what came after 1970—the constant criticism of his eight years as governor by his successor, John J. Gilligan, and the Democrats.

"I was in business and successful and needed to be governor again like a hole in the head," Rhodes said of the early 1970s in a Dec. 10 interview. "But they kept after me. Everything that happened, I would get a dissertation from Gilligan on how bad I was as governor as the reason he couldn't be governor."

Rhodes hungered for vindication. He was making more money than ever before. But at age 65 in 1974, he yearned to cleanse his reputation and win again. Had it not been for Gilligan, "I would never have gotten back in," he said.

His image problems of 1970 are part of the reason why Rhodes wanted a statute of himself erected on the Statehouse lawn before leaving office Jan. 10, many in Columbus believe. He never again would trust his place in history to historians and incoming Democrats.

———————

Rhodes became not just a winner again, but a survivor.

The Life magazine charges were laid to rest. No one ever found solid evidence of a bribe. The campaign fund charges were largely a rehash of Democratic charges in 1962 that Rhodes had taken $54,000 from his state auditor campaign fund for personal use in the mid-1950s, without paying income taxes. After negotiating with the IRS, he paid taxes on $18,000 and returned $36,000 as loans.

Kent State was tougher to deal with. Rhodes consistently has refused to discuss his feelings about the tragedy and his role in it, usually citing pending litigation or the possibility of it. But his closest aides and friends say it affected him deeply.

Chan Cochran, a former executive assistant, said he has heard Rhodes call the shootings "the blackest day in my life" in private. Howard Collier, his budget director and longtime aide through four administrations, said Rhodes feels "personal remorse."

Cochran said future historians with a more objective view will "conclude that Kent State or something like it was bound to happen somewhere" because of nationwide tensions over the war in Vietnam.

Others are less charitable about Rhodes' actions and inflammatory statements about student unrest that he made during his campaign against Taft. Rhodes used "bad judgment," said Ohio AFL-CIO secretary-treasurer Warren Smith, echoing the opinion of many Rhodes critics. "I don't think he was opposed to manhandling a few students."

At the heart of the criticism of Rhodes' role in the KSU disaster was that it could have been avoided if he had heeded the advice of those law enforcement and campus officials who wanted to avoid a confrontation with the students.

————————

Rhodes still refuses all but the most oblique comments. "I was tried for a long time," Rhodes said Dec. 10 about media criticism and courtroom trials.

In the courtrooms, Rhodes made some bizarre statements. In a 1974 deposition given to U.S. District Court, Rhodes made an unusual reference to campus agitators as "night riders." Steven Sindell, attorney for the parents of slain students, questioned him:

Sindell: Who are the night riders?

Rhodes: They are the burners, violence.

Sindell: They ride in the night, is that it?

Rhodes: Yes.

Sindell: Is that going back in history or are you talking about currently in 1970?

Rhodes: Well, I would say the greatest menace to the night riders was Hopalong Cassidy.

Before 1970 and Kent State, Rhodes had lost for governor twice—once to state Treasurer Don Ebright of Akron in the 1950 Republican primary and once to Democratic Gov. Frank Lausche of Cleveland in 1954. From Lausche, he learned how to win a race for governor.

Lausche was the best politician Rhodes ever saw, other than himself. "Lausche was gifted," Rhodes said in the recent interview. "Lausche could answer a question in such a way that there was three sides to it. Everybody was satisfied." Asked if he learned his similar talent from Lausche, Rhodes said: "I was never that good. I wished I was."

Rhodes said he also learned from Lausche what Celeste learned from losing to Rhodes in 1978. He "realized Ohio is a big state. You have to run and lose first," Rhodes said.

"I never had any objection to being a loser. How can you be a good winner if you're not a good loser?"

Rhodes: A snake hunter in Akron

Governor Rhodes didn't think he was getting the kind of support out of Summit County that his 1975 ballot proposals for $4.5 billion in bond issues deserved. Democratic legislators, the Beacon Journal, community leaders—everyone was skeptical.

"Akron needs these bonds," Rhodes told a meeting of legislators and other leaders in his office. He painted visions of highways, mini-domed stadiums, a state office building for Akron, public works of all sorts.

"Any schoolboy knows Akron has the worst downtown in Ohio," Rhodes told the group, including Summit County legislators. "I was in downtown Akron recently and had to kill three snakes just to get to the First National Tower."

Rhodes a virtuoso with the press

Ask Jim Rhodes about his relationship with the press and he'll say: "There's no use in trying to tell a reporter what to write or trying to tell some editor to endorse somebody. You can't do it."

Inevitably, at some point he will add: "I've never been a candidate for editor."

All true, perhaps. But only half-true if you listen to veteran reporters. "Rhodes plays the press like a fiddle," says Lee Leonard, veteran UPI Statehouse correspondent. "He knows how we're going to handle each story, what will produce headlines, and he knows the value of timing.

"It's a standing joke around here that we can expect some major bleat out of the governor's office on the eve of a holiday like Thanksgiving or Christmas. He knows there's a lot of space to fill."

In his sporadic news conferences, Rhodes handled reporters' questions coolly with a spate of sentence fragments and malaprops that alternately charmed, outraged and befuddled even the best of them.

"Rhodes is the Casey Stengel of the gubernatorial fraternity," national columnist Jules Witcover once wrote, likening the governor's verbal goulash to that of the immortal New York Yankee manager.

Former Beacon Journal politics writer Abe Zaidan, who covered the governor for years, once described his close encounters with Rhodes this way: "An interview with James Allen Rhodes is like trying to bring a lumbering old barge into harbor on the end of a kite string. You are usually left holding just the string."

Under fire, Rhodes was the master of hyperbole. When critical reporters hit him on his many golfing trips to Florida, noting that he used to rap former Gov. John Gilligan for his weekend trips to Michigan, Rhodes replied:

"I am the only governor in the history of Ohio who has visited every museum, every cultural center, every state fair, every park and every attraction that we have in the state of Ohio. I am the only governor who has visited every ski lodge—and—and every ski and snowmobiles in the state of Ohio. I visit every place in the state of Ohio where there's action."

As baffled journalists pondered how Rhodes had managed to visit "every ski and snowmobiles," he was off again establishing his tourism credentials:

"What we have in the way of parks and recreation and other facilities for people to stay overnight, when you go to any other state or surrounding states or the Tetons or any of the national lodges that they have—they're all tool sheds. We're the only place that they have an indoor swimming pool outdoors."

Such eruptions were not only hard to punctuate; they also forced reporters to grope for follow-up questions while they were trying to decipher the answer to the first.

"Then, he waits until everybody's in a catatonic state and says, 'What else! Ask me anything!'" said Robert Drumheller, president of the Ohio

Legislative Correspondents Association. "Rhodes' verbal skills are not the best," said Leonard. "But he turns garbage into gold."

But if he caused trouble for reporters, Rhodes also knew how to handle some of the state's newspaper editors. He could always count on his hometown paper, the Columbus Dispatch. The Wolfe family, which owns the paper, had supported Rhodes since his days as mayor of Columbus in the 1940s.

Some Republican-oriented newspapers, like the Cincinnati Enquirer and small-town papers, endorsed him repeatedly, too. But others required persuasion.

One of Rhodes favorite gambits, dating back to the 1960s, was doling out Governor's Awards to editors and reporters, appointing some news executives to university boards of trustees or other state boards. He would also play on a newspaper editor's desire to see his town grow and prosper. "What do you want? What can we do?" Rhodes would ask.

The Ohio landscape is dotted with state office buildings, highways, medical schools and other projects Rhodes promised or delivered around newspaper endorsement time in election years.

In 1974, newspaper editors were investigating and criticizing each other over whether Rhodes had made deals for endorsements. Dayton Daily News editor Jim Fain, never a Rhodes fan, charged that Rhodes "bought" the endorsement of the Toledo Blade in the 1960s by promising publisher Paul Block a medical school at the University of Toledo.

Fain also charged that the Beacon Journal "let its enthusiasm for a medical school there lead it to endorse Rhodes in 1970." Block denied it. Fain's comment about the BJ endorsement of Rhodes "was an outrageously wrong conclusion," wrote BJ columnist James Jackson, who had participated in nearly all BJ endorsement sessions from 1940 to 1971.

Rhodes also denied recently he ever made a deal with BJ editors of the era. Then he noted that BJ editors endorsed his opponents in both the primary and general elections of 1974 and 1978. Reeling off a list of building and public projects his administration built in or around Akron, he said, "We never held it against a city because they didn't endorse. We did more for Akron and they always endorsed our opponents, even in the primaries."

Reminded that the BJ had endorsed him for governor in 1966 and for senator in 1970, Rhodes said, "I thanked John Knight. I was very courteous. But then Ben Maidenburg, he was the greatest industrial development in the history of Ohio."

Rhodes praised Maidenburg, the now-retired Beacon Journal publisher, as well as Block and Tom Vail, publisher of The Plain Dealer, as the editors who were "the most interested in getting jobs for their community."

———————

Still Rhodes' relations with the media were never easy. To an aide he cautioned: "The press are like dogs in heat. If you stand still, you get screwed. If you run away, they chase after and bite you in the ass."

Reporters pursued Rhodes on his income tax problems in the 1950s, his performance during the Kent State shootings of 1970 and his handling of a myriad of state issues. Many dug into his financial dealings and his friends' land holdings around state projects.

John Deardourff, Rhodes' media consultant in the 1974 and 1978 campaigns, said, "He has extremely serious doubts about the objectivity of the press, and you have doubts about his candor and veracity. That creates a schism that is unfortunate for both. His basic posture is that he is safer to assume the press is antagonistic."

One of Rhodes' favorite quips is about Richard Nixon and his relations with the press in the wake of Watergate.

"Nixon was out in California on the beach, and found out he could walk on water," Rhodes said. "After he walked out 15 feet and came back, he called over the reporters to watch him. He walked out again and the headlines the next day said, 'Nixon can't swim.'"

Quotable Rhodes

On his love for Ohio sports: "Woody Hayes once introduced me as the biggest athletic supporter in the state of Ohio."—*Jim Rhodes Roast, Columbus, 1982.*

On his popularity in the Republican Party: "The Democrats used to say I wasn't fit to sleep with the hogs. The Republicans defended me and said I was."—*Columbus, 1982.*

On George Voinovich, who served as Rhodes' lieutenant governor before he ran for mayor of Cleveland: "George was the greatest lieutenant governor in the history of Ohio. He got out in six months and never bother anybody. The other lieutenant governors were always checking with my doctor about my health every six months."—*Cleveland, 1982.*

On cuisine in his home in Jackson County: "Jackson is the Shaker Heights of Appalachia. A seven-course dinner down there is a possum and a six-pack.—*Wedgewood Country Club, Medina County, 1970.*

Advice to Governor-elect Richard Celeste: "The only two jobs where you start on top are digging a hole and governor."—*Columbus, Nov. 6, 1982.*

On the rejection of his $4.5 billion bond issues by voters in 1975: "It's not what you accomplish. It's what you put before the people. We have no failures. We're talking about 500,000 people out of a job. We've had no setbacks. We'll have programs. We've always had programs."—*BJ interview, Columbus, 1976.*

Ducking a question on whether he would run for the U.S. Senate in 1982: "I'm not considering anything, and I know it's difficult to say that."

When it was pointed out he had not answered yes or no: "I don't generally answer yes or no."—*Columbus, press conference, 1981.*

On whether state officials steered Honda Motor Co. to a central Ohio site for a new plant: "You can't tell the Japs anything."

Asked if they would be offended by the word "Japs": "They won't mind. Japs are Japanese. They call us Yankees, whatever that is. I don't mind being called a Yankee." (He apologized a few days later.)—*Columbus press conference,1977.*

Joking to a predominately Jewish crowd at a black-tie celebration of Israel's 30th anniversary: "Once when I was staying in a hotel in Tel Aviv, the housekeeper kept asking me, 'What was your name before you changed it?' Finally, after the tenth time she asked me that, I told her 'Rhodes-enberg.'"—*Ohio Theatre, Columbus, 1978.*

On his 16 years as chief executive: "We have done more than any other 10 governors."

Later in the same press conference: "We are not in a state of ego."—*Columbus, 1978.*

Arguing for a forensic mental health center in the Hough area on Cleveland's East Side: "It would be good because if they broke out of it and found out where they were, they'd break back in."—*to Cleveland City Council President George Forbes, 1981.*

Reply to reporter who asked in April 1977 if Rhodes would run for re-election in 1978: "Can you tell me if your wife will be pregnant next year?"—*Columbus, 1977.*

Making the point that caribou herds are shrinking in areas where oil drilling is forbidden in Alaska, but that caribou herds near oil fields are growing: "This proves that in the free-enterprise system, there's more love, more romance and more production."—*GOP state convention, Columbus, 1980.*

Upon learning that about 79 cases of his gubernatorial papers had been taken to a Columbus dump by mistake and buried: "That was all correspondence and there was nothing in that of any consequence—letters between congressmen and the legislature and all that. They've been keeping papers for a hundred years at the Historical Society and I don't think they've had one request from anybody to look at them yet."—*BJ interview, Cleveland, 1982.**

---

* Rhodes lost to Democratic incumbent Richard F. Celeste in 1986 when he sought a fifth term as governor. He is Ohio's longest serving governor, serving a total of sixteen years. He died at 91 in 2001.

Dick Celeste: See Dick Still Run

Akron Beacon Journal Beacon Magazine, November 18, 1990
WILLIAM HERSHEY

It looked like a scene from Dick Celeste's election-year playbook.

Celeste smiled through the sweat beading on his forehead as the sun beat down on the outdoor stage in downtown Columbus.

Green and white ribbons flapped in the late summer breeze. The chorus blared *You're A Grand Old Flag*.

Ohio's two-term governor, a Rhodes Scholar from the Cleveland suburbs, led the clapping.

Next, surely, Celeste would take over.

After all, it was Sept. 6, the start of prime time for Ohio's statewide elections. Celeste had been a statewide candidate every four years since 1974. And on the campaign trail, he always was Mr. Excitement.

"James A. Rhodes!" he bellowed in 1978, punctuating each syllable.

"Pack your bags!" the crowd, coached in the correct response, yelled back.

"No more business as usual," he blared four years later.

But this time there was no shouting. The scene was a dedication, not a campaign rally, and Celeste wasn't even the featured speaker. AFL-CIO President Lane Kirkland had been brought in to dedicate a new building for the state workers' compensation program.

Richard F. Celeste wasn't on the ballot this year. The Ohio Constitution prohibited him from seeking a third consecutive four-year term as governor.

But he has been on his own campaign trail, battling for his place in Ohio history and maybe for a future shot at national office.

It's a tougher race than the four he ran for statewide office.

He can't surprise people like he did in 1974, creeping up on Republican incumbent John Brown to become lieutenant governor.

He doesn't want to lose, even narrowly like he did in 1978 when Rhodes got 49,000 more votes and didn't have to unpack his bags and leave the Statehouse.

And he and his friends know the results won't be landslide wins, like the thrashings he gave Republicans Clarence "Bud" Brown in 1982 and Rhodes in their 1986 rematch.

This time it's a battle between *which* Dick Celeste history will recognize.

His enemies delight in the first—a failed liberal idealist and corrupt partisan who left an indelible stain of scandal on the state.

Celeste and his friends promote, relentlessly, the second—a visionary activist who pulled Ohio out of recession and positioned the state to compete in a world economy.

The first Celeste is easy to find in eight years of newspaper clippings that highlight corruption and cronyism.

Just consider the "search" committee that screened candidates for top jobs in the administration after the 1982 election—James Rogers, Larry McCartney and Roberta Steinbacher.

Rogers became state youth services director but quit and went to prison after being convicted of extorting kickbacks from contractors.

McCartney, Celeste's first patronage chief, pleaded guilty to a misdemeanor charge in a plea-bargain agreement resulting from an investigation of state contracts and a political hiring system.

Ms. Steinbacher, citing health reasons, resigned as director of the Ohio Bureau of Employment Services, amidst controversies over no-bid telephone contracts and the handling of sexual harassment complaints in her department.

"It (the Celeste administration) hit the ground in a big mud puddle and kept sinking for eight years," says U.S. Rep. Paul Gillmor, a

Republican from Port Clinton who was first state Senate minority leader and then Senate president during Celeste's first four years.

Such references irritate the governor, who's pushing hard for the second Celeste. He touts Ohio—and himself—at building dedications. He has organized national conferences on children, affirmative action and other topics to bring experts to Ohio and to let them know all the virtuous things that he has done.

In speeches across the state and across the nation, Celeste brags about how far Ohio has come in eight years. He refers to Ohio as a national leader in job creation, in caring for the mentally ill and in uniting business, labor and universities to fashion an economy for the 21st century.

It's easy to forget what Ohio was like when he took office, Celeste says.

"This state was in very deep trouble," he says. "We had more people out of work than during the depths of the Great Depression; three-quarters of a million people were out of work."

Not only was state government out of money, it didn't work. The rest stops along Ohio's interstate highways illustrated this. They consisted of a couple of outhouses and maybe a water pump.

Celeste used money from the sale of vanity license plates to install indoor plumbing and other amenities. "We don't need to have outhouses on our highways," he said.

———————

No critic ever accused the governor of doing nothing. He can't sit still. He acts, whether the problem is a $500 million budget deficit—something he faced upon taking office—or stinky rest stops.

It's *how* Celeste acted that sparks fierce debate.

His answer to the budget deficit was a controversial 90% state income tax increase, some of which since has been rolled back. He made permanent a temporary 50% increase enacted when Rhodes still was governor and then added 40% on top of that.

He rammed his tax plan through the Democratic-controlled legislature without consulting Republican leaders. Oliver Ocasek, then a Democratic state senator from Northfield, had to return from Florida, where he was recuperating from an automobile accident and keeping a vigil over his seriously injured wife, to cast the deciding Senate vote.

Celeste's actions revealed a partisan, self-righteous approach, which would mark his two terms, according to Gillmor and other critics.

Gillmor says he held out an olive branch to Celeste, but the governor ignored it.

"I went down to see Dick Celeste because we knew we had a financial problem," Gillmor says. "I said we are willing to work together to work through it in a cooperative way.

"… To that I never got a response. But I got an indirect response when they came out with this extreme partisan 90% tax increase."

Celeste contends that the Republicans started the partisan fighting, even before he took office.

First, there was Rhodes' "temporary" 50% tax increase. It was scheduled to expire at the end of March, soon after Celeste took office—not at the end of June when the state's budget year ended. As a going-away present, Rhodes had forced the new administration to make a quick decision on how to get Ohio through the final three months of a budget for which Rhodes was supposed to have been responsible.

And there was the Morris Jackson episode.

In the 1982 elections, Democrats wrested control of the state Senate from the Republicans, winning a slim 17–16 majority.

Gillmor and other Republicans went to work on Jackson, a Democratic senator from Cleveland. Jackson was bitter about how other Senate Democrats had dumped his friend, Ocasek, as their leader two years earlier and replaced him with Harry Meshel of Youngstown.

The Republicans promised to make Jackson president with their support, putting the Democrats back on the outside.

So Celeste went to work on Jackson.

"Morris Jackson voted with the Democrats and Harry Meshel became (Senate) leader," Celeste says, "and I played a very active role in making sure that all 17 Democrats stayed together then and stayed together during the course of the next two years."

Despite these Republican tricks, some Celeste advisers think, in hindsight, that he could have handled the tax increase differently.

"I think what we did as part of the political process was not very astute," says Joanne Limbach, Ohio's tax commissioner through both Celeste terms. "We charged in kind of like a bull…the loyal opposition has a right to disagree…to be informed."

Even though the final vote might have been the same, the administration would have benefited by bringing Republicans into the process, Limbach contends.

"I think the tone would have been different," she says. "I think there would have been more understanding."

Dick Celeste had other problems besides balancing the budget. They defied the understanding even of his friends.

In the early years of his two terms, hardly a week went by when some scandal or at least a scandalette didn't seem to seep out of the administration.

Sometimes, it was a temporary embarrassment, like when the liquor control director improperly invited representatives of liquor companies to a fundraiser for John Glenn's presidential campaign. Celeste ordered the donations returned.

It wasn't so easy to fix giant-size foul-ups, like the phone contract and sexual harassment messes that shoved Ms. Steinbacher, a longtime friend of the Celeste family, from her job as director of the employment services bureau.

Who was in charge of the governor's office anyway? critics began to ask.

In fact, in the first year and a half, Celeste himself tried to run the office. Unlike Rhodes, he didn't have a chief of staff. It was an omission he later corrected.

John Mahaney, a cigar-chomping business lobbyist who helped Celeste defeat an attempt to repeal the 90% tax increase, puts the problem bluntly.

"As I've been quoted before, he was a very poor administrator," says Mahaney, president of the Ohio Council of Retail Merchants. "He himself was not an administrator and he did not hire a hatchet man to be the administrator of state government."

The people making trouble for the governor throughout state government did not live in fear of their political lives. Celeste, Mahaney says, is "incapable of firing anybody."

Others, however, believe the problem went beyond this.

Celeste and his Democratic allies took office with the notion that state government belonged to them and to those who contributed to

Celeste's campaign. After putting up with Rhodes for 16 of the previous 20 years, their time had come and they were going to take whatever they could get.

In a prelude to what has become known as Columbus' "pay-to-play" system, friends and contributors were rewarded with no-bid contracts. Supporters of Celeste's political allies were rewarded with jobs, whether qualified or not.

Curt Steiner, a former Republican state Senate staffer who was George Voinovich's press secretary in this year's gubernatorial campaign, explains: "Their attitude was, 'We're the Democrats. We won the election. We get to walk off with all the goodies. We get to take care of or friends. That's what we're here for.'"

Worst of all, says Jim Tilling, the Republicans' top staffer in the state Senate, the Celeste crowd insisted that what they did was right.

"Their attitude was that they were so much superior to the previous administration, that they could do whatever they thought was right," Tilling says. "And, somehow, if they did it, because their motives were pure, then the course of action they took was correct.

"In a crude way they had the philosophy that the ends justify the means."

Apologists for Celeste still contend that misdeeds in his administration weren't much different from those that occurred under Rhodes during his four terms. Celeste's problems just got more publicity, they say.

Brian Berry, executive director of the state Republican Party, won't concede past GOP misdeeds, but he rejoices at the big target Celeste made for the Republicans.

"He's been fun," Berry says, "because we always imagine Celeste, when he's on TV or walking somewhere, with a big bull's-eye on him… He was like the reverse Teflon. He was the Velcro governor."

Celeste acknowledges that his activist approach and his reputation before taking office as an idealistic reformer—earned or not—may have raised hopes.

"When Dick Celeste was first elected governor, people had very, very high expectations of him," he says. "In many respects, it's a compliment to me. It probably carries a certain burden with it."

But that doesn't mean Celeste has enjoyed being a bull's-eye.

"I feel that some of the things that have been alleged about the Celeste administration are simply wrong and unfair," he says.

"We didn't invent unbid contracts. The reality is unbid contracts were far more widespread before we came in. We've increased, before there was any issue about it, the number of things that are bid and have worked at that."

What Celeste and his aides also have worked at, ceaselessly, is promoting Celeste. Maybe there's nothing wrong with that, but does it ever stop?

Tilling remembers 1985 when Celeste, in perhaps the best example of bipartisanship in his eight years as governor, was working with Republicans in the state Senate to solve the state's savings and loan crisis.

"I think one of the interesting things about it was that at the height of this crisis, they had TV crews in there filming his response," Tilling says. "One of the big problems is that they have always been far more concerned with the PR value of public policy than with its substance."

That accusation grates on Celeste, especially when it comes to the savings and loan crisis.

He says that neither he nor the Republicans and Democrats in the legislature ever got the credit they deserved for speedily handling the problem caused when Home State Savings Bank of Cincinnati collapsed and drained the state insurance fund.

No depositors lost money, and the state recovered nearly all it spent to bring the crisis to a speedy end. Celeste contrasts what happened in Ohio with the ongoing national savings and loan mess in Washington, which seems to have more episodes than an afternoon soap opera.

Even Gillmor applauds Celeste for how the Ohio cleanup was handled.

"For the most part we did work well together," he says. "On balance it came out very well."

But, like everything else Celeste was involved in, the scandal had a political dimension. Home State was owned by Marvin Warner, a political ally and major contributor to Celeste and other Democrats.

"Remember this," Gillmor says. "But for the special treatment Marvin Warner got from the Celeste administration, there never would have been a Home State crisis. What the (Commerce) department did to let Home State get overextended like that is what caused the crash."

"There's never been a shred of evidence that Marvin Warner or the people at Home State got special treatment," counters Celeste. If there was special treatment, it came from officials in the outgoing Rhodes administration, he says.

And so it goes when Statehouse Democrats and Republicans discuss Celeste. Even on a problem on which they both worked, the sliver of common ground is narrow.

It is possible to find people outside state government with good words for Celeste. Some are fellow Democrats like Louis Stokes of Shaker Heights, dean of the Democrats in Ohio's delegation to the U.S. House of Representatives.

Unlike Rhodes, Celeste took an active interest in what went on in Washington and in how legislation such as the Clean Air Act, with its acid-rain control provisions, affected Ohio.

"It has everything to do with being a good governor," Stokes says. "On legislation which is going to hurt your state, you want to make sure your delegation is aware how it's going to hurt."

Something else Celeste did impressed Stokes. For the first time, a governor aggressively recruited women and minorities for the top positions in state government.

Some, like the jailed Rogers, turned out to be lemons.

But Joanne Limbach, says business lobbyist Mahaney, is "as fine a tax commissioner as this state has ever had."

Yet shortly after Celeste appointed Limbach, the governor received a letter from a business person demanding that he appoint "a real tax commissioner" to the job.

Such a comment highlights the courage it took in a political climate as conservative as Ohio's to appoint a well-qualified woman to a job traditionally held by a man, competent or otherwise.

Dagmar Celeste should get as much of the credit for the appointment as her husband, the governor, says Limbach, a former Tuscarawas County commissioner. "Dagmar was always the voice for people to be brought into the process, like women and minorities," she says.

Sometimes both Celestes push harder than they need to and it backfires. That happened last April when Dagmar attended a dinner of a gay and lesbian rights group in Cincinnati and quoted explicit language from radical lesbian author Andrea Dworkin. When news of her comments got into the state's major newspapers about two months later, reaction was not favorable.

"They (the Celestes) somehow feel they have to intellectually justify their support," Limbach says. "… She did not have to show off her knowledge of the theoretical side of gays by quoting Dworkin."

Controversies involving both Celestes sometimes have obscured the administration's real achievements, says political scientist John C. Green, a Republican.

The governor made innovations in health care, expanded programs for the elderly and increased spending for education, says Green, director of the Ray C. Bliss Institute of Applied Politics at The University of Akron.

Also, Green says, Celeste spent state public works money where it was needed—in communities such as Youngstown still reeling from the recession that gripped the state when he took office.

"It wasn't just throwing money around," says Green. "There was a sense that public monies that were going to be spent anyway ought to be spent to help with the rate of joblessness."

If there is no consensus on the job Celeste has done, comparisons can be made. Celeste won't like Mahaney.

"If he were to be remembered, it would be kind of like Dick Nixon," Mahaney says. "You know, he had these bad things happen, but he was a very bright guy and on balance did a good job."

Nixon? That's a fighting word for a "progressive" like Celeste, whose admirers would much rather compare him to the late John F. Kennedy.

It's probably enough to send him back on the real campaign trail, if he hasn't already planned on it. At 53, he's two years younger than Ronald Reagan was when Reagan first was elected governor of California.

And, even Celeste's critics agree, he is good at campaigning—probably better than anyone in Ohio.

Steiner, the former Republican Senate aide, remembers seeing Celeste at 1982 county fairs, those extravaganzas of corn dogs, cotton candy and prize hogs. The city boy was right at home among the cow pies.

"Somehow everybody at the fair would know he was there," Steiner says. "He just is charismatic. He'd talk to the operatives of the opposing campaign and charm them out of their pants. You'd walk away from him, knowing that Dick Celeste represented everything that you were philosophically against and say, 'He's really a great guy.'"

Celeste won't say what his political plans are, but he categorically rules out nothing, even following the Jim Rhodes' example and running for governor again after sitting out a term.

Bull's-eye on the back or not, Steiner has no doubt that he'll see Celeste at another county fair.

"People will want to take Dick Celeste out of politics," Steiner says. "But you can't take the politics out of Dick Celeste.

"He'll be back."[*]

---

[*] Celeste never sought elective office again after leaving the governor's office in 1991. He served as United States Ambassador to India from 1997–2001 and as the president of Colorado College from 2002–2011.

Nancy Hollister: Hollister Takes Office

Ohio's first woman governor will preside for 11 days
until Bob Taft's inauguration

Akron Beacon Journal, January 1, 1999
JAMES C. BENTON

With a bit of humor and a pledge to provide a smooth transition over the next 11 days, Nancy Putnam Hollister became Ohio's 66th governor yesterday.

Surrounded by her husband, Jeff, four of their five children and one grandchild, Hollister took the oath of office from Supreme Court Justice Evelyn L. Stratton at 12:06 p.m. yesterday—a half-hour after George V. Voinovich resigned so that he could be seated in the U.S. Senate next week.

Hollister, the first woman governor in Ohio's 195-year history, will hold the job for the remainder of Voinovich's second term. Bob Taft will be sworn in on Jan. 11 to the four-year term he won last fall.

Hollister's speech contained thanks and praise for Voinovich and made connections between parts of the state's history and the family histories of the three people who will serve as governor by the middle of the month.

"In the span of 11 short days, three people will hear the title 'Governor of Ohio,'" she said. "The first, a grandson of immigrants from the ethnic neighborhoods of east Cleveland. The third, a descendant of one of America's most political families. And the one in the middle, a person from Marietta, southern Ohio, a member of one of the state's pioneer families."

Before the oath, Stratton said she had been asked to administer the oath of office by Chief Justice Thomas Moyer. "It's a good thing, because he fell and broke his arm, and he can't raise his right hand," she said.

Senate President Pro Tem Robert Cupp, R-Lima, told the audience that some people had said it would be "a cold day" before a woman became Ohio governor. "How did they know?" he asked, referring to the cold snap across Ohio.

Hollister drew a few laughs when she described what she would do during her term.

"Let me be clear about my plans," she said. "I will offer no major initiatives. I will offer no pardons. I will sponsor no major legislation. But most importantly," she said, a hint of a smile belying a sarcastically grave tone, "I will spare you the State of the State address."

The humor aside, Hollister vowed she was ready to face any challenges the state may encounter during her term and promised to complete the term with dignity, integrity, a little humor and a "smooth, orderly transition" until Taft and Lt. Gov.-elect Maureen O'Connor are inaugurated.

Hollister immediately was escorted to her Statehouse office, where she and Stratton signed the oath of office. She answered a few questions from reporters and then went into an adjacent conference room to swear in the 29 members of her Cabinet. She also made three judicial appointments and five appointments to state boards and commissions.

She said Voinovich told her she was capable of being governor when he was seeking a replacement for Mike DeWine, who left in 1994 to run for the U.S. Senate.

"We talked about many things, and we had conversations over a six-month period," Hollister said. "And he looked me in the eye and said, 'One of the most important things about being lieutenant governor is that someday, you may have to take this chair. You can handle it.'"

Voinovich drew a standing ovation before taking the rostrum at 11:57 a.m. to give his last speech as governor. In that speech, he offered thanks to many people, including his wife, Janet, legislators, his Cabinet members and the citizens of Ohio.

"It's hard to believe that eight years have gone by since I took the oath of office on Jan. 14, 1991," Voinovich said. "Together, with God's help, we have made a difference for the state of Ohio."

He then reflected on his professional relationship with Hollister, which extends back to the mid-1980s, when he was mayor of Cleveland and she way mayor of Marietta.

"I've always admired Nancy's work ethic, tenacity and determination," he said. "As lieutenant governor, Nancy, you have gone far beyond what I asked you to do."

Asked what he thought of becoming Ohio's first "first gentleman," Jeff Hollister said he thought it was great. But he emphasized the day belonged to his wife. "Nancy is where she is today because she's worked very hard," he said.

The governor, however, is still quiet about what she will do after her term ends. But she said she had not formally met with House Republicans or formally interviewed for the state House seat being vacated by Tom Johnson, R-New Concord, who will resign his seat next week to become Taft's new budget director.*

---

* Hollister served in the Ohio House of Representatives from 1999 to 2005.

Betty Montgomery: To the Moon with Montgomery?

A defining speech in the governor's race

Akron Beacon Journal, May 8, 2005
MICHAEL DOUGLAS

Ask Lee Fisher about Betty Montgomery and her skillful way of defining the opponent in an election campaign.

In 1994, Fisher was the incumbent attorney general. Montgomery the challenger relentlessly reminded voters that she was the candidate with courtroom experience, the former county prosecutor. Put aside that the attorney general isn't a prosecutor in the traditional sense, or even close. Montgomery jabbed. Fisher struggled to respond and lost the race, swept away in a Republican tide.

On Wednesday, Montgomery (now the state auditor) delivered a speech to the Columbus Metropolitan Club. The talk represented a first attempt at shaping her candidacy for governor. She proved adept at defining her two opponents in the Republican primary.

In this instance, the tool wasn't distortion. Montgomery squarely challenged Jim Petro (the attorney general) and J. Kenneth Blackwell (the secretary of state) on the issues and their styles of leadership. The talk revealed a Montgomery who has grown in office(s). If the criticism was sharp, the tone reflected something larger, a candidate thinking tactically, yes, but also thoughtfully about the state as a whole, about the agenda Ohio should follow.

Jim Petro wants to reorganize the structure of state government, dramatically so. He would slash the number of Cabinet agencies from 23 to nine. He would reduce the state work force by 20%, generating as much as $1 billion a year in savings.

His candidacy involves many other elements. This is his signature issue. (He wants to reorganize higher education, too.) Much of the idea has merit, Ohio burdened by layers and layers of government, at last count, roughly 3,600 taxing jurisdictions. Montgomery made the telling point: If the state launches "a massive government reorganization, that will be the only thing we could get done (if at all) and will distract us from our larger, more significant problems."

Perhaps the task would be a snap. Experience suggests otherwise, the state still smoothing the rough edges of the merger that created the Department of Job and Family Services. Montgomery exposed one of the conceits of the Petro plan (championed in other ways by many at the Statehouse): Must Ohioans wait until government functions perfectly, the perfect number of offices, employees and the like, before taking up the necessary investment to become more competitive in the knowledge economy?

If the answer is yes, the day of adequate investment will never arrive.

That is not to say all restructuring should be shelved. Start with Medicaid, a mighty job by itself, achieving efficiencies without harming the poor. Montgomery emphasized priorities, debunking familiar illusions: "We simply can't cut or cap our way into prosperity. Nor can we reorganize our way into a bright new future."

The centerpiece of the Blackwell campaign is a proposed constitutional amendment that would limit state spending to a level driven by inflation and population growth. The concept sounds reasonable. Montgomery explained the dangers, the inflexibility "handcuffing the governor and the legislature…absolving them of responsibility for making tough fiscal decisions, leading to reduced investments in education and higher education at exactly the time that we need smart investments in these very areas if we are to succeed as a state."

Montgomery argued that the Blackwell proposal "may not be illegal, but it's the kissin' cousin of consumer fraud because it promises something that just cannot be delivered." Don't believe it? Ask the governor of Colorado, long a champion of his state's strict constitutional limits on spending, limits very much like the Blackwell plan. Bill Owens now campaigns across the state urging voters to suspend the limits and allow the government to spend an additional $3 billion.

Owens cites essential road projects that have been postponed, and a University of Colorado that has suffered deep and debilitating spending reductions. Ohioans should note a critical difference. Colorado has a growing population. In other words, Ohio would likely have a worse time.

In her speech to the Metropolitan Club, Montgomery made plain the trouble that looms if Blackwell wins passage of his amendment. She called for its defeat. That wasn't the whole of her talk, a mere episode in the negative, no matter how effectively expressed.

The fair question arises: What would you do?

Montgomery unveiled "Success Grants," stipends of $2,000 a year for eligible Ohio students to help pay for the first two years at a state college or university, placing emphasis on science, math and engineering. She admits the modest proposal ($50 million a year) falls far short of the need. She talks about a work in progress. More important, she sets expectations high, referring to "the day Sputnik was launched—and America responded: We're going to the moon!"

Ohio requires no less.

With more than a year to go before choosing the next governor, Ohioans shouldn't expect candidacies to be fully formed. They should be assessing the foundations the candidates are attempting to lay. Montgomery made a passing reference to "a growing bipartisan consensus." In Ohio? Actually, the germ of one may exist. A band of Senate Democrats has put forward even more ambitious plans along the lines of the Montgomery themes. A vital and aspiring political center? Now there's a concept worthy of a governor's race.[*]

---

[*]   After dropping out of the 2006 governor's race, Montgomery unsuccessfully ran for a third term as Ohio attorney general. In 2021, she was chair of the board of trustees at Bowling Green State University and chair of the Jo Ann Davidson Ohio Leadership Institute.

Jo Ann Davidson: The Whole Package

Akron Beacon Journal, December 24, 2000
MICHAEL DOUGLAS

Betty Montgomery tells the story of how Jo Ann Davidson learned to drive. The young woman bought a car, and she practiced on the alleyways of Findlay, the town in Northwest Ohio where she grew up, mastering the machine until the day she was ready to take (and pass) the license exam.

Classic Davidson, the attorney general explained in a video played last month at a tribute to the House speaker on the eve of her departure from the state legislature. Independent. Self-sufficient. "She always figures out a way to get the job done," Montgomery offered in sum.

Yes, she does, and four decades or so later, those same traits, plus plenty of others indispensable to effective leadership, began to make their appearance at the Statehouse. Davidson won election to the Ohio House in 1980, representing Reynoldsburg and other communities near Columbus. By the time her legislative career had collided with term limits, she had become the state's first woman speaker, engineered a Republican majority and delivered a long list of accomplishments, from welfare reform to electricity deregulation.

I've watched Davidson mostly from a distance and disagreed when Republican majorities have taken sound concepts too far—such as reform of product liability and other elements of civil law—or stopped short of what was needed (for schools, most notably). What has long seemed worth admiring has been her approach to leadership. She brings the whole package, an unrelenting capacity for work, attention to detail, patience, decisiveness and a willingness to talk with the aim of forging consensus.

In a time of political shouters and slashers, Davidson has practiced a civil brand of leadership. Oh, she is a partisan, intensely so. What she resists is self-righteousness, the pose that discourages gritty compromise in favor of feeling proud of herself.

Davidson hasn't been interested in credit. She has gone about her work, modestly, quietly, shrewdly, benefiting from years of apprenticeship, learning and preparing for the role.

Compromise can be misunderstood. It isn't the business of hollering for a time and then cutting the difference. It is the legislator's highest craft, demanding subtlety and care, and a dash of looking at things anew. It requires a command of an issue, and that is what has often amazed those around Davidson, her comprehensive knowledge and depth of analysis. She isn't snowed or led astray.

She has cultivated influence through her capacity to look at situations through the eyes of others. She listens. She recognizes what matters to the players involved and then patches together the necessary pieces to create a coherent whole.

Her finest work may have taken place within her own caucus. The Republican contingent in the House has been a divided lot. In the school-funding debate of 1997, the caucus fractured over the question of raising taxes. Davidson rallied, aware that airing differences serves as prologue for decision-making, inviting understanding, if nothing else.

In the end, she stuck with the concept of more money for schools, and though she failed that summer, by late winter, another tax package had been forged, only to lose at the polls. The defeat was resounding. It didn't diminish the legislative skills of the speaker, skills that would again amaze when Davidson wouldn't accept failure in the battle over electricity deregulation.

At one point (in a moment that has become something of a legend), Davidson encountered a gaggle of lobbyists in a restaurant, letting them know that no amount of maneuvering on their part would deter her. They didn't get "the stare" exactly, the icy Davidson device for expressing dismay or disdain, but they did get the message. The speaker would listen. She would also push.

Davidson had a tough act to follow. Vern Riffe preceded her, his birthday parties (nearly $1 million raised each year), his iron fist, his loyal soldiers. All of it seemed the way for speakers. Davidson knows how to raise big money. She knows how to recruit candidates (far better than Democrats do). What she has faced is the bumpy transition to term limits. The speaker's job is much tougher today, especially if they're going to think about and serve the larger interests of the state.

Garry Wills, the historian and journalist, argued in *Certain Trumpets* that leadership is essentially a struggle, "reciprocally engaging two wills, one leading (often in disguised ways), the other following (while often resisting)." He lamented our tendency to see leaders as one of two types: the superior man or woman, so great that we all fall in line, or the weathervane, polling and then ingratiating, telling people what they want to hear.

Leadership is really more complicated. Wills might as well have Davidson in mind. He noted that for leaders to be successful, their skills must match the moment, and they must attract followers. The former is a matter of fortune. The latter, simple though it seems, is more challenging.

In the legislature, Davidson long ago grasped that understanding potential followers was more important than their understanding her. She could then prod and pull, searching for what Wills called "the answerable call." He wrote: "To sound a certain trumpet doesn't mean trumpeting one's own certitudes. It means sounding a specific call to specific people capable of response."

That doesn't foreclose appealing to the better angels in all of us. It does suggest the route can be circuitous and progress halting. It highlights the many skills of a Jo Ann Davidson, her intelligence, her resilience, her capacity to get the job done.

The Davidson style, something to admire, something to emulate, something that will be missed.*

---

* Davidson retired from the Ohio House in 2000 after serving 20 years, including six as speaker. She was the first chair of the Ohio Casino Control Commission and in 2021 was commission vice-chair.

Vern Riffe: "Boss" Riffe Runs a Tight House

If all goes well, Riffe will seek governorship

Akron Beacon Journal, April 6, 1980
MICHAEL CULL

In the dark, empty cavern of the Ohio House chamber, a photographer searched vainly for the lights necessary to his work.

High on the chamber's podium, House Speaker Vern Riffe turned to the light switch. "I'll get the lights," he volunteered. "I operate everything around here."

If Riffe doesn't operate everything in the Statehouse, he comes close. Indeed, Vernal G. Riffe Jr. just might be the most powerful man in the state.

––––––––––––––

Consider:

- He is the absolute master of 61 fellow Democrats in the Ohio House and has the ability to greatly influence the 37 Republicans. His authority in the House means everyone else has to deal with him: the governor, the 33-member Ohio Senate, the hordes of lobbyists.

- But beyond Riffe's institutional power, there is his personal power—power that is his and his alone, power that he has gathered in the 22 years he has been in the state capital.
- He is the center of a network of people who can supply information and support that more than one legislator has described as awesome. Says State Rep. Harry J. Lehman, D-Beachwood: "He is not only the speaker. He is the floor leader, the assistant majority floor leader and whatever other offices we have."

"He set about collecting the maximum authority in the office of the speaker," Lehman said. "It took about three years to consolidate, but he may have started building as far back as the '60s."

Another legislator—one of the many who requested anonymity because of "cowardice and common sense"—noted that Riffe "has contact with an incredible number of people."

"He has an incredible network of informal bases of power," the legislator said. "He finds out from people who know people who in turn know still other people."

Today, Riffe's power might be growing at a still faster pace because he has begun talking about running for governor in 1982. And that talk means that all who deal with Riffe must now consider they might be dealing with the next governor.

Riffe is doing nothing to discourage that presumption. "Under the same circumstances after the 1980 elections as I am in right today, I intend to be a candidate for governor," he says. "If I had to make the decision today, I am a candidate for governor."

He repeated this line in a speech Wednesday to the Portsmouth Area Retail Merchants Association.

The 54-year-old Riffe (whose name rhymes with "strife," which he abhors) had a head start on the road to power. His father, often acknowledged as the greatest influence on him, was mayor of New Boston in southern Ohio for 24 years. Now 79, the senior Riffe is still referred to as the mayor of the small Ohio River town near Portsmouth.

"I was born and raised in politics, born and raised in government," says Riffe in an accent that softens and slows words enough to be southern but well short of hick.

Young Riffe—often called "Junior" or "June" back at his New Boston insurance agency—was sent into the political world armed with a credo: "Always be honest with your fellow man. Have a reason for an action. If you make a commitment, keep it; if you can't keep it, don't make it."

The elder Riffe taught something else, too—not to fear being the boss. The son, sitting in his Statehouse office, finds it easy to recall his father's talks with employees or other politicians. "My daddy would say, 'Wait a minute. We are not going to do it that way. This is the way we are going to do it.'"

Riffe is the boss.

He knows it and is comfortable with it. Everyone else in the House knows he is boss, although not all are comfortable with it. He never seems to hurry, and he never swaggers. In front of the 99 occasionally restive House members, he holds the highly polished wooden gavel—symbol of his power—lightly. It is never far from his hand.

And he looks like the boss, in dark, well-tailored vested suits with a diamond-encrusted tie pin in the shape of a gavel. His tie is always tight, his sleeves down, his white-tipped eyebrows and sideburns neatly clipped. (He also cares how the House members dress: He likes to see the little gold metal lapel pins that say, "Riffe.")

On the political spectrum, Riffe is a moderate-conservative, reflecting his small-town background. More than one Riffe observer notes that he is close politically to Gov. James A. Rhodes, the political master born about 35 miles from New Boston. Like Republican Rhodes, Riffe avoids issues and ideology.

On some things, they are astonishingly alike. For instance, on the importance of business to a state's economy, Riffe observes:

"First you have got to protect industry from the standpoint of jobs with a good business climate. Without industry and a good climate, you do not have jobs. We have got to make the climate as good as we can and compete with other states."

It could have been said by Rhodes.

———————

But Riffe has roots in the Democratic tradition, too, and has an often-demonstrated feeling for the working man: "You gotta protect employees hurt through no fault of their own, or out of work through no fault of their own. They have got to be protected."

According to one critic: "He believes in the little guy, and strongly, but sometimes he just plays to power blocs." Riffe apparently believes enough in the so-called little guy that he backed bills to improve nursing home regulation, to continue a property tax rollback and to allow heating credits for the poor and elderly.

He also backed the Equal Rights Amendment and a resolution to grant more congressional representation to Washington, D.C., the latter a move intended to help the predominantly Black nation's capital.

Thus, Riffe could side with Rhodes to give tax breaks to, say Ford, to build a car plant and, as he did last February, push through an override of the governor's veto of an additional 13 weeks of unemployment compensation.

———————

He has reached out to find allies in the state's populated and industrial areas and can count among his allies representatives from Akron, Toledo, Dayton, Youngstown and Cincinnati.

"Probably one of the reasons I got along with those from big cities is that I gave them help," Riffe says. "If they had a problem, I was there with them."

Riffe's rule of the House is autocratic. Some have charged he is a tinhorn dictator. He is able to use the power of the speaker's office to control his members.

For example, as speaker, he can appoint 34 people to chairmanships and other leadership posts that pay more than a legislator's base pay of $22,500 a year. Each of those drawing the extra pay, perhaps enjoying a bigger office and staff, owes Vern Riffe.

———————

Not only is Riffe master of the House Democrats, his relationship with Republican leader Corwin Nixon, R-Lebanon, say critics, heads off any chance he will be challenged by a loyal opposition: Nixon, 63, is hardly the combative partisan that former minority leader Charles Kurfess was.

A good part of any infrequent Nixon floor speech is given over to thanking Riffe. His vote last year to support the Democratic budget was considered, in the more ideological Republican circles, as near heresy.

"People who desire to scrap it out on issues are leaving," moans one Republican. "Bob Taft, Jim Betts and even (Rep. C. William) O'Neill, to some extent, are leaving. There is no longer a star system for Republicans. Vern has sort of closed the system to us."

Democrats in Riffe's own caucus who are more issue-oriented also chafe under a system where the process and Riffe's control of it outweigh concerns for open discussion of occasionally controversial ideas.

Riffe is good at reading a consensus, some say, but will do little to create a consensus among legislators and the public to change policy. The state's failure to fund adequately its public schools and repair its roads, they contend, is the result of a cozy, make-no-waves deal involving Riffe, Rhodes and Senate president Oliver J. Ocasek.

The unhappy Democrats tend to be young, somewhat liberal and hopelessly outnumbered, especially when Riffe can dip into a friendly Republican caucus to get needed votes.

Yet it cannot be presumed theirs is a better way, according to Lehman, whose liberal credentials are in good order and who has found a way to disagree with Riffe without being disagreeable.

"People with a strong ideological bent have got to decide whether they want media attention, knowing they will not achieve anything," Lehman said, "or grab hold and try to do their best."

Says one Republican who has watched with awe: "Vern finds out where the levers are. He's like Dick Daley. Take Harry Lehman, a well-respected, big-city liberal. Harry's lever is work, so Vern gives him all the work he can handle."

Riffe also derives power by being available to almost everyone at almost any time. If a legislator cannot catch him at the Statehouse, he can try the Neil House bar, where Riffe can often be heard to say, "You want to talk? Why, sure podnuh, come on."

One young legislator sums it up: "He is not talking all the time. He listens. He listens very well."

State Rep. Vernon F. Cook, the Cuyahoga Falls Democrat who might succeed Riffe as speaker said: "Knowledge is power, and he knows what is going on out there. It is a personal network, not a partisan network."

Cook recalls that during a tangled discussion on the state sales tax, various legislators and administration officials tossed out tax receipt figures gathered the previous month or week. "Riffe gets on the phone, calls someone—God knows who—and finds out how much sales tax was collected yesterday."

Above all, Riffe values loyalty. "If there is one thing I demand, it's loyalty," he says. "If you are loyal to a person...anything else might be lacking but you can help them.

"There is not a member of the (Democratic) caucus I have not gone to bat for. I back my people and I expect it in return."

Those who have proven their loyalty to Riffe have been rewarded. "Vern has a cash register in his head," says one critic. "He knows everyone's price."

For instance:

- Rep. Rocco Colonna of Cleveland has been loyal. He wanted a liquor cabinet, then a waiting room for his Statehouse office. He got both.
- Rep. C.J. McLin, a powerful force in Dayton's Black community and head of the Black delegation in the House, has his own office and an aide—perks generally reserved for committee chairmen—even though he is not a chairman.

- Rep. Arthur Wilkowski of Toledo—credited with helping the coup that made Riffe speaker—has an aide and the speaker's support for financing millions of dollars of studies, seminars and travel to promote a high-speed, inter-city rail system that many think is too futuristic and too expensive for these times.

Riffe can punish, too.

A notable example was when Rep. David Hartley, D-Springfield, objected to the unanimous election of Riffe as speaker at the end of the last House session.

Hartley's legislation came to a dead halt in the House and he was not reappointed vice chairman of a committee.

"He paid for that," said Riffe, adding that Hartley bills are now given attention. "He realizes he made a mistake and he had to pay."

———————————

While Riffe's hold on the House is believed absolute, his reach for the governor's office is considered chancy. Although Rhodes himself says, "He'd be a good governor," Riffe might have to contend with Attorney General William J. Brown, former lieutenant governor Richard F. Celeste, and perhaps Ohio Supreme Court Chief Justice Frank D. Celebrezze.

All those are powerful political names, while Riffe, if remembered at all, is mispronounced.

But then, as one Riffe supporter notes, "You don't pronounce in the voting booth."*

———————————

* Riffe retired from the Ohio House in 1994 after serving 36 years, including 20 as speaker. He died in 1997 at 72.

Bill Batchelder: Bill Batchelder in the House

Akron Beacon Journal, December 24, 2014
WILLIAM HERSHEY

Political second comings don't always end well.

Richard M. Nixon and Watergate may be the best proof. After his narrow defeat for president in 1960, Nixon rose from the political dead to win election to the nation's highest office in 1968 only to resign in disgrace in 1974 in the Watergate scandal.

Richard M. Nixon just couldn't escape the shadow of "Tricky Dick."

It's hard to imagine a happier ending, however, than the final session of the Ohio House last week when Medina's Bill Batchelder stepped down as speaker after four years. He left office showered with accolades from Republicans and Democrats alike.

"Ain't he adorable," quipped State Rep. Vernon Sykes, D-Akron, holding up a picture of a young Batchelder, according to the Columbus Dispatch.

Batchelder's career as a legislator seemed over once before in 1999 when he left office after serving in the House for 30 years.

During that first period of service, he was among the Republicans who took control of the House in the 1994 elections, the first GOP majority in 20 years.

But Batchelder did not become the speaker then. That job went to a quiet, hardworking and hard-nosed pragmatist, Jo Ann Davidson.

You have to be old to remember when Batchelder, who turned 72 last week, was young, but when he was young pragmatic did not describe him.

He was the Tea Party long before there was one. An intellectual conservative and follower, among others, of the late Jack Kemp, the congressman from Buffalo and Republican candidate for vice president in 1996, Batchelder delighted in gumming up the works when he thought government got too big for its britches (a word Batchelder might have used).

Davidson and her allies knew this about Batchelder and at least one of them, whom I knew well, suspected Batchelder of from time to time undermining the new speaker of his own party.

Despite such misgivings, Batchelder left the House that first time with well-earned good will. He had bushy eyebrows, black-rimmed glasses and most always a smile. While he didn't much care for government solutions, he knew how to make government work better than those who did. When Ohio had its savings and loan crisis in the mid-1980s, Democratic Gov. Dick Celeste turned to Batchelder, a lawyer and banking expert, for help.

Batchelder agreed and helped put together the deal that kept depositors from losing their money, even if it might have meant holding his nose, intellectually speaking.

But there always was more to that Batchelder than his conservative philosophy and banking and legal expertise. He was one of a handful of lawmakers who was worth listening to when making a speech. Along with a few others like the late Art Wilkowski, a Toledo Democrat who unsuccessfully championed passenger rail for Ohio, when they spoke, the House listened.

Batchelder did not leave public life when he exited the legislature in 1999. He became first a Medina County common pleas judge and then an appeals court judge before his second coming to the House with a victory in 2006.

Maybe Batchelder changed and had become a pragmatist by then. He was enough of one to win an intraparty leadership fight and eventually become speaker in 2011.

But I doubt that Batchelder's philosophy had changed much. When he returned to the House, Republicans did not have to be moderate or even pragmatic to win. They just had to be well organized, which Batchelder, in his own way, turned out to be.

The party had moved to the right and Batchelder felt right at home, working to advance the anti-tax agenda of Republican Gov. John Kasich, once Kasich took office in 2011.

There was one more thing about Batchelder. It reminded me of something my dad told me when I complained about working "hard" as a reporter.

My dad worked most of his life in a factory; that was "hard" work. There was nothing "hard" about being a newspaper reporter—just talking to people, writing down what they said and turning it all into a story.

The same goes for legislators. Their job may require late hours and some arm-twisting, but it is not "hard" in the physical sense.

Batchelder seemed to know this. Unlike some of the sourpusses at the Statehouse, he knew what a privilege and joy it was to have a job that required brain power, not tired muscles. He loved the work.

The Dispatch reported that there were tears in Batchelder's eyes when he stepped down as speaker for the last time. I bet they were soon replaced by a twinkle.*

---

* Batchelder retired from the Ohio House of Representatives in 2014, after serving 38 years, including four as speaker.

Sterling Tucker: Righting Civil Wrongs

Sterling Tucker Helps Light the Way for a Color–Blind World

Akron Beacon Journal Beacon Magazine, January 3, 1993
WILLIAM HERSHEY

Akron's Sterling Tucker arrived in Washington, D.C., in 1956 to run the local chapter of the Urban League. Not long after that, he found himself at a banquet with Vice President Richard M. Nixon.

Nixon and Tucker had their picture taken together, and Tucker took the photo back home to show to his wife and daughter, who still were living in Ohio.

His daughter, Shelly, proudly took the picture to her first-grade class for show and tell.

"That's a very nice picture, but which one is your daddy?" a classmate asked.

Tucker, a Black man, passed that anecdote along to Nixon the next time they met in Washington.

"He just loved the story," says Tucker, 69.

Tucker loved the story, too. He loved it not because it reflected the reality of a racially divided nation. Rather, it projected, as only an innocent child could, the kind of society America should become.

"Kids can say great things," Tucker says. "They can put their finger on the center of things."

Since then, he has worked full time in Washington, trying to create a society as blind to differences in color as his daughter's first-grade classmate was.

It hasn't been easy, and the country hasn't made it yet, he says. "We have to go from color awareness for negative reasons—where we've been—to color awareness for positive reasons—where we're headed, hopefully. And then to color blindness, once we've eliminated all the negativism of color."

That effort has put Tucker in touch with eight presidents, from Dwight D. Eisenhower to George Bush. He has pursued that goal as executive director of the local Urban League, Washington representative for the national Urban League, chairman of the District of Columbia City Council, a high-ranking housing official for President Jimmy Carter and always as a citizen arm-twister. Along the way, he was also chairman of the regional transit authority when the area's widely praised subway system opened.

But he has found the last 12 years of his fight to be discouraging ones. Ronald Reagan and George Bush seemed to say that gains made by the civil rights movement had been bad for America, Tucker says. A new president will be sworn in on Jan. 20. Tucker knows Bill Clinton and he has hopes.

Now in private business as a government and management consultant, he is not looking for a full-time job. But he wants to serve and give advice.

"What I have to do," he says, "is help turn the lights on in America again."

———

Sterling Tucker has been turning on the lights for nearly four decades.

Born at home on West Bowery Street in Akron, he attended Lane Elementary School and graduated from old West High School. He began working for the Akron Community Service Center and Urban League while attending The University of Akron, from which he received a bachelor's degree in sociology and a master's in social psychology.

He and his wife, Alloyce, a North High and University of Akron graduate, still have many relatives in the Akron area.

After running Canton's Urban League for three years, Tucker went to Washington. He met Nixon during the Eisenhower administration, but didn't visit the White House as much as he would in later years.

He got to know Eisenhower best just after the Republican left office.

Whitney Young, then head of the national Urban League, picked Tucker to be the league's representative to go with the late Roy Wilkins, then executive director of the national NAACP, to visit Eisenhower at his Gettysburg farm.

The civil rights leaders wanted Eisenhower to help them win Republican support for civil rights legislation.

Tucker thought the meeting would be a short one. Instead, it lasted three hours and included lunch.

The NAACP had painted Eisenhower as unsympathetic to civil rights, Tucker says. Eisenhower's aide, Sherman Adams, had fueled this feeling by writing in a book that sending federal troops to Little Rock, Ark., to integrate the schools had been one of the president's toughest decisions.

"He wanted to talk," Tucker recalls. "He wanted us to understand that he was a good guy."

Adams was wrong, Eisenhower told them. Sending the troops in had been an easy decision, because he was following the law. Eisenhower said he would help them, and he did, Tucker says.

John F. Kennedy, who succeeded Eisenhower, and Kennedy's brother, Bobby, the attorney general, made Tucker feel welcome.

"I played touch football with them," says Tucker. "They had a great civil rights interest right away. They had a great interest in the community right away."

The president appointed Tucker to a six-member task force to study how the new administration should relate to the local District of Columbia government. At the president's request, Tucker says he also worked with Vice President-elect Al Gore's late sister, Nancy, in developing the Peace Corps.

While Kennedy was in the White House, Tucker was a vice chairman of and helped organize the 1963 civil rights march on Washington that culminated in Martin Luther King Jr.'s "I Have a Dream" speech at the Lincoln Memorial.

Tucker has a special fondness for Bobby Kennedy; he played his touch-football games at Kennedy's suburban Washington home.

"Bobby was a very tough guy—no-nonsense and hard-driving. I think he kind of believed that being right was enough," Tucker says with a laugh.

He laughs because Bobby reminded Tucker a little of himself when he was younger. While working for the Akron Urban League in the 1940s, Tucker testified at a hearing local bus drivers held during a dispute with the bus company. He testified that he supported the union, but also thought it would be a good idea to hire Black bus drivers. There were none.

"They snatched the microphone and took it away and then tried to get me fired," he recalls.

Tucker was right, but his bosses at the Urban League told him that being right wasn't always enough.

The nation's time with the Kennedys was cut short—first by the assassination of the president in 1963 and then by Bobby's assassination five years later.

He remembers being invited to Bobby's home after his death. "Ethel served lunch," recalls Tucker. "One of the kids came up to me and grabbed my hand and said, 'What do you do with a mother who cries every night?' I still remember that."

President Kennedy's death brought to office Lyndon B. Johnson, the Texan with a giant ego and a giant passion to finish the civil rights work that Kennedy had begun.

The new president drafted Tucker to help draw up the battle plan for the war on poverty.

Johnson was suspicious of some with close ties to the Kennedys, but Tucker wasn't in this group. "Johnson liked Whitney Young (the national Urban League head) and knew I was Whitney's man in Washington," Tucker says.

The president loved to hug people, slap them on the back, do anything else to make his point, says Tucker.

"He didn't understand how hard he could hit," says Tucker, who is 5 foot 7 and weighs 149 pounds. "I remember a couple of times he started flailing his arms, and I backed off…I didn't know where they were going to land."

During the Johnson administration, Tucker continued his civil rights work. He remembers sitting in the Senate gallery with Martin Luther King Jr. listening to the debate on the civil rights bill.

Malcolm X was sitting in another part of the gallery. Reporters had been making a big deal of the differences between King and Malcolm, Tucker said.

"Brother Tucker," he recalls Malcolm saying. "Would you tell Brother King not to let the media put words in his mouth. I'll try to not let them put words in my mouth."

"Why don't you tell him yourself?" Tucker recalls asking. Malcolm agreed that would be a good idea. "I went and got Martin Luther King and the two of them went over in the corner and talked."

Before Johnson left office, Tucker also organized the Solidarity Day March in support of the 1968 Poor People's Campaign that erected a tent city in Washington.

The assassinations of both King and Bobby Kennedy in 1968, plus Johnson's decision not to seek re-election, brought an end to the Democrats' hold on the White House.

Tucker was and remains a Democrat, but he's still surprised at how well he came to get along with Nixon.

"The most fun was Kennedy," Tucker says of his relations with different presidents. "The most productive in many ways was Nixon. It was a time when we were trying to make some gains out of the early 1960s."

Unlike the Kennedys, Nixon had trouble relaxing, Tucker says. "Even when he laughed, he seemed tense."

Still, Nixon generated programs that helped Black people establish small businesses and also supported affirmative action programs that set goals for minority employment.

"Nixon was a pragmatist," Tucker says. "We got lots of economic development stuff done for small businesses. That all started with him. You just had to know how to deal with him."

He recalled right before the 1972 presidential election being in the White House office of John Ehrlichman, one of Nixon's top aides, when the president stopped by.

"Sterling, I know that you and the Urban League and the other civil rights people are not happy with me and what I'm doing in this administration on civil rights," he recalls Nixon saying. "I know what needs to be done and how to do it. But first I got to defeat that little son of a bitch."

Nixon was referring to George Wallace, who he defeated along with George McGovern that year.

Tucker also appealed to Nixon. Home rule had not come to the District of Columbia yet. The president and the Congress still ruled the city. Nixon appointed Tucker vice chairman of the city council and signed legislation giving the city the limited home rule it enjoys today.

District residents now elect a mayor and city council and send a non-voting member to Congress.

"Sterling was sterling," says Leonard Garment, now a Washington lawyer and then a domestic policy aide to President Nixon. "He was very reliable, devoted to the needs of the community. One of the reasons why I felt a particular affinity for the work of the Urban League was because of Sterling."

———————

Tucker also was trying to take the Urban League in new directions.

Until the late 1960s, the league primarily had been a service organization, emphasizing job development and serving as a broker between the white business establishment and Black people.

The league needed to help people get jobs and to empower them to speak for themselves, says Tucker.

He organized the New Thrust program, which emphasized community organization and self-help.

It was just what the Urban League needed, says John Jacob, now the national Urban League president. He joined the Urban League staff in Washington under Tucker's guidance.

"Most fundamental to what Sterling did was place the Urban League back in the neighborhoods where we belonged," says Jacob.

The new Urban League programs required money. Tucker helped his Urban League boss, Whitney Young, work with Garment to arrange a meeting with Nixon's cabinet. As a result, Garment says, the Cabinet officers pulled together $120 million from various departments for Urban League projects.

Watergate forced Nixon from office, but Tucker said President Gerald Ford continued to support increased economic opportunities and small business development for minorities.

"I'd known him when he was on the Hill (in Congress)," Tucker says of Ford. "I like him because he was a moderate up on the Republican side of the aisle."

Ford's presidency was brief, ending in 1976 when Democrat Jimmy Carter defeated him.

Tucker's first impression of Carter had come at the Democratic National Convention when the candidate met with 25 Black leaders.

"Everybody made comments about what they thought he ought to do in his administration," Tucker says. "He went back around the room and responded to everyone, calling many by their names."

Carter was brilliant, but brilliance isn't enough to succeed in the presidency, he says.

"The problem is, he came in as an outsider and unfortunately remained one," Tucker says.

Tucker was busy during Carter's presidency. He served on a task force headed by Vice President Walter Mondale on the federal government's relationship with the local District of Columbia government.

At City Hall, Tucker had moved up. After Nixon had signed the Home Rule bill, Tucker was elected citywide as chairman of the city council.

In 1978, he ran for mayor and endured the greatest disappointment of his career. Marion Barry defeated him by 1,564 votes in the Democratic primary, which is the real election in the overwhelmingly Democratic District of Columbia. Barry went on to easily win the general election. Walter Washington, the incumbent mayor, finished a close third in the primary.

Tucker had known disappointment before. In 1971, in the aftermath of Whitney Young's death, he had withdrawn himself from consideration as a candidate for head of the national Urban League. The job went to Vernon Jordan, who has headed up President-elect Bill Clinton's transition.

It was clear to Tucker that support on the board was divided among him, Jordan and a third candidate.

"I saw the thing as being divisive," he says. "I felt in the best interest of the Urban League, it would be best if I withdrew."

This time, however, he believed he, not Barry, was what Washington needed. Barry, who later left office in disgrace after his involvement with drugs, had been endorsed by the Washington Post.

"It (the endorsement) was very important," says Ronald Walters, who chairs the political science department at Washington's Howard University. "It helped Barry in the white wards."

Tucker had been confident he would win.

"I was ready to give it every ounce of my being," he says, still wistful 14 years later.

A member of Carter's White House staff had been in Tucker's hotel suite on election night.

"He said, 'Sterling, you'll get a call from the White House tomorrow morning.' I didn't know what about," Tucker says.

The call came and Tucker showed up to speak with the president at 2 p.m., just 12 hours after learning he'd lost the mayoral primary.

"In effect, he said, 'Sterling, you were my candidate for mayor. I was hoping you'd be my mayor. We were all pulling for you over here. But you never know what happens in politics. There's a spot we've been holding open for several months that everybody says you'd be just right for,'" Tucker says.

The job was assistant secretary of the Housing and Urban Development Department, in charge of enforcing fair housing legislation and civil rights programs.

"The president of the United States is saying 'I want you' and he wasn't asking me to join the military," says Tucker. "That was quite a big pickup."

The pickup lasted until the 1980 elections, when Ronald Reagan swept Carter out of office.

With the change of administration, Tucker lost his job and formed his own consulting business, Sterling Tucker Associates. He didn't lose his access to the White House, but he didn't stop by nearly as much as he had under previous presidents.

"I met him on several occasions and I liked him personally," Tucker says of Reagan. "But I didn't know him as well as I did the others."

His infrequent visits continued with President Bush. Domestic policy advisers sometimes would invite him in to discuss some ideas.

Also, he served for a year in what he called a frustrating job as director of the District of Columbia's war on drugs. He spent more time trying to keep peace between Mayor Barry and the White House than curbing drug use, he says.

"We didn't have the resources we needed," says Tucker. "I didn't like calling it a war on drugs because it wasn't."

One of his last visits was just before Bush launched Operation Desert Storm.

Tucker was having lunch at the White House when the president stopped him. There was an eerie feeling that something was about to happen, he says.

"I turned around and said, 'Hello, Mr. President,'" recalls Tucker. "He said, 'What do you think I should do?'

"I said, 'Don't do it.'" And he said, "I'm getting that kind of advice, too."

The next day, Bush ordered the invasion. Tucker doesn't regret that he spoke up.

"I wasn't sure what we were going to war for, and I'm still not sure why we went," he says. "It didn't seem worth risking the lives of our people."

Tucker, in a persistent, low-key way, never has had trouble speaking up.

He was the fourth oldest in a family of nine children. His dad drove a truck for the city of Akron and his mom took care of the family and did day work one or two days a week.

"I was a very happy kid," says Tucker. "We were always a very close family."

As a schoolboy, Tucker was drawn to the Akron Community Service Center and Urban League, an association that turned into a career.

In the early 1940s, he became the first Black busboy at the old Garden Grill in downtown Akron. He wanted to eat there, too.

So Tucker, a friend and their dates showed up one day and asked to be seated.

"Sterling, are you crazy?" asked the hostess. She asked what they were doing there.

"We got the seats," says Alloyce Tucker, now Tucker's wife and then his date, Alloyce Robinson. "We were determined. We started out quite young."

At The University of Akron, Tucker continued speaking up enough to win election as the first Black member of the student council. His future wife, a North High graduate, was the second.

"He was my campaign manager," she recalls. "We did a campaign with pictures, a speech or two, fliers."

There haven't been any dull moments in their life together, says Mrs. Tucker. Their two daughters, Shelly and Lauren, are adults; they have a grandchild, Shelly's son, Jason.

There were dinners at the White House with visiting heads of state when Tucker was chairman of the city council.

There were goodwill trips to be made overseas at the request of various presidents.

"He's had so many careers. He's been a tremendous success at each one," says Mrs. Tucker.

Even when he has a setback, like the mayor's race, he "doesn't look back. He goes on to another career."

Right now, Tucker is looking ahead—to Jan. 20 and Clinton's inauguration.

"He has the intelligence and indeed the brilliance of a Carter and the political skills of a Nixon, but not of a Johnson," he says sizing up the new man.

Those skills, however, haven't been tested in Washington. And if Clinton needs help, Tucker's ready.

He's easy to find. The new president just has to look for the guy waiting to turn on the lights for the rest of the country.[*]

---

[*] Tucker died at 95 in 2019.

Thaddeus Garrett: Garrett Faces a Tough Job

There's no Republican with any harder task than the Akron resident asked to recruit Black members for the GOP

Akron Beacon Journal, August 23, 1992
CARL CHANCELLOR

The multimillion-dollar pep rally in Houston that was the Republican National Convention is over, and it is time for the GOP faithful to roll up their sleeves and get down to the business of securing a Bush-Quayle victory in November.

There's probably no Republican with a tougher job in this re-election push, except perhaps Pat Buchanan's keeper, than Thaddeus Garrett Jr., senior adviser to the Republican National Committee.

Garrett, who splits his time between Washington, D.C., and Akron, where he is associate pastor of Wesley Temple AME Zion Church, is the man recently tapped by the party of Lincoln to recruit minorities, particularly African Americans, into the ranks of the GOP.

Garrett and I had a long talk during the convention, where he assured me the GOP is sincere in its invitation to Black people.

"The desire is there and has been there in the past to increase Black and minority participation in the party. We have to encompass all constituencies. The problem has been that we lacked a clear road map on how to accomplish that," Garrett said.

Someone looked at that map and decided to take the shortcut during the convention. What I'm a referring to is the constant parade of Black faces to the podium during the convention.

Obviously, the GOP seized on the media exposure provided by the convention to cultivate an image of a party of opportunity for Black people. For me it was a bit too obvious.

In what is being forecast as a tight presidential race, the Republicans know neither party can afford to ignore any voter group.

Garrett admitted he wants to put more Black voters in the Bush column in 1992. When Bush ran for president in 1988, he garnered some 11% of the Black vote.

"The immediate objective is to broaden the president's base of support. But in the long term there has to be a broadening of the party base if it is to remain durable over the next several decades," Garrett said.

For more than six decades, Black voters were staunch Republicans. It wasn't until the administration of Franklin D. Roosevelt that Black people began abandoning the party of the Great Emancipator. From then on Black loyalty has been with the Democrats.

There exists in the Black community, according to Garrett, the perception that there is not a place for them at the GOP table.

Now, I wonder how that notion came about.

Indeed, Garrett said, "In the past Republicans have been identified as anti-minority and that has stuck with the party... But that view has to be changed."

The truth, Garrett told me, is the tool the GOP must use to reshape its anti-minority image.

That truth, according to Garrett, is that Black people share the GOP's conservative position on many issues. "The philosophical kinship is already there."

Garrett cited figures from a recent HBO and Joint Center for Political and Economic Studies poll that found 33% of Black people say they are conservative.

"Thirty-three percent view themselves as moderate and only 27 percent say they are liberal."

Garrett said the truth is that Black people are conservative when it comes to issues of crime and education and that Black people in the poor inner cities want to take charge of their communities, no longer willing to be told how to live by various government agencies.

He gets no argument from me. All you have to do is look at the strong law and order stance of the Black community in Akron, evidenced by overwhelming support of laws like the one on loitering in a known drug area. It should come as no surprise that those most affected by crime want to get tough on crime and criminals.

But while we are talking about truth, there is no running from the fact that many Black Republicans are upset with their party.

As a matter of fact, New York's Freedom Republicans, led by W. Lugenia Gordon, filed a lawsuit against the party over concerns Black voters were illegally being denied membership on the Republican National Committee and being denied delegate slots.

The truth is the speech given by Buchanan, in which he ranted against homosexuals, working women and abortion and said the American dream was embodied in the troopers who stood with M-16s to beat back the South-Central Los Angeles hordes bent on "molesting old people they did not even know." The speech left no more than a white-sheet thickness between him and the Ku Klux Klan.

The truth is that the intolerance of ultra-conservatives in the GOP leadership will only limit the appeal of the party among minorities.

Still, Garrett thinks the party can attract Black voters, particularly those in the middle class, who he says have values that closely align with the GOP.

Further, Garrett says the party must seek and run more Black candidates for office.

"What the GOP has to do, which it hasn't done in the past, is to support our Black candidates at all levels with dollars.

"If we concentrate our resources and get the message out that this party is open to and wants minorities, we will see the results."

It sure feels good to be wanted.

Hey, Bill Clinton and the rest of you Democrats, I hope you are listening.*

---

* Garrett died at 51 in 1999.

Ralph Regula: Pickups, Pragmatism and Polish

Akron Beacon Journal Beacon Magazine, May 28, 1989
WILLIAM HERSHEY

Ralph Regula is in a hurry. It's about noon, which means the Stark County congressman has been at work at the Capitol for nearly six hours.

The routine is the same nearly every day he's in Washington.

A workout in the House gym. A working breakfast. Back to his second-floor office in the Rayburn House Office Building for some paperwork or to work the phones. Over to the Capitol building steps for pictures with constituents.

On this beautiful Washington morning in April, with the dogwoods showing off pink and white blossoms, the tourists include Jeff and Sue First of North Canton and their children, Matthew, 7, and Julie, 9, and a group of senior citizens from the Little Flower Catholic Church in Middlebranch.

"I like to share this place with them," Regula says of the picture-taking. "I enjoy that."

After the photos, it's off to a caucus of House Republicans and then to a meeting of the Select Committee on Aging.

It's almost lunch time when the 64-year-old Regula pulls his bright red GMC Sierra Classic pickup truck out of the Rayburn garage and drives it through a lane between concrete potted plants that are supposed to deter terrorists. He parks it, motor running, right in front of the House steps at the Capitol, site of the recent picture-taking. He easily climbs the nearly vertical steps, dashes in to cast a vote, and is back in the truck and off to a local hotel and brief appearances before two Ohio groups.

"Trucks are my thing," he says with a smile, en route to the hotel.

In the self-effacing manner that Ralph Regula affects so well and so sincerely, trucks are the natural "thing" for a cow-milking son of a Stark County farm. He came to Congress more than 16 years ago after terms on the Ohio school board and in the Ohio House and Senate and, as he likes to point out, after being a member of the 4-H Club.

But others, including observers as diverse as Stark County industrialist W.R. "Tim" Timken Jr. and former U.S. House Speaker Thomas P. "Tip" O'Neill, think Ralph Regula's real "thing" is something other than trucks.

He has mastered the art of making the House of Representatives work for his district and constituents—something that's difficult for any congressman, but particularly hard for a Republican in a House that has been controlled for more than 30 years by the Democrats.

His influence shows through on issues as diverse as quotas on imported steel—he's for them—and, as a senior member of the House Appropriations Committee, in making sure there's enough money appropriated for the Cuyahoga Valley National Recreation Area.

"I think he's one of the great congressmen," says O'Neill, who took Regula along on every overseas trip he made as speaker. "He's highly regarded and respected. Nobody does his homework better than Ralph does."

"I think he's a fabulous representative for our area," says Timken, the chairman of the Ohio Republican Finance Committee. "Out of the 435 (House members) down there, I can't think of one who works harder for his constituency and has a more realistic view of what has to be done to protect the interests of his constituents."

Regula's reputation as an effective congressman has been growing quietly for several years, so it's not as though he suddenly "arrived" as the quintessential lawmaker.

But this growing recognition of Regula's ability coincides nicely with the arrival in the White House of his longtime friend, George Bush.

Regula and Rep. Willis Gradison of Cincinnati generally are considered the Ohio Republicans with the best access to the Bush White House. Of course, in Northeast Ohio, there's no contest. Regula has been the only Republican House member in the region since 1984 when Democrat James Traficant unseated Republican Lyle Williams, the Trumbull County barber.

"Of the 10 (Ohio) Republicans, I guess you'd have to say that he and Gradison are sort of in a special tier," says Frank Lavin, the Canton native who was political affairs director for Ronald Reagan when Reagan was president.

Regula supported Bush against Reagan for the presidential nomination in 1980 and was among the House Republicans who made a political first-aid mission to New Hampshire on Bush's behalf last year after Bush lost the Iowa caucuses.

Bush, in turn, proved his genuine affection in Regula by showing up for a 1986 Stark County fundraiser at Hoover Park, where the then-vice president ate three ears of Ohio sweet corn. Political advisers at the White House that year had tried to reserve Bush's precious time for competitive House races, and Regula, who ended up winning with 76% of the vote, clearly wasn't in that category.

"George Bush did that as a personal favor," Lavin says. "He did that because he likes Ralph Regula. It does show you that as vice president and president he will be responsive."

Though Regula developed a strong enough working relationship with Reagan over the years to have a handwritten note and three candid pictures of him hanging on the wall of his Washington office, he acknowledges the special connection with Bush.

"I'm sure I can pick up the phone and talk to the president any time I feel a compelling need to," Regula says.

But he won't abuse the privilege, Regula emphasizes. Topics likely to rank a personal call, he says, are the Bush administration plans for controlling acid rain and extending America's quotas on imported steel.

Regula wants to make sure the acid-rain plan makes provision for clean coal technology, a must if Ohio's high-sulfur coal is to have a future.

He wants the quotas continued to protect not just the American steel industry but jobs at the Timken company and other Stark County mills.

Though it will take time to tell how much real clout Regula has at the White House, there's no question that he and his wife, Mary, are welcome there.

Mrs. Regula was at the White House once socially during the eight Reagan years—for a state dinner. Less than six months into the Bush presidency, she's been twice to the Bushes' family quarters—once at a session for early supporters of Bush and second for a luncheon for a club to which she and Mrs. Bush belong.

———————

It's clear from listening to Regula and Bush talk that they share a similar pragmatic philosophy, a philosophy that sees a role for government—a pro-government philosophy, as opposed to the anti-government philosophy Ronald Reagan brought to Washington.

"The role of government is to improve the quality of life," Regula says. "Security is not just external. It's the feeling of confidence that you can walk down the street. The feeling that you can go into a drug store and buy a prescription that will not be harmful, that you can go to the grocery store and be sure the FDA (Food and Drug Administration) is protecting you."

John C. Green, director of the Ray C. Bliss Institute of Applied Politics at The University of Akron, calls Regula the "quintessential pragmatic Republican."

"You listen to Ralph Regula at a Chamber of Commerce meeting," Green says, "and you'll hear him say all the obligatory conservative things about how rotten and intrusive government is and how high taxes are. But then he goes on to talk about the real contributions government has made to the business community and in solving social problems."

That's a philosophy that Akron's former Democratic representative, John Seiberling, saw regularly during the 14 years they served together in the House. He credits Regula with providing early support for the Cuyahoga Valley National Recreation Area and with using his position on the House Appropriations Committee to get money for buying more land and operating the park, often against the wishes of the Reagan administration.

"Ralph is a very decent fellow," Seiberling says. "He's interested in getting things done and not just in politics."

He even suggests that if Bush really wants to be the "environmental president" that he says he does, he might look to Regula for advice.

"I have a very high opinion of him on environmental issues," says Seiberling, who was considered one of the House's top environmentalists. "He's a very capable and levelheaded person."

Though Seiberling doesn't agree with Regula's clean-coal approach to the acid-rain problem—it would make more environmental sense to stop mining the coal and find other jobs for Ohio miners, he argues—he does find common ground on the subject with Regula.

"He and I agree on one thing, that any legislation that is passed should not put a disproportionate amount of the cost on Ohio," Seiberling says.

To Regula, being "pragmatic" means using government not just to protect the physical environment, but also to promote a better environment for the human relationships that can bind a society together or, if neglected, tear it asunder.

Since becoming president, Bush has reached out to constituencies such as Black voters who were ignored during Reagan's presidency. But Regula got there first.

During the Reagan years, he worked quietly as a member of the commission set up by Congress to establish a holiday honoring the late Martin Luther King Jr. Today he is vice chairman of that commission.

While Reagan was trying to decide whether King deserved a holiday and Republican Sen. Jesse Helms was trashing the idea, Regula was making regular trips to Atlanta for meetings of the Martin Luther King Jr. Holiday Commission. Coincidentally, it was his friend, then-House Speaker O'Neill, who appointed Regula to the group.

There were other appointees from the House, but none like Regula, says Lloyd Davis, the commission's executive director and a vice president at the Martin Luther King Jr. Center for Nonviolent Social Change.

"Most of them (the congressmen on the commission), if you see them once a year for five minutes, that's generally for a photo opportunity,"

Davis says. "These are all busy people. I understand that. But Regula is just…he's always there."

Davis says Regula has developed a close relationship with Coretta King, the slain civil rights leader's widow. "They're very fond of each other," he says.

Regula is not bashful about telling why he attended the meetings. "I first of all think the message of Dr. King is the right one," he says. "As we achieve change in our society, to achieve it in a nonviolent way is the right way."

This ability to appeal to constituencies that Democrats have come to regard as their own frustrates Regula's opponents.

"Ralph has a good nose to smell the wind," says Stark County Democratic Chairman Roy Gutierrez. "He manages to vote the way his constituents want."

He is also a bit of a smoothie.

John Thomas knew Regula first as a reporter for the Canton Repository and later as communications director for the Ohio AFL-CIO.

"Part of his success is his charm," says Thomas, now publications director for the United Paperworkers Union in Nashville. "He can sort of talk you out of your sandals if you're not careful. Even if he votes wrong from the labor point of view a slim majority of the time, he always has a good answer."

While admiring Regula's political skills, Thomas says that in the 16th Congressional District, which includes Stark, Wayne and Holmes counties, part of Carroll and a sliver of southern Summit, one group of constituents, the Timkens and their steel company, is more equal than others.

Thomas points to 1971 when Regula, a state senator and considered to be a good friend of the financially strapped education community, voted against establishment of a state income tax, the position favored by the Timken interests.

"Ralph voted against the income tax because the Timkens asked him to," Thomas says.

Regula and Timken, however, bristle at that suggestion.

"Ralph Regula wouldn't take orders from anybody, including me," says Timken. "He's his own person as much as anybody I've ever known."

Regula says he voted against the tax because "I didn't have confidence in the establishment of a state income tax. I basically believe that the government that governs best governs least.

"Never have the Timkens put any influence on me. He (Timken) doesn't expect any preferential treatment for his company."

Of course, Regula does listen to the Timkens and tries to help them, just as he tries to help his other constituents. And that's what frustrates Gutierrez, the Democratic county chairman.

"Currently his office provides tremendous service to the constituents," Gutierrez says. "You're going to Europe and you need a passport. He'll have somebody meet you at the airport."

It's not just Regula that Gutierrez has to combat every two years.

"He has a tremendous asset in his wife," he says. "When she's in the district, you'd think Ralph was here. She makes all the meetings. She has ties with all the local constituent groups."

Gutierrez tells about getting some advice on beating Regula in 1984, the last time the Democrats made a serious run at the seat, from Rep. Marcy Kaptur, a Democrat from Toledo. "I said, 'How the hell do I beat this son of a gun,' Marcy said jokingly 'Shoot his wife.' Or maybe she said, 'Get rid of his wife.'"

Mary Regula, who met Ralph at Mount Union College in Alliance from which they both graduated, says she and her husband are a "team, a partnership." She has her own small desk with a phone right in Regula's office in the Rayburn Building.

She pulls her own weight. In Washington, she is president of the Congressional Club, a group for spouses of House and Senate members, and a member of the board of directors of the Capitol Hill Historical Society. It's not unusual to see her leading Stark County tourists around the Capitol.

Mrs. Regula, the daughter of immigrant parents who grew up in the Youngstown suburb of Girard calls herself an "enlightened Democrat." A former history teacher who quit teaching to raise the three children—two sons and a daughter, now in their 30s—she's not the Phyllis Schlafly type of wife frequently heard from during Reagan's presidency.

"I have no problem being called a feminist," she says.

———————

While the Regulas, who've been married for 38 years, like Washington, it isn't home. They have a townhouse in suburban Virginia, but they return nearly every weekend to their 200-acre farm in Bethlehem Township in southern Stark County. It's not far from the farm where Regula grew up, where his brother, John, still lives.

"I don't think I've spent a weekend here (in Washington) in four or five years," Regula says. "It (the trip to Ohio) is like going to the grocery store."

On his farm, Regula gets as excited about the birth of a new calf as he does back in Washington about reaching agreement on a complicated piece of legislation. He arrived on the farm one Sunday in late April and went right to work figuring out how to bottle-feed a newborn calf that had been disowned by its mother.

At home, when he's not tending to his 18 head of cattle, mending fences or bringing in the alfalfa, he is most likely meeting with constituents.

Mrs. Regula has her own schedule. She has developed a series of popular presentations, such as "Christmas at the White House." They've become big hits with local community groups.

His years of service in Congress have given Regula the seniority to merit an office with a spectacular view of the Capitol.

But it is a view that he must earn every two years. And now, with Bush in the White House and his own clout to get things done growing, the incentive for staying there is that much greater.

Gutierrez says he has a "long-range" plan for dislodging Regula.

Fellow Democrat Seiberling doesn't know what Gutierrez' plan is, but he says he knows what it will take to unseat his old colleague.

"An earthquake."*

---

* Regula served 18 terms in the U.S. House before retiring in 2009. He died in 2017 at 92.

John Seiberling: From Lawmaker to Peacemaker

Akron Beacon Journal Beacon Magazine, February 27, 1994
WILLIAM HERSHEY

Bam!

"As they say in the House of Representatives, the House will be in order," says the usually gentle John F. Seiberling, pounding a table for good-natured emphasis.

It is a subzero January day and Seiberling is about to start a class on "The American Congress" in Room 150 of the James A. Rhodes Arena on the campus of The University of Akron.

"Everything in this course is aimed at giving you not just a theoretical view, but a realistic view of the legislative process," Seiberling tells 43 students, some bundled in parkas and others, at 12:30 p.m., still rubbing sleep from their eyes.

The scene is far from the ornate, wood-paneled chamber of the U.S. House of Representatives, where over 16 years Seiberling assembled the pieces of a distinguished legislative career that started with his election as an anti-Vietnam Democrat in 1970 and ended with his voluntary retirement in 1986.

No longer in the pin-striped uniform of the legislator, he wears a taupe sports coat with suede elbow pads and a maroon turtleneck.

But at 75, the passions that moved him in Washington to imagine the magic of a Cuyahoga Valley National Recreation Area and to fight for dozens of other important pieces of environmental and economic legislation still stir.

If Seiberling had chosen to remain in Washington—and he is sufficiently loved in Akron that he might have remained there forever—he probably would be chairman of the House Interior Committee.

Instead, he decided to come home.

Now he teaches at the university, where he is director for the Center for Peace Studies and an adviser on federal relations.

In the community, he is chairing the Akron-Canton Regional Food Bank's operating and capital fund drive. He's also on the board of the Akron Art Museum and of the foundation of Stan Hywet Hall, the Akron estate that his family gave to the community. Seiberling, whose grandfather, F.A. Seiberling, founded the Goodyear Tire & Rubber Co., grew up at Stan Hywet.

Nationally, he is chairman of the board of the Peace Through Law Education Fund, which he helped organize while in Congress. And he's on the board of the Environmental and Energy Study Institute, which he also helped organize.

"He's remarkable," says University President Peggy Gordon Elliott. "He's become the living symbol of the individual's ability to make change, something that is frequently remote from a university student's experience…If he's not an icon, at least he's a symbol of the power of the individual."

John Seiberling didn't use the same exit many others do when leaving Congress, the revolving door that spins them into new Washington jobs as lawyers and lobbyists.

They cash in, literally but legally, on the experience gained on taxpayer-financed jobs, often advising new clients on issues in which they specialized in Congress.

Former U.S. Reps. Willis Gradison, R-Cincinnati, and Dennis Eckart, D-Mentor, who both served in the House with Seiberling, have achieved a sort of Washington-style celebrity status in their new posts.

Gradison, who specialized in health care issues in Congress, made the cover of the National Journal as head of the Health Insurance Association of America, the group battling President Clinton over his plan for health care reform.

Eckart joined the Washington office of the Cleveland law firm of Arter & Hadden, where he counsels clients on some of the same issues he legislated on as a member of the Energy and Commerce Committee. National Journal called him one of the "star rookies in the big leagues of lobbying" whose salary, believed to be about $500,000, is more than three times his annual pay in Congress.

The door Seiberling used when he retired opened directly to the Akron area, into the house on Martin Road in Bath Township where Seiberling lives with his wife Betty.

"When I said I wasn't going to run for re-election…some of my colleagues in the House said, 'Well, you're going to stay in Washington, of course.' And I said, 'Heck, no. I'm moving back to Akron,'" Seiberling recalls.

Why? his friends asked.

"I said, 'Well because it happens to be a very nice place to live, and that's where my roots are.'"

Seiberling's return even prompted accolades from Republicans like Summit County Republican Chairman Alex Arshinkoff.

"One thing you've got to hand to John Seiberling," Arshinkoff says. "He came home to live under the laws he passed."

He compares Seiberling to the late Ray C. Bliss, who came back to Akron after stepping down as chairman of the Republican National Committee in 1969. Arshinkoff says then-President Richard M. Nixon couldn't believe Bliss wanted to leave Washington.

"Those are great men," he says. "John Seiberling was a darn good congressman. If I were a liberal Democrat, I'd say he was a great congressman."

These days Seiberling is turning his attention to teaching, and it's a job he likes.

"I enjoy what I'm doing," he says. "You know, you tend to assume that everybody knows about the events that we went through in our own lives—the Great Depression, the rise of Adolf Hitler, World War II."

"But it's not so, and a lot of these experiences from the times we lived are like an unknown field to the kids today."

One of the courses Seiberling teaches is called "Values and Concepts of Peace and War." And sometimes even he is surprised by who benefits from the course. He tells of a former high school football player.

"I thought he was getting less out of the course than anybody else," Seiberling says. "He was a great big guy."

The student and others in the class heard a lecture on nonviolence from John Looney, former peace education secretary of the Northeast Ohio chapter of the American Friends Service Committee, who's now president of Peace Grows, an Akron-based nonprofit organization that specializes in conflict resolution.

A few days after the lecture, the student went up to Seiberling and said: "You know, this nonviolence really works."

The student had been in a bar when someone started to pick a fight with his friend.

"He said, 'What I would have done normally would have been to just go over and push the guy over and that would have been the end of it,'" Seiberling recalls.

Instead, he tried talking things through in a nonviolent way and "the whole thing quieted down."

Back in Room 150 Seiberling is talking about what's really important in Congress.

"One thing you've got to know is how to count," he says. "Anybody have any idea what that means?"

He answers himself.

"Counting means knowing in advance whether people are likely to support you on a particular issue."

Seiberling, who ranked second in seniority on the Interior Committee when he retired and chaired the Public Lands Subcommittee, never has been a back-slapping joke-cracker, but he tries some Mo Udall humor to make the students really understand what counting means. Udall, Seiberling's longtime friend, was Interior Committee chairman.

Udall would tell about the young woman from the East who came to a dude ranch in Arizona, Udall's home state.

"The first day a cowboy tells the guest about what you ought to know if you're bitten by a rattlesnake in the foot. 'Make a crisscross where the bite is and suck the venom out,'" Seiberling recounts.

But then the woman wants to know what to do if she's bitten where she sits down.

"Lady, that's when you find out who your friends are," the cowboy says.

"I didn't want to find out after the fact who my friends were," says Seiberling, bringing the story back to Washington. "I didn't bring a bill up for a vote unless I had a pretty good idea that I was going to win."

Donzella Anuszkiewicz, a senior in the American Congress class, says the real-life experiences Seiberling brings to the classroom help the students understand the process he's talking about.

"To sit down and give the technical aspect of how a bill is introduced is one thing," she says. "To come back and say, 'I remember this bill'— that's good."

However, she would like the class even more if Seiberling encouraged more discussion.

"There's got to be all kinds of diverse views in that class," Anuszkiewicz says. "You're doing the class a disservice not to allow discussion."

Patricia Reed, another student, is taking the course only because Seiberling is teaching it. She already had him for Values and Concepts of Peace and War.

"He's very different from the professor-type," Reed says. "They teach in theory. His is almost strictly by example. That makes it interesting. You're getting a real view."

Some students, she says, do think Seiberling can be a bit dry.

"I think he can be. It's an hour and 15 minutes. Who can be entertaining for that long?"

————————

There was a sweet reward for years of legislative labor when Seiberling came home from Washington.

His home is inside the boundaries of the Cuyahoga Valley National Recreation Area, a 33,000-acre national park between Akron and Cleveland that is, perhaps, his most endearing legislative monument.

Deer come right up to the picture windows, and giant ash, beech and oak trees blow in the wind just across the road from his house.

He had gazed north toward the Cuyahoga Valley from Stan Hywet as a boy, and the idea began growing that this valley—with its rivers, hills and scenic vistas—should be preserved.

Seiberling and his wife sold 13 acres of their property to the Trust for Public Lands, a nonprofit tax-exempt organization that facilitates the protection of land and works with the park service to accomplish this. The trust, in turn, sold it to the federal government. Also, they donated scenic easements on their holdings, including the five acres they retained around their house. The General Accounting Office, Congress' investigative arm, at Seiberling's request examined the transactions and concluded that the park service gave him no preferential treatment.

He is a willing guide through the valley, even when the temperature is below zero.

"Look at those pretty beech-tree leaves," exults Seiberling, crunching through the snow. "Even brown leaves are nice."

He pulls the hood tight around his head as he leads an expedition through the woods just across the road from his home.

"We'll follow the deer tracks," he says. "Watch out here. It could be slippery."

Seiberling tires of reports that he single-handedly created the park. Other members of the Ohio congressional delegation, as well as Ray Bliss and others, helped, he says.

But Seiberling was more than the first among equals and the people of the Akron area and Ohio know it.

"Hardly a day goes by," Seiberling says, "but what someone comes up to me—and often it's people I don't know. They'll say, 'You don't know me. I just want to say thank you for that wonderful park. We use it all the time.'

"I say, well, thank God. He made it. All I did was get the legislation passed."

Seiberling doesn't yearn to be back in Congress, although he and his wife say they miss their friends in Washington.

"The big change I see in Congress just since I left is the polarization that has taken place, largely because of the extreme right," he says. "You have a nastiness and an accusatory kind of atmosphere that I think must make it very hard to play a constructive role, because every time you turn around someone is trying to make an issue out of even the best of motives, and the news media plays into that, too."

Still, serving in the House had its advantages.

"One of the things I miss most is my staff," he says. "Not only because they were very good friends, but because I got used to having a terrific staff and getting a lot of things done as a result."

Instead of a staff of 19, Seiberling now shares a secretary with two other people.

"I do my own filing, which isn't very good. I open my own mail. I write letters out longhand. I guess I got spoiled with a good staff."

Seiberling benefited economically from his stay in Congress.

In addition to the $30,000 a year he earns at the university, he gets a congressional pension that was $42,866 last year, according to the National Taxpayers Union Foundation, which tracks congressional pensions. He also gets Social Security and a small pension from Goodyear, where he worked as a lawyer before going to Congress.

He is not a Congress-basher or even a basher of those who left Congress and stayed in Washington to make lots more money than he is earning.

"You know, everybody has to decide for himself what kind of career he wants to have or she wants to have," he says. "So I suppose if you've been away from your home base a long time, in some cases there's no other way to make a living except for putting your knowledge about how the Congress functions to work…I don't see anything wrong with that in principle. That's not what I wanted to do, but I was old enough when I left so that I could get a pension and Social Security."

―――――――――

When Seiberling was first elected to Congress, he had a specific goal: to end the Vietnam War.

Among the current Democratic House members from Northeast Ohio, only one—Rep. Louis Stokes, D-Shaker Heights—also had a specific goal in coming to Congress.

Stokes wanted to give Black people in Ohio a representative in Congress. He had helped with a lawsuit that resulted in a 1967 U.S. Supreme Court decision that threw out Ohio's 1964 congressional redistricting plan on the grounds that it violated the one-man, one-vote principle. Stokes ran and won in 1968 in a new district that was 65% Black and 35% white.

For the other Northeast Ohio Democrats—Tom Sawyer of Akron, Sherrod Brown of Lorain and Eric Fingerhut of Mayfield Heights—the U.S. House is just the most recent stop in an adult life that has been mostly spent in appointive or elective office. They are career politicians.

Don't condemn them, Seiberling lectures.

"There's no burning issue at the moment, no Vietnam War. There's no Depression. So people getting into politics because they're angry or overwhelmed by a particular concern is not the case today. But I'm impressed with the quality of the new members of Congress who came in in the last election, particularly those from Ohio.

"The real question is: Are these people who have ideas and principles? My analysis is: The answer is yes.

"There is a new generation there. They have yet to be tested in the same way earlier generations were. And I hope maybe they never are."

Seiberling picked Sawyer out from a host of eager Akron Democrats as the candidate he wanted to succeed him.

"I think we should be very pleased to have a congressman who is so up on things, who is so very conscientious in trying to decide what's in the best interest of the country as well as the people of his district and who, in my view, votes very intelligently on the issues that come before the Congress."

He dismisses differences between himself and Sawyer.

Sawyer agonizes for weeks before making decisions and often is reluctant to talk about the position he is taking or is trying to take.

Seiberling, unlike Sawyer, never had a press secretary, preferring to speak for himself. He answered questions when asked and wasn't bashful about challenging fellow legislators, reporters or anyone else when he thought they were wrong.

"Everybody has his own style," Seiberling says. "His (Sawyer's) is different than mine. In the end it's the results that count. He has his way of doing things. His job, basically, is to accomplish things in the legislature. We're different people."

He also defends the new-generation president but concedes that Bill Clinton seems to learn the hard way.

"I think Bill Clinton has to learn that the practices that may be condoned in a small state like Arkansas in state politics are not or should not be at the presidential level," he says. "I'm not talking about it being illegal. I'm talking about not being concerned about appearances. I think Clinton has undergone an educational process in that respect. I think you have to say he's a fast learner, but he also tends to learn the hard way."

While still in Congress, Seiberling learned some intensely personal lessons of his own, namely that there is more to life than making laws.

Doctors removed a cancerous prostate gland in April of 1985, and the brush with cancer caused him to consider his own mortality.

After the cancer was diagnosed but before the surgery, he said he thought: "Wow. If anything should knock me out at this point, what a mess I would leave my family."

So he came home.

There has been no recurrence of cancer and he has more time for the really important stuff in life.

That last year in Washington was a difficult one on the family front, too.

His middle son David, now 39, was arrested for breaking and entering in connection with thefts at the Old Trail School and Hale Farm in Bath Township. In 1987 he was sentenced to prison and required to undergo treatment for drug abuse.

David is now studying for a master's degree in journalism at Kent State University and "seems to be maturing and becoming good at the field he has chosen," Seiberling says.

His oldest son, John B., 42, is in Washington working for a company that does telemarketing for environmental organizations.

His youngest son, Stephen, 37, is in Durham, N.C., where he recently got a master's degree in environmental science from Duke University and is now working for the Nature Conservancy.

Seiberling has time now to reflect—and to share those thoughts with a new generation. He tells his class in Room 150 why members of Congress like to be subcommittee chairmen.

"He (a chairman) has a lot more fun… Once more, if he gets white hair, as I did by the time I left Congress, all the staff around the Capitol gets to address him as 'Mr. Chairman.' When that happens, you feel you've finally arrived.

"Maybe it was just that I had white hair. Anyway, it made me feel good, sometimes."[*]

---

[*] Seiberling died in 2008 at 89.

Louis Stokes: A King of the Hill

Akron Beacon Journal Beacon Magazine, January 14, 1990
WILLIAM HERSHEY

Lt. Col. Oliver North, six rows of service ribbons on his olive-green Marine uniform, had turned the Iran-Contra hearings inside out.

North was supposed to be the target of critical questioning that would yield answers to one of the century's great foreign policy mysteries.

Instead, with a gap-toothed grin, mournful eyes and flag-waving bromides, he had put the 26 senators and House members on trial before a national television audience. He had successfully cast himself as the patriotic victim of an un-American witch hunt.

But North's performance on July 14, 1987 didn't faze one member of the joint committee, a balding Cleveland-born House member. Louis Stokes also had worn *his* uniform to the hearing room, a cavernous sardine can packed with television cameras and wall-to-wall bodies.

Stokes' uniform was a well-tailored business suit, a shirt and tie and well-shined shoes—the clothes of a professional lawmaker.

North may have earned the right to wear his uniform through undisputed combat bravery. But Stokes also had earned the right to wear his. He had carried newspapers, shined shoes, stocked shelves, served his country in war, gone to night school while working to support his mom during the day, and finally used the courts to make his country live up to her ideal of representative government.

His testimony has been "chilling" and "frightening," Stokes told the self-confident North.

"Officials who lied, misrepresented and deceived. Officials who planned to superimpose upon our government a layer outside of our government, shrouded in secrecy and only accountable to the conspirators. I could go on and on, but we both know the testimony, and it is ugly. In my opinion it is a prescription for anarchy in a democratic society," said Stokes, sounding like the courtroom lawyer he was before coming to Washington.

Patriotism belongs to all Americans, he lectured North.

"Colonel, as I sit here this morning looking at you in your uniform, I cannot help but remember that I wore the uniform of this country in World War II in a segregated army.

"I wore it as proudly as you do, even though our government required Black and white soldiers in the same army to live, sleep, eat and travel separate and apart, while fighting and dying for our country. But because of the rule of law, today's servicemen in America suffer no such indignity."

Stokes was almost finished.

"My mother, a widow, raised two boys. She had an eighth-grade education. She was a domestic worker who scrubbed floors. One son became the first Black mayor of a major American city. The other sits today as chairman of the House Intelligence Committee.

"Only in America, Col. North. Only in America. And while I admire your love for America, I hope that you will never forget that others, too, love America just as much as you do and that others, too, will die for America, just as quick as you will."

––––––––––––

Louis Stokes was elected to the U.S. House in 1968, the same year Martin Luther King Jr. was assassinated. Stokes became Ohio's first Black congressman. There hasn't been a second.

On the eve of the national holiday celebrating King's birth, the nearly 22 years since his death have seen the flame of hope, ignited by his dream for a just and color-blind America, sometimes flickering, occasionally burning brightly and at other times almost snuffed out.

In Stokes' congressional office, a shrine to Black achievement with pictures of achievers from every walk of life, the flame has burned steadily, quietly and each year a little brighter, as Stokes, with little fanfare, broke through barriers and unwritten stereotypes that preceded him.

In 1970, he became the first Black person to serve on the powerful Appropriations Committee. Now he's the seventh-ranking Democrat on this money-dispensing panel.

In 1977, when turmoil engulfed the special committee appointed to investigate the assassinations of Martin Luther King and President John F. Kennedy, House Speaker Thomas P. "Tip" O'Neill turned to Stokes to take over.

In 1980, O'Neill named Stokes to the House Ethics Committee, which he later headed. It was a demanding and sensitive assignment that encompassed a sex and drug scandal involving congressional pages and the investigation of Democratic vice presidential candidate Geraldine Ferraro's finances.

In 1987, the same year he served on the Iran-Contra committee, Speaker Jim Wright named Stokes chairman of the House Intelligence Committee, entrusting to him the nation's espionage secrets.

Until Stokes, 64, assumed these jobs, Black congressmen, for the most part, had been relegated to posts limited to serving their big-city, minority constituents. They were "Blacks" first and House members second.

"The first Blacks elected (to Congress) this century were all machine politicians," says John C. Green, director of the Ray C. Bliss Institute of Applied Politics at The University of Akron. "Stokes and others really have had to fight that image."

William H. Gray III of Philadelphia came to the House in 1979, 10 years after Stokes. This year Gray was elected majority whip, the first Black representative to hold this leadership post, third in the chain of command behind Speaker Thomas Foley and Majority Leader Richard Gephardt. Before that, Gray had been chosen as the first Black person to chair the Budget Committee and the first Black person to chair the House Democratic Caucus.

"I often tell people that my success, rising in the leadership of the Congress, has been as the result of the leadership of people like Lou Stokes," Gray says.

"Lou demonstrated his ability to lead as chairman of the assassinations committee and as chairman of the Ethics Committee. When I decided I was going to try to run for the chairman of the Budget Committee, there was a foundation there. There were people who said, 'You know, Lou Stokes did a heck of a job. Hey, these African American congressmen can do more than be advocates for their own constituency groups.'

"…I am the majority leader of the United States House…because of the leadership of Lou Stokes."

Gray says the foundation of quiet, broadly based competence that Stokes laid down over two decades also helped create the political climate that led to David Dinkins' victory last year as the first Black mayor of New York City and Doug Wilder's apparent victory as the first Black governor of Virginia, the one-time cradle of the Confederacy.

Among House members, Stokes has gained respect not only from fellow Democrats but across the aisle.

Bob McEwen, a conservative Republican from southern Ohio whose hawkish views on foreign policy contrast with those of Stokes, served on the Intelligence Committee when Stokes chaired it.

"I don't think there has been a member of the committee or the chairman of a committee who has been more responsible than Lou Stokes was," McEwen says. "I have the utmost trust in Lou Stokes. I would trust his word. There aren't a dozen of members of Congress I would put the level of trust in that I have for Lou Stokes."

———————————

Stokes wanted the tough committee chairmanships he was handed.

"It was important to me," he says, "to try and carve out a special niche, so to speak, in the Congress that would be centered around respect for the service I gave as a whole congressperson. I didn't want to be looked at just as a Black congressman, as someone who is to be relegated to issues that just affect minorities."

Not that Stokes turned his back on the special needs of Black people—not only those in his district, but across the country. His district includes Cleveland's East Side and eastern Cuyahoga County suburbs.

In Stokes' early years in Congress and to a lesser extent today, he and other Black members had two constituencies.

"Actually, a Black congressperson goes to Congress not only representing his own district," Stokes says, "but also in the unique capacity of having to give representation to a national constituency of Blacks, Hispanics, other minorities and the poor."

At first this meant that, among other things, Stokes had to try to win appointments to U.S. military academies for qualified young Black candidates from the South. There were no Black members from Southern states and the whites wouldn't help.

"A deserving young person could get appointed to one of those academies by Louis Stokes from Ohio, and the academy would turn its head and not acknowledge that this youngster did not live in my congressional district, but lived in Mississippi," says Stokes, who now lives in Shaker Heights.

The number of Black members in Congress has grown from 10 when Stokes first came to Washington to 23 today, including Southerners Mike Espy from Mississippi and John Lewis from Georgia.

But Stokes' national constituency still has special needs. Why has life expectancy for Black people stood still and even declined during the '80s while white people lived longer? Stokes has become the Congressional Black Caucus' health expert, convening workshops and seeking out experts to answer this and other questions.

Ironically, Louis Stokes never planned to go to Congress. That was supposed to be a job for younger brother Carl, the family politician.

A new 21st Congressional District, 65% Black and 35% white, had been created as a result of a 1967 U.S. Supreme Court decision that threw out Ohio's 1964 redistricting plan on the grounds that it violated the one-man, one-vote principle. (According to Stokes' office, the racial makeup of his district is about the same today.)

Carl Stokes had been interested in running for Congress, and Louis Stokes, as chairman of the NAACP's legal redress committee, directed the courtroom battle.

By the time the high court ruled on Dec. 4, 1967, however, Carl had been elected mayor of Cleveland. He wasn't about to run off to Washington.

Louis by then was one of Cleveland's rising young trial lawyers. He had taken to the U.S. Supreme Court not only the redistricting case but a second case that established police standards for frisking suspects.

The leadership group that had won the fight to create a district that could be won by a Black person needed a candidate. The group turned to Louis Stokes and Kenneth Clement, a politically active Cleveland physician. Louis Stokes remembers a Sunday morning meeting at brother Carl's house.

"Carl went into his kitchen, as I recall," Louis says. "He talked at length with Kenneth Clement. Then he came out of the room and he said, 'Kenny doesn't want to go, So, Lou, if you're interested in going, we'll go with you.'"

After talking it over with his wife, Jeanette, and four children—his family now includes three grandchildren—Louis Stokes decided to make the race.

He won that first election with 75% of the vote and has continued to win big, most recently with 86% in 1988.

If Louis Stokes deferred to Carl in running and in other early political decisions, it wasn't that way in the rest of their life together, says Carl, now a Cleveland municipal judge.

"He's the usual jerk that big brothers are," Carl says. "He didn't like me wearing his clothes and tried to boss me around."

Carl, however, found his big brother's weak spot. "He (Lou) has suffered all his life from nose bleeds," he says. "When I found out that if you hit him in the nose and it would bleed…"

A few bloody noses did not prevent the brothers from forging a strong bond that endures today. Their father died when Louis was 3 and Carl 1, leaving their mother, Louise, to raise the two boys.

"Over the years, Lou was the closest thing to a man figure in the house," Carl says. "Mom would learn to trust him and confide in him. She would leave him in charge of the house. I would do what he said—not willingly."

The two brothers developed in different ways. Carl was the outgoing politician; Louis the nose-to-the-grindstone lawyer.

"Where I tended to be impatient and impertinent," says Carl, "he was, to the contrary, very restrained and sober."

Ironically, it is Louis, not Carl, who has had the longer career in politics. That doesn't bother Carl.

"I guess many people have been surprised that neither Lou nor I have ever been jealous of one another," he says. "I just take great pride in him."

Louis, in turn, attributes his political success and the success of other Black people since the 1967 Cleveland mayoral race to Carl.

"Carl was the nucleus," Louis says. "He was the one who inspired Black political achievement all over the country.... So many people over the years remember me as Carl Stokes' brother and it never disturbed me because I was proud of my brother and I'm proud of him today."

There were others who inspired Louis Stokes on his way to Congress. Foremost of these was Isadore Apisdorf, who hired Stokes when was a 16-year-old high school student to be a stock boy at an Army-Navy store in Cleveland.

Stokes explains: "One day this gentleman (Apisdorf) sat me down and said, 'Louis, I got an idea. I don't want you to hold this experiment against me if it doesn't work. I have a theory that a colored person'—at that time we used the term 'colored'—'ought to be able to sell to a white person the same as white people sell to colored people.'"

Now this was during the early 1940s and such a practice was unheard of, even in Northern cities like Cleveland.

"The next thing we knew," Stokes recalls, "he liked my work so much as a salesman that he hired a young white fellow as the stock boy and made me a full-time salesman."

Only one white customer questioned the arrangement. Apisdorf, who was Jewish, intervened.

"He took him (the customer) by the shoulders," Stokes says. "He said, 'We don't want your business in here,' and he literally threw him out of the store. He (the customer) was a big guy, but he just literally threw him out."

Apisdorf kept track of Stokes as he graduated from high school, served in the Army and returned to Cleveland to go to law school at night while helping his mom by working as a typist for the U.S. Treasury Department during the day. Apisdorf singled out outstanding Black lawyers with downtown offices as role models for Stokes to follow.

"He would say, 'Louis, one day you'll be just like those outstanding men,'" Stokes says.

Their last meeting came a few years ago—just before Apisdorf's death.

"I recall one of the last things he said to me was, 'Louis, you should be president of the United States.' And he meant it."

Though Louis Stokes must likely never will sit in the Oval Office, he has earned the unelected title of "consummate insider." That's a label reserved for a select few in the House or Senate.

These "insiders" usually are senior members who have figured out how to work the committee system and the whole legislative process for the benefit of their districts. Many, like Stokes, are almost secretive about their behind-the-scenes bargaining.

"When Stokes does his 'insider' business, his work pulling strings and arranging things, he does it by being very moderate and not strident in his style," says Green, the Bliss institute director.

Stokes flexed his "insider" muscles just before the House recessed last year; he was one of several House members who slipped in hefty grants for their districts in the spending bill for the Housing and Urban Development Department. HUD Secretary Jack Kemp was livid, protesting that the grants weren't judged on their merits against other projects.

But Stokes is unrepentant about the $800,000 he took home for anti-drug programs at a Cleveland Metropolitan Housing Authority project.

"My constituents sent me to Congress for me to be able to represent them and get things done for my congressional district," he says. "They have kept me here so that I would be the beneficiary of a seniority system and be able to acquire the power that comes with seniority...So I'm not going to ever apologize to anyone for taking money back to my congressional district."

Stokes has had little to apologize for over the years, but he did slip in the spring of 1983. On the way home from a late-night House session, he was ordered off the road by police in suburban Maryland, who said he failed a roadside sobriety test.

No charges initially were filed against him, though the incident received extensive news coverage.

Then at a demagogic press conference-revival at Olivet Baptist Church in Cleveland, Stokes proclaimed that he had had nothing to drink that night and lashed out at the media.

"I always knew that someday racism and bigotry in the media would raise its ugly head against me, too," Stokes told supporters who yelled, applauded and burst into singing *We Shall Overcome*.

Dick Feagler, a Beacon Journal columnist and Cleveland television personality who has observed Cleveland politics for years, accused Stokes of "trying to make *Roots III* out of a traffic arrest."

After the press conference, Stokes was charged with driving under the influence of alcohol. He testified at his trial that he "had a couple of drinks" while waiting to vote on the night of the incident but that he was not intoxicated. He was eventually convicted and fined $250.

Stokes, who never has had a reputation as a big drinker, put the incident behind him by not appealing the verdict, though he still proclaimed his innocence.

"I was very emotionally involved, disturbed about the way the media was pursuing the matter," he says now, "and I think my reaction at that time was more in the nature of responding to the way I felt that the media had been hounding me relentlessly and improperly. As I reflect back on it now, I think I would have handled it differently."

The incident had little effect on Stokes' ability to get things done in Washington.

"Lou's a solid type of individual," says Rep. Ralph Regula, whose district chiefly covers Stark and Wayne counties and who serves with Stokes on the Appropriations Committee. Although a Republican, Regula was endorsed for a state Senate seat by Carl Stokes during the 1960s when he and Carl served in the state legislature together.

Louis Stokes, Regula says, has been true to his political beliefs over his career—another reason he has built up such a reservoir of trust.

"He's an honest-to-goodness liberal," says Regula, who likes to think of himself as an honest-to-goodness pragmatist. "Lou doesn't do things because they have political appeal. People respect that."

Stokes' brand of liberalism fell out of favor during Ronald Reagan's presidency, with Democrats scurrying off toward a fuzzily defined "political center." Stokes wants to bring those Democrats back.

"The thing that made the Democratic Party great was the fact that it was the party of the common person in American," Stokes says. "The elderly, the poor, minorities, all of those who gravitated to the Democratic

Party did so out of a sense that there was a line of demarcation between the Republicans and the Democrats."

———————————

Louis Stokes has combined service to his constituencies with devotion to fulfilling Martin Luther King's dream.

"His (King's) name is a constant reminder to us that if we indeed love America, we ought to be able to make the kind of sacrifices that will enable us to have more brotherhood in this country," he says.

Now the dean of the 11 Democrats in Ohio's delegation to the House, Stokes plans to keep doing his part.

"As long as I have the good health I've been blessed with and I still feel as committed as I feel at this time…to run up and down the streets in my congressional district and attend to all the problems and other things that are required of me in this job; as long as I continue to feel that way, I'll continue to run," says the consummate insider who made a difference.*

———————————

* Stokes served 15 terms in the U.S. House before retiring in 1999. He died in 2015 at 90.

John Glenn: Crying Out A Message of Doom

Akron Beacon Journal Beacon Magazine, February 26, 1989
WILLIAM HERSHEY

Lobbyists in somber gray suits jostle with late-arriving reporters for standing-room-only space at the packed Senate committee hearing.

Ohio's John Glenn is at work becoming a national hero for the second time.

He first became a hero with his historic space flight almost 30 years ago.

This time he's trying to save the nation from the scourge of radioactive and toxic wastes that have built up over nearly four decades at the nation's atomic weapons plants.

Amazing courage, unmatched physical stamina and a little luck drew attention to Glenn the astronaut. He lifted American spirits with his three-orbit voyage around the earth on Feb. 20, 1962. When he emerged safely from his cramped Friendship 7 space capsule, the nation puffed out its chest and recaptured some of the self-respect the Soviets had stolen from us with their successful space flights.

He was then a space-age Daniel Boone, blazing a new path for the country in what may be the real last frontier.

Today Glenn the senator is more like Paul Revere or maybe a biblical prophet of the Old Testament, shouting out a modern-day warning:

We are risking our national defense and poisoning ourselves and our environment with the messes that we have created at the nuclear weapons factories.

"It does us little good to protect ourselves from the Soviets and the Soviet nuclear threat," Glenn preaches whenever he gets the chance, "if at the same time we poison our own people."

If the truth were told, John Glenn probably felt more at ease scrunched inside his space capsule than he does in front of news conference microphones. If you want to get on the newscasts, you must condense your opinion into 30- or 60-second "sound bites." That's all the time television news is likely to give a senator or anyone else. If you can't do it, the reporter will find someone who can.

Although he's better now than he used to be, Glenn still is no master of the sound bite. He continues to see the world in complicated shades of gray and wants to carefully examine each hue. It's hard to get anyone's attention that way, especially if you're talking about an issue as complicated as the nuclear weapons complex. It's what Glenn calls a "MEGO" subject—short for "my eyes glaze over."

The crowd at last month's hearing indicated that Ohio's self-effacing prophet of potential doom finally had gotten the nation's attention—at least for a day. Seven lights flooded the dark-paneled hearing room with the brightness demanded by television cameras.

When you are a pilot or an astronaut, you do a lot on your own. But as a senator working to solve a complex issue, Glenn needs to move not only public opinion but also a massive government bureaucracy.

At the hearing, five of those television cameras showed up to watch Chairman Glenn and the members of his Governmental Affairs Committee grill Energy Department officials on what's being done to clean up the disasters at the plants and make their future operations safe.

The video turnout didn't match the 41 cameras that came last year for a press conference on military-base closings—a Pentagon record. But at least Glenn wasn't alone, as he often had been in the past when he tried to break through the secrecy that clouded operations of the nuclear weapons factories.

The nation was beginning to take notice, and Glenn was even thanked for the wake-up call.

"Mr. Chairman, if they gave a Nobel Prize for public service, you'd deserve it," gushed Joseph I. Lieberman, a first-term Democratic senator from Connecticut.

Glenn had come upon the nuclear mess in the course of doing a public servant's run-of-the-mill business. He was responding to complaints from his constituents.

It was 1979 and the constituents were employees at the government-owned uranium enrichment plant in Piketon in southern Ohio. The workers were on strike, complaining of health and safety violations at the facility, where uranium is prepared for use in civilian nuclear power plants and the Navy's nuclear reactors.

"Like almost everybody else, I guess I thought that DOE (the federal energy department) must be taking good care of this waste and the radioactive material," Glenn recalls. "The more I learned about it, the more I found out that this was not the case."

Glenn learned that the nuclear weapons plants had produced small mountains of radioactive and toxic wastes that nobody really knew what to do with. The wastes were stored in ways that could contaminate the soil and ground water and threaten the health of plant workers and neighbors. Sometimes radioactive dust was blown directly into the air.

Equally alarming, he discovered that records of what workers and communities were exposed to are incomplete. The rush to produce the weapons became an excuse for work habits that ignored and shortchanged health and safety guidelines.

Dr. Anthony Robbins, who was director of the National Institute for Occupational Safety and Health in 1979, remembers the problems his agency encountered before it could get the information it needed to look into problems at the Piketon plant. The agency is the arm of the Health and Human Services Department that conducts research on occupational safety and health issues.

"There was all sorts of stalling and delays in terms of access to the plant's and the workers' records," Robbins says.

As Glenn began to look at similar complaints at other defense plants, he discovered this pattern of secrecy that had enabled the government and plant operators to overlook the health and safety regulations they should have been following.

The Cold War threat from the Soviet Union had sent the nation into a frenzy of weapons production, Glenn found, and safety was at best a distant afterthought.

"I shared the concern," Glenn says. "You know, 'the Russians are coming, the Russians are coming.' And so we have to have that production to prevent some dire catastrophe."

But in the process, another potential catastrophe was created.

"How do you take care of this waste?" Glenn asks. "Oh, God, dig a pit back there and put the stuff in it. That's all right."

It wasn't all right, of course. The nuclear weapons complex is huge, with 17 major plants and numerous smaller ones covering a land area larger than Delaware and Rhode Island combined.

Ohio has three major and one smaller weapons sites, more than any other state. They are: the Feed Materials Production Center at Fernald, near Cincinnati; the Mound Laboratory in Miamisburg, near Dayton; the Gaseous Diffusion facility near Piketon in southern Ohio and the RMI Co. Extrusion Plant, the smaller facility in Ashtabula. They are mainly chemical and metal-working facilities, not nuclear reactors. At these plants, the radioactive materials are enriched and shaped—middle steps in the process of fashioning ore into the ingredients for nuclear warheads.

Since 1981, the General Accounting Office, the investigative arm of Congress, has issued 50 reports on environmental, safety and health problems at the nuclear weapons plants. Many of these reports were requested by Glenn.

And each new report by the GAO or other investigative agency seems to uncover a new outrage.

At the Fernald plant near Cincinnati, for example, there was the problem with the big filters that were supposed to keep uranium dust from being blown over southwestern Ohio. An alarm sounded when there was a problem with the filters.

"The push for production was so strong that the alarm goes off, and how'd they take care of that emergency?" Glenn asks. "Instead of shutting the plant down and correcting it, they turned the alarm off."

With each new disclosure, Glenn's outrage began to build. But it was an outrage peculiar to Glenn.

Unlike ban-the-bomb advocates, Glenn, a Marine fighter pilot in World War II and Korea, has and continues to support a nuclear deterrent. He's convinced that we must have the nuclear weapons plants and that they can be operated safely.

That puts him at odds with critics of the weapons plants such as Robbins, who is now a professor of public health at Boston University and the treasurer of International Physicians for the Prevention of Nuclear War.

"I don't see how you can build them safely," Robbins says.

In time, Robbins believes that Glenn may come to the same conclusion. Right now, however, he is glad that the senator has taken the lead on cleaning the plants up and making them safer.

"My impression is that in some ways Glenn is ideal," Robbins says, "because no one questions his commitment to doing what's right in this area. Though he may not be a hawk, he certainly is someone who is considered a supporter of the military."

That reputation helped Glenn in prodding the Reagan administration to make a start in cleaning up the weapons complex. In a speech to the National Press Club in December, former Energy Secretary John S. Herrington admiringly called Glenn "a leader" in the efforts to make the plants safer.

According to one well-placed source, Glenn helped Herrington in the former secretary's attempt to find out more about what had gone on at the weapons plants. The pressure from Glenn, a Senate committee chairman, was the justification Herrington needed to press ahead in the search for both information and the necessary funds to work on the overwhelming problems.

No one in Washington questions Glenn's knowledge of the issues confronting the weapons complex. If he's had a problem bringing these issues to the nation's attention, it's the same problem that plagued him when he ran for president in 1984.

"John Glenn is a flat person," says Bruce Freed, a legislative consultant who used to work for Democratic Rep. Mary Rose Oakar of Cleveland. "He's not a dynamic person. He doesn't have a feel for the jugular and a sense for the dramatic that an Al Cranston or an Al Gore has."

This judgment is harsher than some would make of Glenn, but it's not meant to reflect on Glenn's ability. "The man technically knows these issues," Freed says. "He understands them. Unfortunately, it's the hot ones who jump in and know how to garner the media attention."

Fortunately for Glenn, and perhaps for the nation, the media finally has begun paying attention to him.

Most noticeable has been the New York Times, with its national circulation and strong Washington presence. Other papers, including some in Ohio, had been reporting on problems in the plants in their states and regions. But last year the Times began reporting the story from a national perspective. It became clear that the same sorts of problems were occurring at plants across the nation.

"You have a major paper that has been pushing it," Freed says. "You'll have other papers following along. You have the TV news picking it up. The fact that the Times has decided to become crusading again means that Glenn now has an outlet."

The coverage by the Times has helped raise public awareness of the issue just at the time when the problems seem worse than ever.

The system's biggest reactor at Hanford, Wash., which produces plutonium, has been closed since January 1987 for safety reasons. Since the nation has an ample inventory of plutonium, the situation at Hanford isn't as serious as the problem with the plant at Savannah River in South Carolina.

The South Carolina plant, the nation's only source of tritium, a perishable radioisotope used in nuclear bombs, has been closed since last April for safety reasons. At some point tritium production must resume or the United States will begin a sort of involuntary disarmament, a scenario Glenn dreads. At Glenn's committee hearings last month, John Ahearne, chairman of an Energy Department advisory committee on weapons plant safety, questioned whether the department ever will be able to operate the plant at the safety levels required of commercial nuclear power plants.

And at those same hearings, Colorado Gov. Roy Romer said that his state will shut down a plant in Rocky Flats by May unless a new site is found for hazardous wastes from that facility. The wastes used to be shipped to Idaho, but in October Idaho sealed its border to further shipments, causing a buildup at Rocky Flats.

Glenn had hoped that the Reagan administration was getting the message about what he called a "ticking time bomb," not a bad attention-getter for the low-key Glenn. More needed to be done about the plants and that meant spending more money. Cleanup alone may cost more than $100 billion over 20 or 30 years, Glenn says.

But Reagan didn't get Glenn's message. His proposed budget for 1990—a budget that new President George Bush can modify—called for spending just $315 million for cleanup. That's only about one-fourth of what the Energy Department's own officials had estimated was needed.

So now Glenn is going after Bush on the cleanup issue. Bush wanted Glenn's Governmental Affairs Committee to hold early confirmation hearings for Richard Darman, his nominee for budget director.

Fine, Glenn said. Darman's hearing began on Thursday, Jan. 19, the day before Bush was inaugurated. Besides talking about the budget deficit, Glenn took Darman to school on the nuclear weapons complex.

Reagan's $315 million for cleanup "may well buy the blueprint paper and not a whole lot more," Glenn told Darman.

Then in case Darman and Bush didn't get the message that he was serious, Glenn scheduled his committee hearings on the weapons complex for Bush's first week in office. He wants the new president to know that he thinks the crisis at the nuclear weapons complex demands as much attention as the savings and loan problem, Central America or any other issue.

"It is an attempt to keep the heat on," says Glenn spokesman Dale Butland, "and to ensure that the cleanup of the weapons plants receives a much higher priority in the Bush budget than it did in the Reagan budget."

———————

In the Senate committee room, Glenn's hearings have gone into their second day. Most of the television crews have left to cover confirmation hearings for John Tower, Bush's controversial choice as secretary of defense. John Glenn is by himself again, as he has been for much of his crusade.

But he hardly seems to notice. Glenn questions each witness in detail. First there are Govs. Richard F. Celeste of Ohio, Cecil Andrus of Idaho and Romer of Colorado. All have bomb plants in their states and Glenn

wants to know what is going on. Then there is Ohio Atty. Gen. Anthony
J. Celebrezze, Jr., who fashioned a federal court-approved agreement
giving the state the authority to regulate cleanup at Fernald.

There also are representatives from the U.S. Environmental Protection Agency and the National Academy of Sciences. Ahearne, chairman
of the Energy Department's safety advisory committee, also testifies.

The hearing starts at 9:30 a.m. and it is nearly 1 p.m. before Glenn
finishes. He is 45 minutes late for his next appointment, and that's before
a television reporter ambushes him in the hallway.

Some of the headline-grabbers have begun nibbling away at the issue,
but so far it still belongs to Glenn.

"I don't think anyone yet has gotten out and stolen the march in that
area, but there have been some who have been trying recently, I've noted,"
Glenn had said a few days before the hearing.

Let them march along with him, he said. "I don't mind. I'm just glad
the thing is likely to get some attention and get cleared up.

"That's where I get my kicks."*

---

* Glenn is the only Ohioan elected to four consecutive terms in the U.S. Senate. He
retired in 1999 and died in 2016 at 95.

Howard Metzenbaum: Going Out in Metzenbaum Style

Akron Beacon Journal Beacon Magazine, November 13, 1994
WILLIAM HERSHEY

Howard Metzenbaum is leaving the U.S. Senate after 19 years, and, as usual, he's doing it his way—at the same rocket pace that has propelled him through his half-century political career.

To some, Metzenbaum is a political dinosaur. Unlike many of his more modern colleagues, the Democratic senator from Ohio doesn't always have his finger in the air, calculating the varied interests of voters and financial supporters.

"Today, politics is about fear—fear of the 30-second attack ad, fear of special-interest groups," Metzenbaum said in a recent speech. "If you are afraid, you can't lead. Too many in this town are so fearful for their political lives that they forget about helping the people who sent 'em."

It is clear that Howard Metzenbaum is not afraid. And nobody really believes that people have seen the last of him.

Just five days after his Oct. 7 "farewell" in the Russell caucus room, Metzenbaum summoned reporters to his office in the same building to announce his plans for the future.

At 77, 12 years past the retirement age for most Americans, this self-made millionaire from Cleveland's East Side announced he will become the first-ever chairman of the Consumer Federation of America, a non-profit coalition of 240 pro-consumer groups with 50 million members. He will serve without pay.

Metzenbaum was in vintage form, filled with outrage and demanding attention.

After long years of crusades, "Headline Howard" knows that outrage makes little difference if it doesn't get any attention.

So C-SPAN was on hand to record news of his new position for nationwide broadcast later that day. And Metzenbaum delayed the start of the press conference to await the arrival of the Associated Press reporter, whom he scolded for being tardy.

"I'm excited about doing this," Metzenbaum said. "I kid you not that I had some concerns about what I would do with myself when I leave the United States Senate."

Then, with uncharacteristic understatement, he added:

"I'm an activist."

Metzenbaum's causes have remained the same for nearly half a century.

In many ways, his new job sounds just like his old one, in which he championed gun control, workers' rights and consumer protection.

Now, he expects to protect consumers against what he considers to be the greed of banks, savings and loans, insurance companies, cable television companies, major league baseball owners, food makers, drug companies and other Metzenbaum villains too numerous to list.

And he has a new favorite outrage that he wants to put near the top of the federation's priority list—child labor.

"Americans buying products made with child labor in India, Bangladesh, Pakistan, Honduras, China and various other places… I think it's an abomination for these fancy sweater houses, dress houses, Persian rug manufacturers to have their products made by kids from anywhere from 5 to 14 years of age at absolutely sub-, sub-, sub-standards wages," he said.

The final hearing Metzenbaum conducted as chairman of the Labor Subcommittee highlighted atrocities in overseas sweatshops that would make even the most ardent free-traders blush—children working in

Indian carpet factories for $1 a day, 12-year-old Peruvians mining for gold and then dying of malaria, and 8-year-olds in Bangladesh hung by their hands if they work too slowly in garment shops.

The United States should prohibit the importing of goods made under such conditions, Metzenbaum said, adding that, at the very least, labels should say how the products were made.

"I think consumers have a right to know what they're buying," he said, "and then make up their minds as to whether they want to purchase products made by kids anywhere from 5 to 10 years old."

As Metzenbaum's press conference continued, delight alternated with outrage. His beeper went off:

"I'll be right with you, Bill," he said, grandstanding with an offhand reference to the president of the United States. "He bothers me all the time—won't leave me alone."

Steve Brobeck, the consumer federation's executive director, said the organization is thrilled to have Metzenbaum coming aboard, although he gently pointed out that the 40-member board of directors, not Metzenbaum, will be setting priorities.

But Metzenbaum will give the federation the one thing it has lacked—a celebrity who will be sought out for television news appearances, Brobeck explained.

"This is just great news for consumers," he said. "For nearly 20 years the senator has been our champion in the United States Congress. Now he's going to continue his consumer advocacy, only with the consumer federation."

Years from now, if Metzenbaum ever leaves this world and not just the Senate, his tombstone should be carved with an apt instruction:

"He Would Not Go Away."

And, in smaller letters, it should say:

"He Did Not Turn the Other Cheek."

In his final days on the Senate floor, he persisted, unsuccessfully, in trying to bring to a vote his legislation to eliminate the antitrust exemption for major league baseball. Even friendly Democrats tried to get him to stop.

He can't seem to help stepping on toes.

"He's done it to me," Michigan Sen. Carl Levin, a Democrat and Metzenbaum ally, said at the Russell building reception.

Throughout his long career, Metzenbaum never has retreated willingly and has always returned to fight another day.

His opponents in the Ohio Senate found that out back in 1948. He had expected to be chosen majority leader after Democrats gained control of the body. But his reputation as an ultraliberal—communist sympathizer, some said—and the anti-Semitism of the time prevented that from happening. Five Democrats turned against him.

He saw to it that all five eventually were defeated.

"I would not forget something like that," he said.

Republican Robert Taft Jr. found out about Metzenbaum, too. Taft defeated Metzenbaum in Ohio's 1970 U.S. Senate race, but six years later Metzenbaum turned the tables and defeated Taft.

In between, he got to the Senate for a year in 1974 when Gov. John J. Gilligan appointed him to the seat left vacant when Republican William Saxbe resigned to become U.S. attorney general.

John Glenn defeated Metzenbaum that year in the Democratic primary, but Metzenbaum leveraged that bitter loss into a victory for himself and Ohio.

Together with U.S. Reps. John Seiberling (D-Akron) and Ralph Regula (R-Navarre), Metzenbaum had been pushing in Congress for creation of the Cuyahoga Valley National Recreation Area. After losing to Glenn, Metzenbaum asked his fellow senators for a favor:

"I lose the election to John Glenn and I had the balance of the year to serve…and I say to them, 'Come on guys—give me this national park.'"

The senators agreed, but President Gerald Ford still had to be convinced. So for perhaps the first and only time in his career, Metzenbaum joined forces with the late Ray C. Bliss of Akron, the former Republican national chairman, who lobbied Ford on behalf of the park.

Metzenbaum caught up with the president by phone to ask for a going-away present.

"I had to reach Jerry Ford on the slopes of Vail (Colorado) and ask him to sign it," Metzenbaum recalled. "I said, 'Mr. President, I know you're having fun out there. The House and Senate have a bill to create a national park, and this is my piece of legislation, and it would mean so much to me if you would sign it.' He signed it."

Metzenbaum didn't tell Ford that he'd be back. He returned to Washington in 1977, while Ford left the White House after losing to Jimmy Carter.

———————

An overriding purpose always has fueled Metzenbaum's comebacks. He has been on a lifelong crusade to help the underdog, those he deems to be the victims of unfair power structures.

Starting as a Cleveland labor lawyer in the 1940s, he worked for civil rights for Black Americans and for labor rights for American workers.

"He was involved in the politics of labor unions when it was a real movement, not just a set of interest groups," said political scientist John C. Green, director of the Ray C. Bliss Institute of Applied Politics at The University of Akron. "Movement politics breeds a certain kind of energy, being on the outside and having to fight your way in."

Even after making his fortune, Metzenbaum has always been on the little guy's side.

These days, he views consumers—himself among them—as being on the outside while giant transnational corporations try to maximize their profits, exploit child labor and, when possible, avoid paying their fair share of taxes.

He is and always has been a populist as much as a liberal.

"To be a populist is to be a guy who speaks for all the people," he said. "A liberal might not be speaking for all the people but might be standing up for the right to burn the flag."

(Metzenbaum, of course, has defended flag-burners and fought efforts to punish them.)

His outrage never gets stale. He keeps in touch with the times, said political scientist Green.

"I contrast him (Metzenbaum) with Ted Kennedy, who in some sense has been passed by," Green said. "His (Kennedy's) tenaciousness was much more a matter of style. When liberalism passed out of favor, he became extremely marginal."

Green, a Republican, believes Metzenbaum still is in tune with Ohio voters. Had Metzenbaum sought a fourth term, he would have won, Green said.

In all those he has championed—Blacks, working people and now consumers—Metzenbaum has seen himself, a poor kid from Cleveland who had to work his way through Ohio State University and then make his own way in a business world that wasn't particularly hospitable to a young Jewish lawyer.

Even now, Metzenbaum sees himself, despite the millions he made in developing airport parking lots and other investments, as an outsider.

"It just hurts me to see people who aren't being fed or clothed or educated, who can't have decent health care," he said. "It actually hurts me. I guess sometimes I wish I could wave a wand and make things better for so many of the have-nots."

At another farewell party, this one thrown by Mother Jones magazine to honor him as a "Congressional Hell Raiser," editor Jeffrey Klein explained why he liked Metzenbaum.

"Once he became a senator, he did something that I think was remarkable," Klein said. "He betrayed his class."

Metzenbaum's response?

"They never let me in that class," he said.

Metzenbaum roared through his final days in the Senate, attacking foes real and maybe sometimes imagined.

A few days before the Russell building reception, he appeared on *Crossfire* with John Sununu, White House chief of staff under President George Bush.

The combative Sununu kept interrupting Metzenbaum.

"Are you going to hold your tongue...or do I have to punch you in the mouth to shut you up?" Metzenbaum told him.

For days afterward, members of Metzenbaum's staff joked that they hoped Sununu wouldn't show up at the farewell party. (He didn't.)

And, the debate in the Senate's final days of 1994 over Metzenbaum's legislation to make transracial adoption easier also—to put it mildly—energized him.

The bill, which passed, prevents child welfare agencies from discriminating against prospective parents solely on the basis of race or national origin.

It was aimed at resolving an emotional national debate pitting groups such as the Association for Black Social Workers, who fear that the widespread adoption of Black children by white parents will destroy the children's racial identity, against those who contend that the most important thing for a child is to have parents, no matter what their skin color.

Some of the early supporters of the proposal complained that Metzenbaum had caved in by allowing the final version to say that agencies may consider "cultural or racial-identity needs" as one factor, but not the only factor, in adoption. This will allow agencies to bar white couples from adopting Black children—the very thing the legislation was intended to stop, these Metzenbaum critics said.

But Metzenbaum insisted that officials of the federal Health and Human Services Department had assured him that that won't happen.

"If they screw up over this, they will pay," Metzenbaum said in an interview. "If they break their word to me, I swear I'll break their necks."

———————

On a pleasant October day, with the trees on Capitol Hill decorated red, yellow and orange, Sununu's mouth and the necks of the bureaucrats at the Health and Human Services Department seemed safe.

Metzenbaum, in his office for an interview, appeared downright grandfatherly. Grandson Zachary Hyatt, the 7-year-old son of Susan and Joel Hyatt, and Danny Johnson, the 8-year-old so of two former Metzenbaum staffers, Joel and Mimi Johnson, were playing together on the floor under Metzenbaum's smiling gaze.

Earlier Metzenbaum and his grandson had visited the White House. The senator was as excited about that trip as he was about his new job with the consumer federation. Although President Clinton wasn't in the Oval Office when they visited, Leon Panetta, the White House chief of staff, was there with his parents.

"He (Panetta) introduces me to his parents and I introduced him to Zach," Metzenbaum said. "And Zach stands there in front of the (president's) desk and takes a picture."

Metzenbaum and his wife Shirley have four grown married daughters and eight grandchildren. All the grandchildren except for the youngest, Jason, just 8 months old and the son of daughter Amy Metzenbaum and spouse Joel Yanowitz, have spent time in the Senate with Metzenbaum recently.

"Just so that they have some feel of what being a senator is about, not what they read in the paper," he explained.

Family is important to Metzenbaum, and at the heart of this affection is his wife of 48 years, Shirley. She figures importantly in his retirement plans.

"I think we'll take some trips we've talked about taking," he said. "I'd like to sail the Greek islands. I've been trying to explore that a little bit. I think we might take a trip to Israel. I've always had a hankering to go to Australia. We'd also like to go back to the south of France."

Shirley Metzenbaum knows her husband better than anyone—well enough to doubt the likelihood of taking all those trips. During their 19 years in Washington, there was always a Senate vote or a staff meeting or something to keep him at work.

Shirley knows there will never be a retreat to the rocking chair.

"That wouldn't be Howard," she said.

———————

Howard Metzenbaum has been in politics for 50 years. Here's what he thinks about some of the people he has met:

Bill Clinton: "I think he's able, committed, concerned, gutsy, but has not as yet been able to convince the American people that he is all of that, plus more. But, also I think he's the greatest rebounder in politics."

George Bush: "Rather shallow, not an intellectual giant. Nice guy, kind of guy I could imagine playing an enjoyable round of golf with, although he probably would beat me handily."

Ronald Reagan: "Vastly overrated. Didn't know that much about what was happening in government but is still probably popular enough that he might even get re-elected if he ran again."

George Voinovich: "A politician who doesn't alienate many people. Doesn't accomplish that much. Doesn't rock the boat."

James A. Rhodes: "Straight-talking, no 'ifs' and 'ands.' Always got along well with him."

John Glenn: "Highest integrity, sincerity, strong commitments, intellectually honest and a caring, concerned human being."

Bob Dole: "Nice guy personally, sometimes a little too nasty politically."

Jesse Jackson: "One of the best speakers in the country. Sometimes I become concerned about why he arrived at certain points he has arrived at. Sometimes I've had strong disagreements with some of his positions, but not normally so."

Ross Perot: "Not stupid. Reasonably intelligent, but too anxious to get his publicity, using his own money for that purpose."

Rush Limbaugh: "Hustler, making a lot of money."

Louis Farrakhan: "An embarrassment to his people and a dangerous force in America."*

---

*   Metzenbaum died in 2008 at 90.

Mike DeWine: When a Family Man Heads for the Hill

Akron Beacon Journal Beacon Magazine, January 1, 1995
WILLIAM HERSHEY

It's late October, and Mike DeWine's "Road to Victory" campaign bus is confidently bouncing along the state's highways. Inside, Bill Schenck happily endures the bumps, the cookie crumbs and music that ranges from Patti Page to 10,000 Maniacs.

Schenck, the Greene County prosecutor from Xenia, wouldn't be anywhere else. After all, DeWine, who will be sworn in Wednesday as Ohio's 53rd U.S. Senator, has been his close friend and political ally since the 1970s.

It's been a friendship defined by loyalty, perseverance and hard work— the same qualities that helped DeWine, 47, defeat Democrat Joel Hyatt in November.

"You work with Mike DeWine and what you find is real—real inner strength and integrity. He does caring, giving things for the people around him," Schenck says.

Schenck knows.

In June of 1976 he and DeWine formed a law partnership in Xenia. Earlier they had worked together as assistant prosecutors in Greene County, just east of Dayton.

Schenck, now 48, had left the prosecutor's office in 1973 to enter private practice in Dayton. DeWine quit in 1975 after he discovered that the prosecutor, a Democrat, had planted a listening device in DeWine's office.

DeWine decided to challenge his old boss for the prosecutor's job, and he invited Schenck to help run his campaign. Schenck returned to Xenia, but by July of 1976 he became too sick to work.

"I had a form of colitis," he explains.

DeWine told him to rest up at a tobacco farm Schenck's uncle had in Virginia.

"You take whatever time you need…and just rest," Schenck remembers DeWine telling him. "Find a good doctor and see what's wrong."

He had left DeWine in a bind, with a new law practice and a campaign to run. Yet DeWine even offered to pick up 75 open files Schenck still had from his practice in Dayton.

"He (DeWine) took every one of my files, notified every client that I was undergoing some physical difficulty…if they needed anything to call him and he would take care of it," Schenck says.

That wasn't all.

"Mike DeWine took care of every one of those cases or at least maintained them and sent me every single penny from every single case," he continues.

The payments to Schenck amounted to several thousand dollars, money he needed for his mortgage, car payments and other expenses.

"What it told me was here is a guy who really cares about me," Schenck says. "This guy is not some political opportunist who uses people. This guy reaches out and takes care of the people who are around him."

Schenck returned to Xenia in August of 1976 and DeWine was elected prosecutor. Then in 1980, he won a seat in the Ohio Senate and Schenck became Greene County prosecutor, the job he still holds.

DeWine shrugs off what he did for Schenck.

"He was my friend," DeWine says. "That's it."

But Bill Schenck isn't Mike DeWine's "best" friend. That title belongs to DeWine's wife Fran.

DeWine and Ohio's other U.S. senator, Democrat John Glenn, (their nasty 1992 Senate race notwithstanding) have one thing in common— both married childhood sweethearts.

Glenn met his wife Annie when both were toddlers back in New Concord, Ohio.

The DeWines hooked up in first grade in Yellow Springs, home of Antioch College, not far from where they live today in Cedarville, about 20 miles east of Dayton.

By high school, they were inseparable. Mike drove Fran to school in a Model T Ford that they still have.

They were Roman Catholic conservatives growing up in a liberal college town, and together they campaigned for Barry Goldwater against Democrat Lyndon Johnson.

They married while attending Miami University in Oxford, from which both graduated.

Before a cheering Columbus crowd on election night, DeWine beamed as he introduced his wife as his partner, his best friend, and the mother of their eight children.

"No one deserves this victory more than she does," DeWine said. "No one has worked harder; no one has sacrificed more."

Fran DeWine has been a stay-at-home mom, but not in a father-always-knows-best household.

"Mike and I basically make decisions together," she says. "He always asks my opinion. If he doesn't ask, I give it to him anyway."

On the campaign trail she wore an "I Like Mike" button, only the "Like" was crossed out and "Love" was written in.

DeWine has always had women in top staff positions. The partnership he forged with his wife is one reason why, says Laurel Pressler, who managed DeWine's recent campaign and will be chief of staff in his Washington office.

"It really taught him throughout his life that women are just as strong as men," she says.

———————

A cookbook, *Fran DeWine's Family Favorites*, was a hit on the campaign trail this year, just as previous versions were in other DeWine campaigns.

It is filled with recipes like "Mother's Tex-Mex Dip," "Amish Barn Soup," "George Voinovich's Pan-Fried Walleye" and "Mike's Favorite Sausage Gravy and Biscuits."

Copies were snatched up quickly in small towns and in big cities— Akron and Cleveland included.

This year's edition was dedicated to the DeWines' daughter, Becky, who was 22 when she was killed in a car accident on Aug. 4, 1993, shortly after graduating from the College of Wooster in Wayne County. Becky's death brought the campaign and the DeWine's cheerful family life to a temporary halt.

"My first reaction was that I was not going to run," DeWine says.

But he and Fran, with input from their other children, decided he should try.

Patrick, 26, the DeWine's oldest child, provided the best reason for getting back in.

"It's not going to do anyone any good if you don't run," he told his father. "Nothing is going to be accomplished if you don't run."

DeWine found he could get through the days on the campaign trail, although it did nothing to lessen the pain. Nothing will ever do that, DeWine says.

Mark, the DeWine's 7-year-old son, summed up what the loss meant to the family.

He told his mother he thought Becky was in heaven. Mrs. DeWine agreed. Then he said "heaven is better than here," and Mrs. DeWine agreed again.

A week later, Mark brought up the subject again.

"You know, Mom, the trouble with heaven is your friends and family can't go up, and you can't come down," he concluded.

"That's really it," Mrs. DeWine noted during an interview before the election. "She doesn't get to call me anymore… (but) she is here with us. I always think when I'm doing something on the campaign or anything, what would Becky think?"

Fran DeWine and several of the children popped on and off the bus as DeWine made 100 stops in 60 counties during the last 10 days of the campaign.

Their presence put extra zip in DeWine's step and brought a smile to his face, particularly when he pointed to Fran and told crowds that she was a grandmother. Their daughter and son-in-law Jill and Bill Darling, have a 1-year-old son, Albert.

"Mike DeWine's family is the most important thing in the world to him, period," longtime friend Schenck points out.

The couple have been able to provide their children with the kind of family life that is becoming increasingly rare in America. Both sets of grandparents live nearby and they all frequently get together for family gatherings.

DeWine's roots run deep in Greene County. His great great-grandfather, Dennis DeWine, came to southeast Ohio in the 1840s to escape the potato famine in Ireland. He worked on the railroad and ended up farming. His son, Tom, also became a farmer.

DeWine's grandfather, George, farmed as a boy. But when he came home from fighting in World War I, he opened up a feed store in Yellow Springs. The business prospered under DeWine's father Dick, who sold the company when he decided to retire more than 10 years ago.

The company was so prosperous, Mike DeWine's interest in it made him a millionaire, with a net worth of about $2.4 million today.

DeWine's wealth has made for a comfortable family life in a spacious 19th century farmhouse. But their lifestyle is defined more by DeWine's plaid shirts and Fran's home-cooked meals than by tuxedos and candle-light dinners. His favorite food is ice cream, especially banana from Young's Dairy near the DeWine home.

"Mike DeWine is not a man who is impressed by material wealth or material things," Schenck says. "He is not motivated by money or trying to impress people."

———————

Some Republicans weren't always impressed with DeWine—a fact that irritated DeWine supporters last year.

"Influential Republicans suggested that he didn't have the charisma, the looks. That he's too short, blind in one eye," griped one high-ranking Republican source and DeWine ally, who asked not to be named.

DeWine is 5 foot 6 inches tall and had a cataract removed from his right eye as a baby, leaving him with only very limited peripheral vision in that eye.

And he is not "senatorial," if that means silver-haired, tall and distinguished-looking. Congressional Quarterly magazine, in a post-election issue, described him as having a "lopsided grin and revenge-of-the-nerds persona."

Of course, none of that has anything to do with whether he will be a good senator, notes Summit County Alex Arshinkoff, a steadfast DeWine supporter.

In the primary, Art Modell, the owner of the Cleveland Browns and Canton Industrialist W.R. "Tim" Timken backed Dr. Bernadine Healy, former director of the National Institutes of Health. Akron developer David Brennan supported state Sen. Eugene Watts, R-Galloway. Aviation consultant George Rhodes also was in the race.

DeWine won easily, with a hefty 52% of the vote.

Gov. George Voinovich, whom DeWine has served as lieutenant governor for nearly four years, calls DeWine the most underestimated politician in the United States.

Jim Nathanson found that out the hard way. Nathanson, former political director for the Republican National Committee, helped run Dr. Healy's unsuccessful campaign against DeWine. She was attractive, articulate and television-savvy, but finished a weak second place.

"(DeWine) is just tenacious. He goes at it," says Nathanson, now a Dayton-based political consultant. "More importantly, Mike's great strength is that he knows how to relate to the party cadres. Even Voinovich can't do that very well. (DeWine) can go to the counties, talk to the people in the party. They feel that he's one of them."

As a U.S. senator, the bigger question for DeWine now is whether he can forge the same relationship with Ohio's diverse population, and whether he has the vision to look out for interests as different as steel mills and grain farms.

Democrats, who regard DeWine as a hardworking political accident, are skeptical.

"What are his accomplishments? What's he done?" says former Ohio Democratic chairman James Ruvolo. "There's nothing to point to. I don't want to prejudge the guy. He hasn't had any accomplishments in his professional life."

DeWine disagrees. He points to passage of a drunk-driving law in the Ohio legislature, to a federal law making it easier for children to testify against child abusers, to helping Voinovich give law enforcement more tools to fight crime.

But Mike DeWine differs in a major way from his predecessor. Democrat Howard Metzenbaum was a New Deal liberal who thought the federal government should play a large and direct role in improving the lives of ordinary Americans.

"One thing I've learned is that the federal government is not going to solve most of our problems," DeWine says constantly.

State and local governments know better than Washington about what's needed to solve most of America's problems, he says.

His answer on welfare reform? Give the states federal block grants and let them figure out how to feed hungry children and get parents back to work and off the public dole.

Crime prevention? Again, give the states their share of federal taxes and let them figure out how to punish the guilty and keep the innocent safe and out of trouble.

On crime, he differs from some conservatives who say no level of government—state, local or federal—should spend much money trying to prevent crime through after-school tutoring, feeding and recreation programs.

DeWine's stand on that issue is consistent with his pledge to make children his number one legislative priority.

"Children in this country are in crisis," he said on election night. "One-third of all births are illegitimate…and in our cities, it is two-thirds of all births. The poverty rate among children is the highest of any age group. The most vulnerable members of society are also the least well off."

DeWine says programs that can make a difference are like those operated by the United Methodist Center in Youngstown, which provides Golden Gloves training, after-school activities for good kids and programs to help those in trouble. The center designs programs to meet the specific needs of the predominantly African American and Hispanic population that it serves.

Millicent Counts, the center's executive director, is a big DeWine fan—and not just because he helped the center get a $36,000 grant.

"He is a very warm and caring person," says Counts, a Democrat who voted for DeWine. "Not only did he come (to the center), he brought his wife and daughter, Anna."

DeWine's roots in southern, rural Ohio won't stop him from serving the whole state, she says. "We made ourselves known to him. He listened. I think he'll do wonderful. I think he'll be sensitive to the needs of urban areas as well as rural areas."

As a senator, DeWine will have nearly 11 million Ohioans to listen to. But they should not expect to change his mind on some issues.

He opposes abortion, except in cases of rape, incest or when the mother's life is in danger.

He supports capital punishment.

And he doesn't like government interfering in business. When DeWine served in the U.S. House from 1983 to 1990, he voted against legislation requiring companies to give workers 60 days' notice before they lose their jobs in a plant shutdown.

Although his Senate service is just starting, DeWine already knows how he wants Ohioans to remember him:

"I hope they do say that Mike DeWine knew Ohio. Mike DeWine loved Ohio. Mike DeWine always knew where he came from and Mike DeWine always fought for Ohio families."

That may be asking a lot of himself.

But Mike DeWine has been underestimated before.*

---

* DeWine was defeated for re-election to a third term in the U.S. Senate in 2006. He was elected Ohio attorney general in 2010 and re-elected in 2014. He was elected Ohio governor in 2018 and was serving in that office in 2021.

Sherrod Brown: Brown Takes on the Role as Challenger

Democrat hopes contrast with foe put his party back in power

Akron Beacon Journal, September 3, 2006
CARL CHANCELLOR

For U.S. Rep. Sherrod Brown, this year's run for the U.S. Senate has to seem like some sort of upside-down *deja vu*.

It was 1994 when Brown—then a freshman congressman representing the 13th District that included Lorain—faced a strong challenge from a popular officeholder, Lorain County Prosecutor Greg White.

Brown was the incumbent, but the race was handicapped as a virtual toss-up, owing to Brown's Democratic Party posting low approval numbers and many of the party's incumbents being deemed vulnerable.

Given the dissatisfaction with Democrats going into the 1994 midterm elections, the GOP leadership, headed by Newt Gingrich—chief architect of the Contract with America—were eagerly anticipating a takeover of the House and Senate.

Brown held off the White challenge.

But many of Brown's Democratic colleagues lost their seats, giving the GOP control of Congress.

That was 12 years ago.

Now, fast-forward to 2006.

Today, at 53, Brown is the challenger taking on the incumbent, two-term Sen. Mike DeWine. And just like in 1994, the party out of power—this time the Democrats—is salivating over the prospect of retaking the House and Senate. Pundits are predicting a close race, again attributed to the increasing unpopularity of the party in power—the GOP.

So what did Brown learn from that hard-fought 1994 race that he plans to apply to his 2006 challenge of DeWine?

Sitting at a patio table in the backyard of his Avon home with the sleeves of his Oxford shirt rolled to the elbows and the chatter of lawn mowers in the background, Brown paused to consider the question.

"I don't know if there is anything specific…I don't know if White made any mistakes," he began, thinking back to the race.

"The parallels are that one party controlled everything in 1994 and people were unhappy with it…One party controls everything now and people are unhappy with that situation."

According to Brown, the GOP worked hard to get a reluctant White to enter the race. He recalled that for most of 1993 the Lorain prosecutor fended off their overtures and denied rumors that he would take on Brown.

Likewise, Brown initially indicated he wouldn't challenge DeWine, despite polls showing Ohio's senior senator was vulnerable. That led to the announcement by another Democrat—political newcomer Paul Hackett, a Cincinnati lawyer and Iraq war veteran—who later yielded to party fears of a messy primary and withdrew after Brown declared.

Brown—who took flak for his about-face leading to Hackett's messy exit—said family issues that he wouldn't discuss sorted themselves out.

Unlike the race this year, however, Brown noted that while White ran an aggressive campaign, "he had never been in a federal race."

Ultimately, Brown said, it was a combination of White's lack of experience and Brown's taking a page from the GOP playbook issuing his own contract with the 13th District that led to Brown's victory. In that contract the congressman pledged to fight for jobs, fair trade, the environment and congressional reform.

"I guess what I learned (from the 1994 race) was that it is important to show the contrasts," Brown said. "I want voters to walk into the polls this November and be certain about the differences between me and Mike DeWine. I owe it to the voters to make that contrast very clear."

Brown reached down to scratch the head of the family's pudgy pure-bred Pug.

"I call her Rufus, but her name is Gracie. But she looks like a Rufus," Brown said, teasing his wife.

"He knows I don't like that name," said Connie Schultz, 48, a Pulitzer Prize-winning columnist, who had joined her husband in the backyard.

Taking an unpaid leave of absence from her job as a columnist at the Cleveland Plain Dealer, Schultz has been doing her part to make sure Ohio voters know the distinctions between her husband and DeWine.

Spreading Brown's Message

For most of the spring and summer she traveled the state in a leased sky blue Chrysler Pacifica, with the goal of visiting all 88 Ohio counties to spread the gospel according to Brown.

In mid-July, she was in the southern Ohio town of Piketon, meeting with former factory workers who were being retrained to become boiler-makers. On that hot and sticky afternoon about three dozen men and women filled the Boilermakers Union Hall Lodge 105 to hear what she had to say.

"I know where you come from. I know the blood running through your veins," said Schultz, who talked about being the daughter of a union man with a utility company.

"I married Sherrod Brown two years ago because he fights for workers. He fought NAFTA and he fought CAFTA," said Schultz, speaking of Brown's opposition to free-trade agreements he says have cost Ohio thousands of manufacturing jobs.

"My husband wears a canary pin in his lapel which was made by Steel-workers," she said, noting that coal miners once used the tiny birds to determine if the air in the mine was toxic.

"The government wasn't looking out for workers," she said. "The mine bosses weren't protecting miners. The miners had to protect themselves."

Her husband wears the pin, she told them, to remind him of the continued struggle for economic and social justice.

As if on cue a woman in the audience jumped to her feet and praised Brown's careerlong efforts on behalf of workers.

"That's my man," Schultz declared.

Important Early Lessons

Her man grew up in Mansfield on a 200-acre farm that had been in the family for four generations. His father, Charles, was a respected doctor and his mother, Emily, grew up in Georgia.

"Dad taught us about fair play. And, mom, even more than my dad, taught us about social and economic justice. She was involved in the civil rights movement," said Brown, the youngest of three boys. He attributes his political activism to his mother.

In high school Brown organized a march to recognize the first Earth Day in 1970. Later that year he enrolled in Yale University, where he got his first taste of politics working on George McGovern's 1972 campaign for president. Two years later it was his turn to run.

"My political career started right out of college. It was 1974 and I was still a senior in college when I got a call from the local Democratic chairman, who asked me if I wanted to run for the state legislature. I said sure. I would have never thought of running but he asked me. So I moved back home after graduation to run…As a matter of fact I won the primary while I was still in college," Brown said.

"I didn't get very many votes in the primary. But you don't need many when you're unopposed," he said with a smile.

Brown, with the help of his entire family—including his brother Charles, who dropped out of law school to run his campaign—beat the Republican incumbent. He would serve eight years in the legislature before making a successful bid for Ohio secretary in state in 1982.

"I was in that office for eight years and I only left that office because they beat me," said Brown, who shook his head in what seemed to be a try at dislodging the memory.

"The guy who beat me was Bob Taft," he said.

Looking at his long political career, which has included seven terms in Congress, Brown said he never "made a conscious decision that this would be something I would do for 30 years. But I'm certainly thankful because I like what I'm doing."

Brown said he decided to give up his seat in the House for a chance to fight for the issues he believes in on a larger stage.

"In the Senate you are confirming cabinet members and judges…voting on treaties, but more than that you are speaking for an entire state. You have the ability to put issues in the public agenda much more easily that a House member. When a senator talks about an issue it gets more attention."

Talking about the issues

The issues Brown has talked about in his campaign against DeWine are health care, education, jobs, trade policy and, increasingly, the war in Iraq.

"I voted against the Iraq war," Brown said proudly, charging that the way Bush misled the country into that war "was a disgrace." He criticized what he termed DeWine's "rubber-stamping" of the White House's "failed" agenda in Iraq. He said the U.S. needs a winning exit strategy for Iraq that will bring American troops home starting in October.

"I'm disgusted with the way Tom DeLay, Bob Ney, and Mike DeWine have sold out and betrayed the middle class," he said. "…The American people know they have been betrayed. That's why the Mike DeWines of the world are in trouble this year…."

"The people look at what government has done in the last five years," Brown said, "and they see a drug bill that favors the drug companies. They see an energy policy that is all about oil companies making more money. They see a government that has refused to pass a minimum wage bill for 10 years but has given six pay increases to itself."

For 13 years, Brown has refused the health insurance policy offered House members until Congress passes universal coverage. He has also been an outspoken critic of the Medicare Part D prescription drug program and a staunch supporter of environmental protections.

"When I'm sworn in in January '07 the voters will already know exactly what I am going to do because I will have already talked about it," Brown said. "There won't be any question about where I stand."*

---

* Brown unseated Republican incumbent U.S. Sen. Mike DeWine in 2006. He was re-elected to the Senate in 2012 and 2018.

Contributors

William Hershey is a retired Beacon Journal Washington correspondent, and Columbus Bureau Chief. He is the author of *Quick and Quotable: Columns from Washington, 1985–1997,* and co-author (with John C. Green) of *Mr. Chairman: The Life and Times of Ray C. Bliss,* both published by The University of Akron Press.

James C. Benton is a former Beacon Journal Columbus Bureau reporter, a PhD historian, and in 2021, director of the Race and Economic Empowerment Project at Georgetown University. He is the author of the forthcoming book *Fraying Fabric: How Trade Policy and Industrial Decline Changed America* (University of Illinois Press).

Carl Chancellor is a former Beacon Journal reporter and columnist, and in 2021 Vice President of Editorial for the Center for American Progress.

Michael Cull is a former Beacon Journal Columbus Bureau Chief and a retired state government official.

Michael Douglas is a retired Beacon Journal editorial page editor.

Bob Dyer is a retired Beacon Journal columnist and reporter. He is the author of three books: *Omar!: My Life On and Off the Field* (cowritten with Omar Vizquel); *The Top 20 Moments in Cleveland Sports* and *Blimp Pilot Terrorizes Akron*, all published by Gray & Company.

Steve Hoffman is a retired Beacon Journal politics writer and editorial writer.

Doug Oplinger is a retired Beacon Journal reporter, Business Editor and Managing Editor, and in 2021, the project coordinator for Your Voice Ohio, a coalition of news organizations that engages Ohioans in conversations on important topics.

Brian Usher was a Beacon Journal politics writer and Columbus Bureau Chief, and also served as press secretary for Gov. Richard F. Celeste; he died in 2011 at 65.

Dennis J. Willard is a former Beacon Journal Columbus Bureau Chief, and in 2021 was a public affairs consultant.

Index

Printed in the United States
by Baker & Taylor Publisher Services